Contested Sudan

The political economy of war and
reconstruction

Ibrahim Elnur

Routledge
Taylor & Francis Group

LONDON AND NEW YORK

First published 2009
by Routledge
2 Park Square, Milton Park, Abingdon, Oxon, OX14 4RN

Simultaneously published in the USA and Canada
by Routledge
270 Madison Avenue, New York, NY 10016

Routledge is an imprint of the Taylor & Francis Group,
an informa business

© 2009 Ibrahim Elnur

Typeset in Times by Keyword Group Ltd
Printed and bound in Great Britain by MPG Books Ltd, Bodmin

British Library Cataloguing in Publication Data
A catalogue record for this book is available from the British Library

Library of Congress Cataloging in Publication Data
Elnur, Ibrahim.
Contested Sudan : the political economy of war and reconstruction /
Ibrahim Elnur.
    p. cm. – (Durham modern Middle East and Islamic world series)
    Includes bibliographical references and index.
    ISBN 978-0-415-47645-4 (hbk : alk. paper) – ISBN 978-0-203-88798-1
        (ebook) 1. Economics–Political aspects–Sudan. 2. Postwar
        reconstruction–Sudan. 3. Sudan–History–Civil War, 1955–1972.
        4. Sudan–History–Civil War, 1983–2005. I. Title.
    HB74.P65.E48 2008
    962.404'3–dc22   2008020355

ISBN 10: 0-415-47645-3 (hbk)
ISBN 10: 0-203-88798-0 (ebk)

ISBN 13: 978-0-415-47645-4 (hbk)
ISBN 13: 978-0-203-88798-1 (ebk)

Dedicated to the memory of Osama Abdel Rahman Elnur (1942–2007) and Fatima Elrasheed Abdel Rahman (1958–2007)

Contents

Illustrations

Tables

Maps and figures

Boxes

Preface

Rather than emphasize its overstretched one million square miles, Sudan is increasingly associated with conflicts, humanitarian crises and instability. A plethora of writings echoes a certain requiem of the conflict-ridden country. This book is not yet another requiem but an attempt to understand the dynamics of the unmaking and possible directions of the making of an alternative Sudan. The book's emphasis is on an alternative conceptual framework for understanding the processes that led to the erosion of the structural foundation of post-colonial Sudan and the emergence, out of the wreckages of conflicts, of new political and socio-economic terrains. War produces new forms of multilayered and overlapping urbanities, rural structures and extensive and interactive local, translocal and transnational networks that are constantly reshaping institutions and unleashing new transformative potential. A new North and a new South were born with little resemblance to the pre-war ones.

Understanding such a transformative potential and its dynamics is an essential step towards building a sound integrated framework for addressing post-war reconstruction. The book, thus, addresses questions related to how conflict produces new economic forms ranging from militarized to informal economic structures, which are perceived as temporary expressions of the grotesque violence and marginality produced at the height of violent conflict. Central to the answer of these questions is how 'war economies' emerge out of a 'before' and reshape new sorts of economies in the 'after'. Furthermore, the book addresses issues related to how war produces massive demographic changes. What are the implications for local productions of place and space? How do relations (economic, political, social and cultural) between the urban and the rural get reconfigured? And what are the relationships between transnational and global trajectories and the remaking of the local social contract? While pre-conflict terrains are neither retrievable nor conducive to lasting peace, the major task is to explore synergies and linkages between conflict-produced political, socio-economic terrains, development and lasting peace. The central hypothesis is that, beyond tragedies and looming miseries, war and prolonged conflicts, in particular, are transformative. Harnessing such transformative potential is central to successful post-conflict peace building and development.

The fieldwork that formed this text was carried out over more than a decade ago. The initial interest was focused on internal displacement resulting from war. Much of the findings on the impact of population displacement owes to extensive surveys undertaken by the Displaced Population Study Group (DPSG) collaborative research project that was hosted by Juba University (1990–1995). This was followed by two shorter follow-up works undertaken by the author. A one-semester release by the American University in Cairo was instrumental in making possible full-time work in the early draft of this book. A generous guest researcher grant from the Office of International Relations, excellent working conditions provided by the Centre for Development Studies (CDS) and intellectually motivating atmosphere created by both faculty and students at the CDS at the University of Bergen at large made my stay in Bergen fruitful and very productive. The excellent Sudan collection at the CDS-Middle East and Islamic Studies library was a great help in closing gaps and identifying important supportive literature. The greatest help came indeed from the unfailing support from CDS colleagues. I am particularly grateful to the following colleagues. Professor Terje Tvedt introduced me to his rich collection on Sudan including fieldwork material on Southern Sudan. His collection on NCA work on Southern Sudan (1972 onwards) was extremely relevant to my work and saved me valuable travel and research time in Oslo. Professors Leif Manger, Shon O'Fahey, Gunnar Halland, Paul Opocku-Mensah and, last but by no means least, Anwar Osman Magid were a constant source of help, support and intellectual motivation. Kristin Holst Paulsen and the CDS's administrative staff spared no effort at making my stay smooth and pleasant. I am heavily indebted to the AUC who offered me intellectual refuge long before a job. Cyrus Reed, the late John Gerhard and Tim Sullivan were all a source of encouragement and support. I am much indebted to the Ford Foundation for supporting the research on IDPs. I am deeply appreciative of the non-failing support of Richard Longhurst, Emma Playfair and Humphrey Davis. In 1993, when it became clear that researching a war-displaced population was a security taboo, Barbara Harrell-Bond generously hosted the whole DPSG group, including myself, Yassir Yacoub and the late Fatima Elrasheed, at the Oxford Refugees Centre for six months.

I am most indebted to my research partners at RWCMEA (War Torn Communities in the Middle East and Africa), particularly to Martina Rieker who shared with me the challenges of coordinating the activities of this group for over five years, and to Ann Lesch, AbdelGhaffar Ahmed, Hamit Bozarslan, Eileen Kuttab, Shahrazad Mojab and Ciraj Rassool who gave useful feedback on the early theoretical framework. Feedbacks and comments from my colleagues at the Department of Political Science at the AUC were of great help. I am equally indebted to the excellent research assistance provided by Amira Ahmed, Joseph John Viscomi and Hadeer Shafie. Hadeer particularly survived the over-demanding job of identifying missing links and references in my writing-fatigue phase. My family, my wife Rajaa and my siblings Loaie, Ruaa, Nazim and Rawie, have been a never ending support even when it meant accepting my absent presence even when I was physically among them.

While conceptually I avoided the requiem, in real life I was not able. Tragically, two people who directly and indirectly influenced the process of writing this book died as I was revising the manuscript. Fatima Elrasheed, my student, colleague and co-researcher, a fine academic, Sudanese and Darfurian, passed away. We shared together the challenges and insight of researching the impact of forced internal displacement during the harsh years of Islamist ascendancy (1990–1993) and we took refuge in Oxford fleeing the constant harassment until we finalized our project. The tragic humanitarian crisis in Darfur must have been beyond her capacity to endure. Osama Abdel Rahman Elnur, a cousin, friend and outstanding student of Meroitics and Nubian history, was a great source of inspiration as he courageously fought malignancy to complete his Nubian Electronic Project and update the ARKAMANI website. To the memory of both this book is devoted. They are both sorely missed.

Ibrahim Elnur,
Cairo, AUC
March 2008

Abbreviations

CPA	Comprehensive Peace Agreement
DPA	Darfur Peace Agreement
DUP	Democratic Unionist Party
ECA	East Sudan Peace Agreement
FRELIMO	*Frente del liberacaco do Mozambique*, Mozambique Liberation Front
GoNU	Government of National Unity
GoS	Government of Sudan
GoSS	Government of Southern Sudan
IGAD	Intergovernmental Authority on Development (Djibouti, Eritrea, Ethiopia, Kenya, Somalia, Sudan and Uganda)
JAM	Joint Assessment Mission (UNDP, WB, GoS, SPLA)
JEM	Justice and Equality Movement (Darfur)
MNFP	Ministry of Finance and Planning
NCP	National Congress Party (Turabi faction after 1999 NIF split; before, PCP: Peoples National Congress)
NDA	National Democratic Alliance
NIF	National Islamic Front
SLM	Sudan Liberation Movement (Darfur)
SPLM/A	Sudan People Liberation Movement/Army
SSDF	Southern Sudan Defence Forces

Part 1

Historical and theoretical foundation

1 Introduction

The making of Sudan: a history of incomplete processes

With 2.5 million square kilometres, extreme ethnic and linguistic diversity, neighbouring nine countries and sharing with them a number of ethnic groups, Sudan's history can be presented either in terms of diversity, an unviable extensity that cannot be harnessed to accommodate a single cohesive national unit, or as a slow build up of such a unit. The long history of the civil wars in Southern Sudan which started on the eve of independence (1955–1972) and the second war (1983–2005) tends to support such a static view of the long history of nation building in Sudan. Alternatively, the history of Sudan can be seen as a long process, albeit incomplete, of incorporating and integrating diverse groups and cultures, in which riverain Sudan acted as a melting point for over two thousand years. Such processes have been marked by never ending migratory flows from all geographical and cultural directions dating back to the ancient Nubian Kingdom.

Northern Sudanese, the features of one nuclear family resembling a complex mosaic of historical cultural mixings, present a more distinct typology of miscegenation.[1] Mazrui's (1973) fascinating article 'The Black Arab in Comparative Perspective' would have been complete if he had expanded his categories. Northern riverain Sudan is certainly a case of symmetrical acculturation characterized by cultural transmission as a two-way affair. Mazrui is right in cautioning the extent of influx of Muslim Arabs suggested by Abdel Al-Rahim (1973): 'the fluidity of genealogies and tribal affiliations exaggerated the degree of biological Arabization' (Mazrui, 1973, p. 62). While the black Arab (Nubianized Arabism) continued to expand its boundaries and redefine such boundaries in a manner that justified the happy story of the ascending miscegenation model, there is a parallel unhappy story that was not told. The Nubiazation of both Islam and Arabism progressed simultaneously with the 'slave mode of production' in riverain Sudan. The ascending miscegenation is a different bitter story and, despite its decay, it left its deep marks in the history of Northern Sudan. Had Mazrui incorporated the parallel process of unhappy ascending miscegenation, he would have been less surprised that 'there are some Arabs, deeply black, whose credentials are usually respected in their Arab genealogies' (ibid., p. 69). 'Descending miscegenation of the United States; ambivalent miscegenation of both America, the divergent miscegenation of apartheid South Africa; and the ascending miscegenation.' In the latter, he grouped Sudan and Zanzibar as a model of Afro-Arab intermingling. Despite commonalities, the Sudanese case exhibits certain unique characteristics that may merit a more distinctive typology. The starting point for this distinctiveness is the matriarchal system of the Nubian Kingdom; as Abd Al-Rahim (1973) stresses, 'their [the Arab Muslim immigrant] readiness to mix, coupled with the matriarchal system of Nubians on the one hand, the Arabian patriarchal organization of the family and the tribe on the other, had to effect not only of facilitating the assimilation of the immigrant and spreading their culture and religion, but also giving them reins of power and political leadership in the host society'. This process of symmetrical acculturation, first of the Nubian elite including their Christian clergy[2] and later the rest, gives the Northern Arabism its distinctive nature.[3] The distinctive characteristic of Nubian miscegenation lies precisely in the fact that it was not based on relation between equals. David Ayalon (2001) in his analytical narrative of the 'spread of Islam and Nubian Dam' shows how the Nubians, a Christian people of military might and skills, defeated the Muslims and were able to maintain their power until the thirteenth century. Quoting al-Baladhuri's evidence: 'The Nubian people fought the Muslims very fiercely. When they encountered them they showered them with arrows, until all of them were wounded and they withdrew with many wounds and gouged eyes. Therefore they were called the "marksmen of eye". They shot at us until [our] eyes were gone. A hundred and fifty gouged eyes were counted. We said, therefore, that nothing is better than making peace with these ones' (ibid., p. 19).

Without going deep into these fascinating corridors of Muslim Arab–Nubian encounters, let me go back to Mazrui's typologies of miscegenation. The major point that I wanted to extract from this rich historical encounter is that both 'Arabism' and 'Islamism' were Nubianized and defined by the riverain Nubian population who gave Sudanese Arabism its distinct dark colour and Islam its Africanized nature in a similar way to that brilliantly expressed by Trimingham (1948): 'The Sudanese received Islam whole-heartedly, but, through their unique capacity of assimilation, moulded it to their own particular mentality; escaping the formulae of theologians, they sang in it, danced in it, brought their own customs, their own festivals into it, paganized a good deal, but they always kept the vivid reality of its inherent unity under the rule of the one God' (ibid., p. x).

It is this dynamic 'Jellaba'[4] multifaceted agency that contributed to the spread of the common 'Sudanization' that emerged out of the process of Nubianization of both 'Islam' and 'Arabism'. The negative 'connotation' and post-colonial writings liking the 'Jellaba' role to the lopsided development and marginalization of non-riverain Sudan is certainly a serious 'reduction' of multiple processes at work into a single one. 'Jellaba' entrepreneurship and its wider agency in the spread of 'Sudanization' was in fact 'inclusive' rather than 'exclusive' in terms of enlarging Sudanization beyond the 'narrower' confines of riverain Sudan. While Islamist scholars played a predominant role in the spread of Islam along the riverain Sudan, it was the active agency of riverain Sudan traders which played an important role in spreading both Islam and Arabism into Western Sudan.

A number of studies provide a wealth of knowledge about such a gradual and cumulative process of 'Arabization' and 'Islamization' (or Sudanization). The riverain traders (commonly known as Jellaba in the West and South Sudan) were most often performing multiple agency roles that transcend the limited notion of trade in areas where money has become essential, especially around the main roads and around important trading centres; the local people have assimilated themselves so thoroughly to the culture and values of the dominant. Several contributors to the study of the Sudanization process (Mazrui, 1971, 1973; Bjorkelo, 1989; Kurita, 1989, 1993) used the term 'Arabization'. 'Arabization' misses an important aspect of the Sudanization process, pioneered by riverain Sudanese, namely that the process of incorporation targeted both 'Arabs' or more precisely non-riverain Arabs as well as non-Arabs. Doornbos (1988) offers a fascinating reading of the cultural agency of the 'Jellaba' traders among other agents who came later (administrators, school teachers and itinerant preachers). The cultural changes among the Masalit in Foro Baranga in the early 1980s, as Doornbos observed, meant a partial abandonment of a Masalit culture including tribal dancing, drinking of local beer (Marissa) and traditional ways of dressing, but also regression in women status. The direction of change was towards adapting 'riverain' Sudan cultural traits restricting women's public role, using cash, shunning alcohol and dressing in a 'riverain' style. Doornbos uses the term 'Sudanization' rather than 'Arabization'. First, Arab Bedouin of Darfur were changing their tribal culture and adopting 'riverain' cultural norms of what Doornbos calls 'Sudanization'. Second, the cultural mode they aspired to follow was a 'riverain' Sudan Arabism not an international one.

It was the Nubianization of both 'Arabism' and 'Islam' that gave the crucial dimension to the agency of riverain Sudanese in the Sudanization process. This particular mode of Sudanization overwhelmed O'Fahey (1995) so much to the extent of equating it with an imagined ethnic group called 'northern riverain Sudanese'. Defining such ethnic groups, O'Fahey suggested: 'The ethnic group in question are the northern riverain Sudanese, living along the Nile between Khartoum and the Egyptian border and between two Niles in the Gezira ... These *awlad al-balad* (sons of the land), to use the older term, possess a common history, medieval Nubia, the Funj Kingdom of Sinnar (1504–1821), Egyptian colonial rule (1821–1885); a common language, Arabic, even if some groups use Nubian; and a common religion, an Islam heavily saturated by Sufism. No other area or ethnic grouping within the boundaries of the present Sudan share the same history and culture with *awalad al-balad*, except in a limited way the Beja of the east. Darfur has its own long history of state formation (the latest state, the Keira Sultanate, existing from 1650–1916); nor was Arabic until relatively recent times the dominant language there, while Islam in Darfur is much influenced by West Africa as by riverain Sudan.[5]

Admittedly, non-riverain 'Arabs' were much easier incorporated through intermarriages but 'Sudanization' was never identical with 'Arabs' or being more 'Arab'. 'Sudanese' were, and continue to be, heavily shaped by the riverain Sudan-dominant Nubian cultural background and their perception of both 'Arabism' and 'Islam'.

Yet, one cannot but agree with Deng (1973) when he quoted at length Salah Ahmed Ibrahim's poem ('Malual') with the comment: 'I quote at length from this poem because it captures the essence of the South/North history, reveals the complexities of identity of the Sudan, and articulates the challenges now facing the Sudanese in the process of nation building' (ibid., p. 70). But as Deng aptly noted, commenting on the 1924 uprising, there were two dimensions to be acknowledged. First the flexibility of the incorporation process of the riverain-led 'Sudanization', which has not only admitted ex-slaves into its ranks but accepted their leadership of the first most important anti-colonial movement. Second, the positive dimension of this flexible incorporation in to the political sphere was not extended to the social realm.

Beyond the ancient history of riverain Sudan, including the first attempt at centralization represented by the 'Loose Confederation of the Fung Kingdom of Sennar' using Crawford's term (Crawford, 1952), there are three significant attempts at the making of the modern political state of Sudan:

1   The Turkish period of 1821–1885
2   The Mahadist period of 1885–1898
3   The Anglo-Egyptian condominium period of 1898–1956

I argue that the Turkish period, largely underestimated, made a significant attempt at establishing the modern political state of Sudan and sowed the early seeds of the modernization project.

The spillover of Mohammed Ali's modernization drive in the Sudan (1820–1885)

In scholarly works, school textbooks and the popular narratives of Sudan and Egypt the two main motives of Mohammed Ali's imperial project in Sudan was the acquisition of slaves for the army and gold (*El Zahab wa Elrigal*). In addition to this, Mohammed Ali's attempt to forge an alliance with the northern Sudan elite was seriously eroded by excessive taxation that dominated not only popular discourses about the '*Turkiyya El Zalma*' (the unjust Turkish) role but also the scholarly work that focused disproportionately on resistance and injustices incurred. This simplistic reading seriously understates Mohammed Ali's grand modernization drive with serious overflows into Sudan. While the commonly held view that Mohammed Ali's motives were essentially related to the acquisition of Sudanese slaves for his new army and exploitation of the country's natural resources holds some credence in the immediate objective, they are overstated. Access to Northern Sudan mediated slave trade and was always possible without direct control and perhaps far more cost effective. Northern Sudan was predominantly a slave mode of production long before Mohammed Ali's conquest. As Willis noted, 'The whole social system of northern Sudan grew to depend on the possession of slaves without whom no property could be developed or family maintained.' Bjorkelo's (1989) description of the socio-political structure of the *Ja'aliyyin* Kingdom on the eve of *Turkiyya* (Sudanese name of Mohammed Ali's rule in Sudan) is aptly representative of the whole Northern or riverain Sudan. Bjorkelo noted that the socio-political structure was characterized by a hierarchy of slaves, commoners (peasants and nomads), merchants, nobles and the king (ibid., p. 4). The village communities were typically made up of a peasant household where differences between households in terms of wealth and status and power reflected the unequal distribution of land, water-wheels, animals and slaves (ibid., p. 4). It is this socio-political structure of Northern Sudan, I will maintain, that is central to the understanding of the failed modernization drive of Mohammed Ali in Sudan. Furthermore, it did not take long before Mohammed Ali realized that the slave supply promise was not that significant. According to Sikainga (1998), 'by the late 1830s, it became clear to Mohammed Ali that the use of Sudanese slaves in the Egyptian army was a failure. Mohammed Ali attended to other sources such as gold, gum Arabic, livestock and ostrich feathers. The slave trade was left to private merchants, particularly after the White Nile opened in the late 1830s' (p. 12).

Attempts at realizing the productive potential in agriculture

Mohammed Ali's emphasis on the realization of the productive potential of agriculture in Sudan became more explicit since the early days of his rule. In a document dated 7 February 1825, Mohammed Ali wrote, 'In order to develop agriculture in "Sinnar" which we have conquered with so much fatigue ... we require skilled men for the task ... Do not neglect this or you will bitterly regret'[6] Similar messages were echoed during his visit to Sudan (1838–1839). Addressing northern Sudanese, the *Pasha* called on them to 'be diligent and exert your maximum efforts in tilling and planting. Agriculture contributes positively to the progress of your country and homeland.' Addressing the ruler, who was attending the meeting: 'As for you *Pasha*, you have to encourage the locals and to persuade them day and night that agriculture and cultivation is the road to wealth and prosperity' (Gadal, 1993, p. 75). The *Pasha*'s modernization package for agriculture was indeed a comprehensive one. It included the introduction of new products and varieties and, in horticulture, new crops including sugar cane, cotton and indigo and a new variety of wheat and corn (Issawi, 1954; Gadal, 1993; Magar, 1993). The indigo factories in the Dongola area experienced some impressive steady growth of output as shown in Table 1.1.

The package also included the introduction of new technologies (metal-blows), the replacement of Sudanese sagias (water wheel) with a technically superior Egyptian one and a whole team of technicians including experienced farmers (Gadal, 1993; Issawi, 1954; Magar, 1993). Educational plans included the training of Sudanese agricultural technicians in Cairo's specialized schools (Magar, 1993, p. 102). Conducive measures were taken to modify the land tenure system to confirm existing ownership rights and to allow for foreign

Table 1.1 Indigo output in the Dongola area: 1833–1837

1833	10,000	*Ugga*
1835	21,416	*Ugga*
1837	50,000	*Ugga*

Ugga is equivalent to 1.248 kg.

Source: Humeida, 1983.

ownership through government claims on non-registered lands that became automatically state-owned lands. Efforts to encourage horticulture included tax holidays which was influential in encouraging both northern Sudanese and foreigners to develop fruit production (see Humeida, 1983, p. 114). Some of these reforms and productivity enhancements constituted the structural foundation of the modern agricultural sector during British colonial rule (1898–1956). Ironically, Mohammed Ali's early experimentation with new varieties of cotton was the basis upon which the British rule capitalized in their attempt to compensate for the disrupted cotton trade with America (Elnur, 1988).

The spillover from state-led industrialization of Mohammed Ali

Early attempts at building modern manufacturing units during the two colonial eras (The Turko-Egyptian era, 1820–1880, and the Anglo-Egyptian era, 1898–1956) were sporadic and had an insignificant impact on the structure of the economy.[7] The earliest of these attempts, during the time of Mohammed Ali, was linked to mineral extraction. In 1830, Mohammed Ali obtained eight iron foundries from England to exploit reportedly rich iron ore deposits in the White Nile province. Eight English artisans and an Egyptian manager contributed to the establishment of the foundry. None of them survived according to Hill (1959, p. 57): 'Death crept in to end a mission which had never had a chance of success.' A second expedition, led by the Austrian mineralogist J. Von Russeger in 1838, and a third, led by Glamorganshire mining engineer John Patric in 1847, equally failed.

The two latter expeditions recommended the improvement of the indigenous smelting techniques: 'The iron was there but, for want of transport and skilled labour, its working would not pay' (ibid., p. 58). Other attempts, aimed at introducing modern mining techniques, were not successful either. In contrast, the introduction of sugarcane plantation and processing was reportedly successful. During the time of Ahmed Basha Abu Adlan (1826–1838), a large cane plantation with a refinery and arrack (local rum) distillery was managed by a German foreman (Hill, 1959, p. 56). Available records do not explain why this industry failed to survive and expand. In fact, sugar continued to be a major import item throughout the period of Turkish rule (see Hill, 1959).

Traditional spinning and weaving was well established before the advent of the Turko-Egyptian occupation and textiles were both exported and imported.

However, the establishment of two modern textile mills and a modern cotton ginnery in Kassala proved to be premature and met little success (Elnur, 1988). By the end of Turkish colonial rule, nothing was left of these unsuccessful manufacturing units. The strongest and the most important impact of the Turkish colonial rule was on the handicraft industries. The need to develop exports and export transportation led to a substantial improvement in boat building, tanning, sagias (bullock-driven water wheels) and the production of agricultural tools, using simple production techniques. During Osman Bey's term of office in Sennar in central Sudan, a group of skilled workers was sent to Sudan to grow opium, indigo and cotton and to tan hides. With them came blacksmiths, masons and carpenters. A strong addition to the ranks of foremen, cultivators and artisans arrived with the appointment of Khurshid as governor in 1826. This was in response to Mohammed Ali's orders to the governors of Egyptian provinces.

The beleaguered Mahadist state

The armed struggle waged by El Mahadi brought an end to the Turkish era by 1885. As Barbour (1961) aptly noted, the Mahadist state 'came about just at the time of the Conference of Berlin, when the whole of the African continent was in the process of being partitioned into spheres of interest between Europe, Sudan became independent of foreign control' (ibid., p. 14). The beleaguered Mahadist state (1885–1898) was obliged to develop many handicraft industries to meet several needs such as those of defence and agriculture. It attempted to develop the embryonic metal fabricating industries that it inherited from the Turkish colonial system. One interesting aspect of the Mahadist state policies is the retention of both physical and human capital inherited from the Turkish era. Personnel operating, printing unit, small arms manufacturing as well as accountants and administrators were employed in positions relevant to their skills voluntary or involuntary, and non-Muslims were actually forced into Islam (see for example Slatin, 1896). Continuous internal and external wars prevented further development, even of these tiny embryonic industries (Gadal, 1982, pp. 133–156). Despite disruptions and discontinuities, Mohammed Ali's modernization drive overflowed into Sudan and left its marked impact. From modern education to improved farming practices and techniques, embryonic manufacturing units and new skills in metal working, there is ample evidence of the initial drive. The Mahadist state's turbulent years were indeed disruptive as far as stable growth of new modern activities. The Mahadist state, however, driven by its pressing needs and endless wars, further accelerated the process of transforming the slavery-dependent mode of production and accelerated the transformation of slaves into workers.[8] The incomplete mission of accelerating this process through wide-scale land reform was driven to its logical ends by the British colonial authorities keen to maximize agricultural output. Mohammed Ali's modernization spillovers were certainly incomplete. Using Marx's celebrated phrase on the incomplete British colonialism of India, Mohammed Ali's colonialism of Sudan was incomplete, but certainly ushered transformations that could no longer be halted. Perhaps the Mahadist state was the most influential in the vast incorporation of Northern Sudan nomads with the riverain Northern Sudanese. Although the Mahadi himself is from the riverain elite, the bulk of his support came from the Arab nomadic tribes of western Sudan. Naturally, the support for Mahadi was not purely religious, as Rose and Dusen (2002) rightly noted: 'Others supported the Mahadi for more mundane reasons: Some had their economic interest harmed when Egypt started suppressing the slave trade in the 1860s and others were nomads who resented the taxes and control imposed by the Turco-Egyptian administration. The nomads formed the bulk of Mahadi army of *jihadya* (holy warriers).' This major incorporation of the nomad tribes into what defines a 'northern entity' was not without simultaneous conflicts within the power struggles in the nascent Mahadist state. With the death of Mahadi and the advent of his successor (the Calipha) from the Beggara nomads from Western Sudan a series of power struggles between the riverain Sudanese and the Western Sudanese nomads took place. The trajectories of this process of incorporation are well recorded in other studies; what matters, however, is that despite conflict a major inclusive process of constantly enlarging northern identity took place. The other process of incorporation took place to the East, incorporating the Beja tribes loosely in the northern entity as defined by the riverain elite. This was a much slower process mediated by the Sufi Islamic sect of *Khatmya*.

The condominium period, 1898–1956

It was the British colonial period that gave Sudan its current territorial entity: the signing in 1902 of a treaty with Ethiopia that established the Southern Eastern Boundary with Sudan, an Anglo-Belgian treaty in 1909 establishing the border with Belgian Congo, and annexed Darfur in 1916 terminating the Far Sultanate.

Colonial lop-sided development

Understanding the current extremely uneven and lop-sided development and in particular the marginalization of both Southern Sudan and Darfur is futile without placing it into its historical context. The British colonial administration laid the foundation for the lop-sided development in the Sudan with the concentration of all developmental projects in the riverain triangle and its adjacent region to the West in Kordofan and to the East in Kassala. Such lop-sided development benefited and reproduced the dominance of old factions of elites (religious and tribal leaders, traders and at a later stage the emerging civil servants and professional groups).

The British colonial administration finished the incomplete process of ending, albeit gradually and tuned to its political alliances with northern elites, the slave trade, a mission that was started half heartedly during the Turkish rule. Yet, the British colonial rule blocked the slow process of incorporation and integration with Central Sudan through the 1922 Passport and Permit Ordinance. The ordinance barred Northern Sudanese from entering or working in the South. The ordinance,

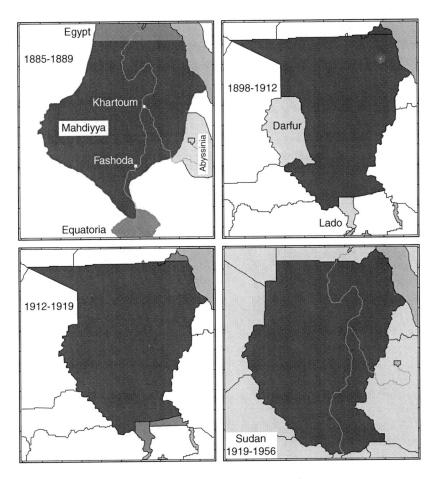

Map 1.1 Sudan's changing frontiers between 1885 and 1956.
Source: http://www.zum.de/whkmla/histatlas/northafrica/haxsudan.html, accessed 28 Feb 2008.

as Sidahed and Sidahmed (2005) noted, 'generally sought to curb the flow of Arabic and Islamic culture through personnel, dress or trade. A church Missionary Society held a conference in 1924 in Rajaf in Equatoria that decided on using English as the main lingua franca in the South in addition to seven indigenous languages' (ibid., p. 22). It is true, as shown in Map 1.1, that in addition to the annexation of Darfur the British administration's vast territories of Southern Sudan were never incorporated in the previous two periods of Turkish and Mahadist rules. The dominant opinion within the administration was favouring the eventual integration of Southern Sudan with British East Africa.

By any stretch of the imagination Southern Sudan was not in any serious sense neither part of any colonial design of cultivating its potential as a supplier of raw materials nor even part of a grand design of making it a 'labour reservoir' for the more visible colonial cultivation project of Northern Sudan. In fact the labour reservoir for the colonial raw material supply economy of North Sudan was essential for West African migrants (see Balamoan, 1981). As Sriam and Nielson (2004) rightly noted: 'In place for twenty years, the policy did little to move the South forward in terms of development or self-rule. In retrospect, it perpetuated the inequality and had devastating consequences for the South when it was incorporated into independent Sudan' (ibid., p. 28).

In addition the marginalization and maintenance of Southern Sudan as a virtual untapped, pre-capitalist subsistence economy was by and large a colonial policy and legacy. Douglas's (2003) conclusion that the origin of the current North–South problem should be seen in the Turkish era (1820–1885) (ibid., p. 7) and the Northern Sudanese involvement in the slave trade (ibid., p. 4) is certainly an understatement of the role of the British colonial administration's Southern policy. The wealth of information made available following the publication of 'The British Document on the Sudan: 1940–1956' in 2002 provided strong criticism of such policies by senior British administrators. A memorandum by Nebold, then civil secretary, 3 April, 1944 revealed such a widely shared criticism among colonial administrators of British Southern policy that 'there is no need to stress to the council the backwardness of Southern Sudan. We have a moral obligation to redeem its inhabitants from ignorance, superstition, poverty, malnutrition, ... etc.' (ibid., p. 25). 'A number of factors have contributed to this in the past: the great distances and poor communications; climatic factors; tribal apathy and conservatism; certain disabilities inherent in mission education ... etc.' (vol. 2, p. 25). In a rare admission of the total failure of the British colonial (North–South) imaginaries, the Governor General of Sudan, in a memorandum dated 12 September 1945, admitted: 'Forty-five years of British administration have not turned the Sudanese into African Englishmen, nor will another twenty years of it. Their form of self-government and standards of public life will be fundamentally oriental, and their national outlook will be Arab and Middle Eastern. The ties of common origin, common outlook and tradition, which play so large a part in binding together the British Commonwealth, cannot influence the Sudanese nation of the future' (ibid., p. 19) (for a wider overview of the British colonial discourse see Appendix 1–1).

The neglect of Darfur in the marginalization of the South during the colonial period and the famous 'Closed District' laws were much publicized while that of Darfur was far less discussed. Yet by the time of independence, Darfur was, on average, worse off than Southern Sudan. Flint and de waal (2005), citing a colonial administration file 'Economic Development, Darfur Province' from the Khartoum national archives, found that the file contained only five entries during the entire period 1917–1980. Thus by 1935 'Darfur had just one elementary school, one "tribal" elementary school and "two" "sub grade" schools' (ibid., p. 31). 'In addition no maternity clinics before the 1940s, no railway etc.' (ibid., p. 13).

It was only in 1946 when the Sudan Administrative conference determined that Sudan should be administered as one country. The conference delegates agreed to re-admit the Northern administration to Southern posts; abolish trade restrictions imposed under the 'closed door' ordinance; allow Southerners to seek employment in the North; and introduced Arabic in the South as the official administration language. According to Abdelgadier (2004), the last two recommendations were resented by the Southerners: the imposition of Arabic and the 'replacement of trusted British district commissioners with unsympathetic northern' (ibid., p. 15). On 18 August 1955 the first civil war started, less than four months before the official declaration of the newly independent state of the Sudan on 1 January 1956.

The colonial legacy

During almost forty years of British colonial rule in Sudan, no attempt was made to establish modern manufacturing (see Appendix I). The railway, first built in the conquest of the country, was expanded to export cotton and provided the only engineering industry. Irrigation projects for cotton led to the establishment of a cement factory to build the Sennar dam but, following the completion of the dam, the factory was dismantled and re-exported. Cotton ginneries remained about the only modern manufacturing activity till the outbreak of the Second World War. Introduction of modern large-scale production of cotton was followed by a systematic policy aiming at the destruction of the local cottage-based cotton industry which had flourished, particularly in the Gezira region, for centuries (see Pollard, 1984, p. 176).

The sudden interruption of international trade, as a result of the war, provided the country with a great opportunity to mobilize its potential productive capacity. Factories producing essential consumer goods (soap, glassware, matches, etc.) were established. The potential shown by the engineering industry was particularly great. The Atbara workshops (with the largest foundry in the country) and the Ordinance and the Public Work Department increased their workforce fivefold, in response to the demand of the local population and allied troops in Sudan and North Africa (Prest, 1948; UPA, 1971; Nimeiri, 1976).

> There was much to do in conversion alone: rail coaches became ambulance trains, [the Sudanese Navy] was formed after two tugs were converted to a mine sweeping role; vans became armoured cars, rail wagons were strengthened to carry tanks instead of cotton. Gun mounting bomb clips and aircraft repair stands were designed and manufactured in Sudan (UPA, 1971). The saw mills in Southern Sudan increased their production almost threefold (from 76 to 219 thousand tons) as wood replaced iron for irrigation pipes.
>
> (Prest, 1948, p. 163)

The war-time flurry of import substitution manufacturing was marked by a simultaneous import substitution orientation in agriculture. Wheat production increased from 8,000 tons (1936–1939 average) to 24,000 tons in 1943, which more than compensated for domestic production and the one lost through the deliberately depressed export prices; expenditure on war-time 'development' was negligible.

With the resumption of normal trade following the end of the war, the Sudan plunged again into the extreme of primary production specialization. Almost none of the import-substitution industries survived the competition of imports nor the deliberate policy dismantling them. The fact that most of these industries were established by the War Supply Department made the latter task easier.

The colonial state and capital accumulation

A detailed analysis of the colonial state policies in the field of administering capital accumulation is beyond the limits of this study. However, an understanding of the historical context that has shaped the particular form of the post-Independence development process is needed.

Throughout the first phase of colonial rule (1898–1925), production for exchange value was substantially increased, but almost totally in the form of petty commodity production (Khalafalla, 1981, p. 36). Unlike other colonial experiences, particularly in East Africa, private foreign capital did not succeed, for historical reasons, in establishing plantation and mineral activities. Hence, the private foreign capital activities of the large British companies concentrated in the sphere of circulation were mainly that of foreign trade and finance. Resident foreign capital, of European and Middle Eastern origin, dominated the wholesale trade and small and medium enterprises in manufacturing. Indigenous capital was, by and large, confined to retail trade, small and medium enterprises in services and a modest share in wholesale trade. There was a deliberate policy to restrict indigenous capital activities to certain fields. Furthermore, the colonial state set a ceiling on credit for indigenous capital (The Credit to Natives Restriction Ordinance, 1909). However, preparing the country for political independence, the colonial state's policy was dramatically changed, and promotion of indigenous capital accumulation in agriculture was initiated.

Such a policy was motivated by the direct needs of the colonial power as Cowen (1983, pp. 142–149) has elegantly shown in the case of Kenya, but was also influenced by the growing nationalist movement in post-war Sudan. From the early 1950s onwards, the private cotton schemes owned by indigenous capital grew at an unprecedented rate as shown in Table 1.2. Mechanized rain-fed farming, which started in the early 1940s, also contributed to the enlargement of the scale of indigenous capital accumulation. However, its dramatic rate of growth relates to the post-Independence period.

Except for the mutiny that started in Torit in August 1955, that signalled the beginning of the civil war in the South, an orderly post-colonial state emerged. The nascent independent state was built on a relatively stable institution, limited but manageable flows and almost clear boundaries between the small niche urban space and the vast ocean of traditional agriculture and modern small-scale irrigated agriculture. Compared to other emerging post-colonial states in Africa,

Table 1.2 Development of indigenous capital cotton cultivation: 1941–1956

Year/Average	1941/42	52/53	53/54	54/55	55/56
Area in 000 Feddans	15	50	57	92	106
Production in 000 Kantars	55	203	249	384	480

Source: Barclays Bank, DCO, 1955, The Sudan Economic Survey.

the Sudan enjoyed a well-developed civil service, a well-developed educational system, a vibrant civil society and political organizations and a commercial elite with a long history but all situated in the riverain central Sudan. Failure to expand such a state in an inclusive manner that would have facilitated or accelerated the process of incorporation and integration of the rest of the country is the subject matter of this book.

The book

Through the example of Sudan as a site for both failed modernity and the longest civil war in the history of Africa (Southern Sudan) as well as the recently escalated humanitarian crisis in Darfur, this book attempts to bring a new understanding of the dynamics governing the formation of post-conflict spaces in their multiple forms and layers (new economies, new urbanities, new diasporic experiences and new conditions and foundations for articulating an alternative social contract).

Part 1 of this book is concerned with the historical background of the Sudan and the conceptual foundation of the analysis of the war and post-war situations. As seen, the introductory chapter of this book provides a necessary historical prelude for understanding the post-colonial unmaking of the Sudan. As opposed to the static description of the Sudan diversities, the introductory chapter provides an overview of the-state-building process in the history of the Sudan, suggesting a slow but cumulative process, albeit an incomplete one, of incorporation and integration throughout a long history dating back to Nubian kingdoms.

The analysis in this book emphasizes that the several instances of irreversibility produced by war are a direct result of abrupt and massive flows affecting not only population but also their institutions, assets, skills, entrepreneurship, and means of production and reproduction of social classes. It, therefore, questions the validity of the main assumptions underlying the conventional approach to post-conflict reconstruction: that reconstruction is an act of retrieving the pre-war situation, that war is a temporary instance of disequilibria, the localized nature of war effects, and finally its emphasis on macro variables or alternatively negligence of the vital and profound impact of micro variables. War produces new forms of multilayered and overlapping urbanities, rural structures, extensive and interactive local, translocal and transnational networks that are constantly reshaping institutions and unleashing new transformative potential. Understanding such transformative potential and its dynamics is an essential step towards building a sound integrated framework for addressing post-war reconstruction. The book asserts that the interlocking nature between crises leading to wars and prolonged conflicts and the political, socio-economic new spaces shaped by war are fundamental for understanding the dynamics governing post-conflict reconstruction and the success or failure in realizing the transformative potential unleashed by such dynamics.

The book is premised on a complete departure from the conventional thinking about reconstruction. It suggests that war, itself a complete departure from the unilinear progression of modernity, triggers multiple processes and transformative potentials that cannot be readily predictable. Chapter 2 provides an overview of the current debates that inform reconstruction thinking. It goes further to suggest that war typically produces a number of irreversiblities that render the notion of retrieving old political and socio-economic formations obsolete. These irreversiblities are central to the understanding of both the challenges and potentials of post-war transition to peace and reconstruction.

Part 2 of the book is the crisis-making processes in post-colonial Sudan. Thus Chapters 3 and 4 of this book are devoted to the crisis making of post-colonial Sudan. The two chapters analyse the processes that led to the unmaking of the Sudan. The focus is on two periods of active state intervention in the economy and society which radically transformed the process of capital accumulation. The central argument of both Chapters 3 and 4 is that both Nimeiri's period (1969–1986), in particular its post-Infitah (open door policies) period of agrarian strategy, and the post-Islamist ascendancy (1989–2005) were central to the understanding of the process of crisis or the unmaking of post-colonial Sudan. The immediate post-independence period (1956–1969) witnessed a remarkable continuity of the colonial policy particularly with regard to the agrarian strategy and the mechanism of extraction of surplus and control over the vast traditional substance of rural economy. The immediate post-colonial state (in both its parliamentary and military phases) continued the colonial pattern of expansion in irrigated modern agriculture, and encouraged expansion in mechanized rain-fed agriculture, but without undermining the structural foundation of the vast traditional agricultural sector. The immediate post-colonial state was able to manage smoothly through the same indirect colonial policy, various flows between the small manageable urban economy, modern agriculture and the vast ocean of traditional agriculture, while still maintaining a manageable extraction of surplus from this vast but relatively stable traditional agriculture through manipulation of taxes on external trade. Conflicts and manageable competition over resources were resolved through well-functioning traditional communal-mediation mechanisms.

This is not a suggestion of a static notion of sustainability and manageability. As long as the traditional subsistence economies and communities are kept in a stagnant situation; additional untapped resources are available to accommodate natural population growth; and no significant transformative potential was triggered neither through local agency nor through an external one; such tranquil sustainability of the colonial mode of indirect rule may still be viable. This is, however, based on a relative notion of sustainability. No colonial or post-colonial administration is capable of preserving such a manageable stagnation for an unlimited span of time. This is particularly true with regard to the post-colonial authorities, whose legitimacy is most often than not based on their ability to provide education facilities, primary health care, veterinary services and some additional infrastructure that facilitates people's movement. Even if these usual 'initial' development gains are kept to the minimum and extremely uneven in their distribution across the regional and urban–rural divide, they trigger transformative processes that reduce the manageability and sustainability of the inherited colonial cost-effective indirect rule. Let us recall that the Southern Sudan problem erupted a year before formal independence and was in part a result of some 'hastily' introduced programmes addressing decades of the colonial administration's strategy of 'keeping the South as it is'.[9]

Nimeiri's 'Grand Bread Basket' strategy, and in particular its aggressive expansion of mechanized agriculture, created the basis for an ecological crisis that eroded the structural foundation of the traditional rural economy. The mid-1980s Sahelian droughts escalated such a crisis and the policy of politicization of the communal leadership further accentuated such crisis. The 'Islamist' regime rising to ascendancy on this crisis, benefiting from its outcome (influx of rural population in urban spaces) and direct politicization of communal structures and ethnicity, brought such crisis to its conclusion. The privatization of the state apparatus speeded such a process leading to the state's virtual collapse.

Chapter 3 provides an in-depth study of the crisis making in post-colonial Sudan. It emphasizes Nimeiri's period of 1969–1985 as a period that led to erosion of the structural foundation of the post-colonial 'modernity project'. Chapter 4 examines the ascendancy of the National Islamic Front (NIF) and factors that contributed to such ascendancy. It examines how the Islamist-dominated regime of 1989–2004 triggered processes that brought the crisis to its ultimate conclusion. The chapter addresses the impact of increasing international isolation of the regime and how this isolation exacerbated the process of stagnation and shrinkage of the economy and the state, leading to further repression of wages, increased outflows of skills and capital, proliferation of conflict perpetuated by the deepening of the crisis in the economy and society, and the NIF's own policies of divide and rule.

Part 3 of the book is entitled 'Re-negotiating a Sudan'. The title is hoped to bring together various means (violent and peaceful) and notions of re-negotiating an alternative Sudan/s. Chapters 5, 6 and 7 of the book are devoted to the war-produced economy and society with a focus on challenges to the peace-building processes. Chapter 5 is based on empirical data from war-torn Sudan examining changes resulting from war and the relevance of the transformative potential thesis. It examines the implications of the processes perpetuated by massive rural to urban population flows that produce new urbanities and ruralities and new institutional setups. Concurrently, local, translocal and transnational diaspora experiences usher in new transformative potentials.

Chapter 6 in this part is premised on a central argument that reconstruction is shaped greatly by the processes through which civil war ended and far less, if at all, by the initial conditions that triggered it. Consequently, the chapter is an essential prelude for understanding the political terrain emerging out of negotiated settlement in the Sudan: new collisions, partnerships and various actors representing national, regional and international interests are all actively playing a role in the reconstruction process. The chapter maps out the sources of fragility in the peace-building process and challenges of governance in the post-war situation as well as the challenges of democratic transformation.

The following chapter, Chapter 7, looks at the war-produced economy characterized by new forms of multilayered and overlapping urbanities, ruralities dominated by overwhelming informalities, and extensive and interactive local, translocal and transnational networks that are constantly reshaping institutions and unleashing new transformative potential. The chapter maintains that understanding such transformative potential and its dynamics is an essential step towards building a sound framework for addressing post-war reconstruction. In so doing, the chapter places heavy emphasis on the issues related to rural transformation, addressing the root causes of the crisis in primary production, as well as land tenure reform, as the key to sustainable peace and successful reconstruction. The chapter also addresses the often-neglected war-driven multi-layered urbanities, which are the site for both potential threats to peace as well as progressive and development-enhancing potential. The specificities of negotiated settlement have also been highlighted.

The final part, Part 4, is a conclusion that provides, not just a summary of the arduous processes of re-negotiating a Sudan, but also some attempts at comparative assessment of various plausible future scenarios.

2 War and the transformative potential

Towards an alternative conceptual framework for analysing post-civil wars

When chaos begins classical science stops.

(James Gleick, 1987, p. 3)

'... since we did not regard him as our enemy ... we had hidden nothing ... But Duke Bernhard's troops broke into our land and plundered us completely of horses, cattle, bread flour, salt, lard, cloth, linen, clothes and everything we possessed. They maltreated the people, shooting, stabbing and beating a number of people to death ... They set alight the village and burnt down five houses and five stables.'
A Protestant shoe-mender living in a village near Ulm in Bavaria narrating the events when Duke Bernard of Saxe-Weimar, then in Swedish service, was fighting the Protestant cause.

(Herberle, 1978[1975], p. 31, cited by Outram, 2002, p. 250)

The coming war is not going to be the first.
It was preceded by wars and wars.
The last war ended by victors and losers. Among the losers ordinary people starved.
Among the victors ordinary people starved.

B. Brecht (translated by Suliman, 1999)

War is a typical case of chaos,[1] producing unpredictable patterns; new dynamics of changes in society and economy; complete disruption of usual linearities; and new forms of societal organizations and networks. We may mourn the death of old tools designed to measure both normalities or linearities or alternatively look at the new situation as a paradigm shift and attempt, as was already done in meteorology and mathematics of uncertainties, to develop a conceptual framework that accommodates war-produced uncertainties. Furthermore, if civil wars and prolonged conflict are triggered by failed modernities,[2] then post-war political, social and economic terrains should be the sites where alternate and viable modernities should be explored.

This chapter maps out the theoretical debates that inform current attempts to theorize both war and post-war situations. It critically examines the dominant conceptualization of war and post-conflict reconstruction. The chapter asserts that, despite convoluted and diverse scenes of 'protracted conflicts', a certain level of generalization is both plausible and necessary. The following analysis emphasizes the limitations and in most cases the irrelevance of the conventional approach to reconstruction. Such an approach is based on narrowly defined engineering-economic notions of rebuilding devastated areas. It asserts that war and especially prolonged civil strife produces a number of irreversibilities in the socio-economic structure and triggers new dynamics for societal change. These irreversibilities are a direct result of abrupt and massive flows affecting not only populations but also their institutions, assets, skills, entrepreneurship and means of reproduction. Therefore, it questions the validity of the main assumptions underlying the conventional approach to post-conflict reconstruction, which include: the 'retrievability' of a pre-war situation, that war is a temporary instance of disequilibria, the localized nature of war effects, and finally its emphasis on macro variables or negligence of the vital and profound impacts of micro variables. It is not difficult to see that the 'irreversibility' and 'irretrievability' that undermines the validity of viewing war as an instance of temporary disequilibria apply equally to other spheres of political, social and cultural spheres. It is at this juncture that the inadequacy of the term 'reconstruction' becomes glaringly clear. As Lake noted in many cases the issues are of 'construction rather than reconstruction, building rather than rebuilding, politically as well as economically' (Lake, 1990, p. 16). Back in 1935 Pareto noted that 'whenever authority, whether in the form of public authority, declines, little states grow up within the state, little societies within society'.[3]

War produces new forms of multilayered and overlapping urbanities, ruralities, and extensive and interactive local, translocal and transnational networks that are constantly reshaping institutions and unleashing new transformative potential. Understanding such transformative potential and its dynamics is an essential step towards building a sound integrated framework for addressing post-war reconstruction.

The dilemma of theorization

Theorizing war and post-war situations continues to present a dilemma for scholars working in this field. Given the over-diversified nature of the communities torn by war in terms of stages of development, initial pre-war socio-economic conditions, the relative strength of the state (failed, collapsed or simply not functioning) and impact of war, the problem of theorization with any level of viability seems to be a formidable task. In other words, given such convoluted and diverse scenes of 'protracted conflicts', what would be the level of general-ization that will not reduce the explanatory rigour and validity of an analytical framework? As some argue, such attempts should be abandoned altogether in favour of case-specific framework for analysis (e.g. African- or Balkan-specific conceptual framework).

Earlier attempts at laying foundations for a general theory of conflict were entrenched in debate based on alleged dichotomies between structural (political, social and economic inequalities) and psycho-cultural (based on 'the beliefs about self, others and behavior'; Utterwulghe, 1999, p. 129), in explaining the root causes of protracted social conflicts. Other debates (Rose, 1993; Warren, 1993) were very much focused on psycho-cultural factors, their relative weight and how they contribute to the emergence of conflicts, the processes of conflict escalation and resolution. Azar (1983, p. 90) suggests that structural victimization affects some groups disproportionately and 'it is at this juncture of actual physical and psychological deprivation that structural victimization burst into hostile and violent action'. Both Rose (1993) and Utterwulghe (1999) were critical of such a characterization of the links between structural and psycho-cultural factors and how the interaction between them leads to conflict. Utterwulghe emphasizes the differences between the structural causes of conflict that emanate from power structures and is defined largely independent of the perception of the participants as opposed to the 'subjective' psycho-cultural factors based on the participants' perception of themselves, others and their respective behaviours. In his opinion, it is the competing interest of groups that constitutes the prime motivation of conflict, subscribing to Rose that the emergence of conflict depends on the relative strength of the social, economic and political organization of the society and the strength of the ties within communities. Thus, if 'economic and political discrimination and weak ties of kinship exist in a society, the chances of conflict between groups will be higher' (ibid., p. 3). Suliman (2000), addressing the environment-driven wars in Sudan, suggests that the struggle for control over resources (land, water and oil) was the direct cause of the second civil war that started in 1983 in Southern Sudan and that of Darfur in Western Sudan. Identity was important but was not the initial and direct cause: '... as war continues identity becomes a material cause of war' (ibid., p. 17), turning from a 'perception' to an 'inversed perception'.

The process of complex interaction between various variables pertaining to both structural and psycho-cultural domains can only be understood within a system that mediates between them through institutions, both state and non-state. In that sense, protracted social conflict can be seen as an ultimate conclusion of a failed development model, not just a failed state. Goldman's (1983) visionary insight on the outcome of the crisis in the former USSR was an early unrecognized contribution to conflict theory and indeed to the institutional approach where links between institutions, institutional change and economic performance occupy a central place. In his 1981 'Peking Lectures', Goldman predicted three possible scenarios for the outcome of the Soviet model crisis. All three scenarios lead to a 'pressure cooker' effect on the political, social and ethnic fabric of the USSR and formerly Centrally Planned Economies.

Recent studies on the transition in Eastern Europe provide an interesting analysis and an extension to Goldman's notion of the mechanisms through which such a 'pressure cooker' effect works.[4] Verdery (1993) examines the linkages between the process of bureaucratic allocation resources and the rise of ethno-national conflicts in Eastern Europe. She suggests that ethno-nationalism was actively reproduced at one or another place in the operation of socialism and in people's daily experience within it. The crux of Verdery's argument is that, as a result of competition for the resources in the 'economy of shortages', in a socialist system based on federal structures in which nationality is the federating principle (USSR, Yugoslavia, CSSR), ethno-national mobilization might occur as it does in other systems in which ethnic grounds influence the distribution of state-allocated goods. Consequently, 'with the fall of the communist party rule, ethno-national resentments flare up in an environment maximally unpropitious to managing them, an environment devoid of any intermediate institution for channeling ethnic sentiment for settling disagreements peaceably or for offering alternative means of expressing one's grievances' (ibid., p. 183). A similar path of explanation was echoed by Melvin (2001, p. 3), who summarizes three studies on regional civil war in the former USSR and concluded: 'The pattern of regional conflicts stems from the form of political modernization that was developed in the region during the twentieth century. Within this programme, national communities were regarded as bearers of political privileges in the ethnically defined republics, which constituted the building blocs of Soviet federation.' As a consequence, 'With little or no alternative civil or regional institutions or identities to counter this narrow focus, conflict for control over the state rapidly emerged, based often on exclusive ethnic and national identities. In the public sector dominated economies of the regions access to the resources of the state (including public employment) also became a strong incentive to attempt to seize control of the state' (ibid., p. 4). Both Verdery's and Melvin's analysis transcends the exploration of the structural foundation that triggers ethno-national conflict to offer an understanding of the sources of instability in post-conflict settlements based on ethno-national representation.

On the initial conditions that trigger civil war, Walter (2004) states: 'Civil wars will have little chance to get off the ground unless individual farmers, shopkeepers, and potential workers choose to enlist in the rebel armies that are necessary to pursue a war, and enlistment is only likely to be attractive when two conditions hold. The first is a situation of individual hardship or severe dissatisfaction with one's current situation, the second is the absence of any nonviolent means for change. An analysis of all civil wars ending between 1945 and 1996 suggests that a higher quality of life and greater access to political participation have a significant negative effect on the likelihood of renewed war' (p. 371). Referring to Rothchild and Groth (1995) and Kauffmann (1996, 1998), Gurr (2000, p. 66) observes that 'cultural identities – those based on common descent, experience, language, and belief – tend to be stronger and more enduring than most civic and associational identities'. Moreover, once war breaks out, ethnic identities and hatred tend to become cemented in ways that make cooperation and coexistence between the groups even more difficult and these are the wars that are likely to recur over time (p. 372).

Broad political economy approaches: an overview

Admittedly, this is a broad category employing a plethora of analytical frameworks and looking at the diverse sites of civil wars at the country, regional and global levels. The range is certainly wide – from Wallerstein's (1989) world-system analysis predicting that after the fall of Berlin 'violence and conflict would proliferate because underdevelopment and regress could no longer be imputed to supposedly inappropriate policies' (ibid., p. 3), to the voluminous literature on how post-cold war loss of aid and conditionality imposed by neo-liberal reform packages speeded up the process of state decay, to the neo-patrimonialism arguing that the root causes of contemporary violence and conflicts are founded in the maladjusted nature and dynamics of internal systems following the end of the cold war and the economic decline that followed the two oil price-hikes of 1973 and 1979 (Clapham, 1989; Allen, 1999; Richards, 1996; Reno, 1997; Bratton and de Walle, 1994, among others). However, all these approaches have much in common in terms of their perspective on the interaction of internal and external variables and what types of processes they trigger as they interact. Central to these studies is the process of state decay and how this process in turn provides an understanding of the emergent post-war political and socio-economic terrain. State survival strategies were greatly shaped by the unfavourable conditions resulting from external shocks and declining aid following the end of the cold war patronage. Thus, in the words of Ahorsu (2004), 'The non-viability of the patron–client relations was additionally exacerbated by the post-cold war loss of aid and other grants and in some situations to the withdrawal of hitherto ideological patronage' (ibid., p. 11). In conclusion, the Neo-patrimonialists see that the institutionalization of the neo-liberal political system, economic reform and economic conditionalities undermined the viability of the patrimonial state, eventually bringing its demise through civil war and prolonged conflict.

Empirical interpretations of civil wars

The most influential empirical studies modelling conflict risk were undertaken by Collier and others (Collier, 2002a, 2002b; Collier and Hoeffler, 2002, 2004; Elbadawi and Sambanis, 2000, 2002). On the economic causes of civil wars, Collier and Hoeffler find more support for the 'greed theory' than they do for the 'grievance theory'. The authors also find that primary commodity exports, large diaspora and high geographical dispersion contribute directly to the risk of civil wars, while male secondary school enrolment rate reduces this risk. Democracy, income inequality, ethnic dominance and polarization were found to be insignificant. Elbadawi and Sambanis suggest that lower dependence on natural resources and income together with failed political institutions were the major factors causing a higher incidence of war. Variables pertaining to ethnic dominance, democracy, geographical dispersion, male secondary school enrolment and religious factionalization were found to be insignificant. A more recent study of the causes for civil wars in Asia and Sub-Sahara Africa (Krause and Suzuki, 2005) found that, in both regions, civil war is less likely to occur with increased economic development and trade openness, while mixed autocratic-democratic regimes raise the likelihood that states will experience civil war. Ethnic and religious factionalization was found to be statistically insignificant in sub-Saharan Africa. However, in Asia ethnic factionalization is likely to cause civil war. According to their findings, a change from a fully institutionalized autocracy to a mixed autocratic-democratic regime is most strongly associated with a greater risk of civil war onset: 'The substantive effect, however, is much greater in Asia than in sub Saharan Africa' (ibid., p. 172). Overall Krause and Suzuki's findings support earlier findings by El Badawi and Sambanis (2000) on the effect of poorly developed political institutions on civil war onset in sub-Saharan Africa. However, Krause and Suzuki, unlike earlier studies, examine oil export dependence specifically rather than all primary commodity dependence. Their findings suggest that sub-Saharan African states with oil dependence are more likely to experience civil war onset than states without it, but the effect does not hold in the case of Asian states.

The critique from within the approach, i.e. empirical literature on civil wars, questions the validity of the death-toll definition of civil war (Sambanis, 2001) and assesses the fragility of a number of empirical results through sensitivity analysis (Hegre and Sambanis, 2005). They concluded that while their results on income and growth agree with Collier and Hoeffler's (2004) theory they 'find that the political variables – institutional instability, incomplete democracy, undemocratic neighbourhood – are very important and increase the risk of civil war' (ibid., p. 25). Additionally they find a weak association between civil war and oil export dependence. Using a sample of sub-Saharan Africa over the 1960 to 1996 period, Gyimah-Brempong and Corley (2005) find that the incidence and severity of civil war incidence has a robust, negative and statistically significant effect on growth rate per capita income but they 'are unable to find any significant relationship between the level of income and the incidence of civil war in SSA countries after controlling for other variables that are correlated with income levels' (ibid., p. 270).

On the 'road map' to reconstruction: a critique

However, the recent World Bank document 'Breaking the Conflict Trap' is increasingly becoming a 'road map' to reconstruction or a universal package for a new 'Washington consensus' on reconstruction. Based on earlier mentioned quantitative studies, 'civil war occurs when an identifiable rebel organization challenges the government military and resulting violence results in more than 1,000 combat-related deaths with at least 5 percent on each side' (Collier *et al.*, 2003, p. 11). The inadequacy and arbitrariness of the operational definition suggested by Small and Singer (Small and Singer, 1982, pp. 214–215) was pertinently noted by Licklider. First, Licklider noted that such a definition lumps together revolutions aiming at controlling the central state apparatus as well as war of session and some coups (Argentina and Bolivia); and second, that international involvement is not included in the definition, a factor that may indeed be critical in determining the course of the war (Licklider, 1995, p. 682). Dismissing all other explanations of civil wars, the report states: 'Those on the political right tend to assume that it is due to long standing ethnic and religious hatred, those in the political centre tend to assume that it is due to the lack of democracy and that violence occurs where opportunities for peaceful resolution of political disputes are lacking and those on the political left tend to assume that it is due to economic inequalities or to deep-rooted legacy of colonialism' (p. 53). 'The key root cause of conflict is the failure of development. Countries with low, stagnant and unequally distributed per capita incomes that have remained dependent on primary commodities for their exports face dangerously high risk of prolonged conflict' (p. 53). Civil war is development in reverse. In simple words, envisioning reconstruction needs is not seen as an outcome of a careful reading of the emerging political, economic and social terrains or of the dynamics produced during the course of civil wars, but with an implicit assumption of a *tabula rasa*.

On the one hand, this is surprising because such links between war and some far-reaching societal transformative processes are part and parcel of early writings on war including founders of the political economy. On the other hand, civil war, in particular a prolonged case, reveals a very complex interactive relation between the root causes of it and the dynamics it produces during the period leading to war itself, during the war and naturally in the period following the cessation of hostilities. Such convoluted terrains of place and space, located within a specific historical and social context, can hardly be captured by a generalized typology. Indeed much of the criticism directed towards Collier *et al.* (Breaking the Conflict Trap) model of conflict emphasized that several variables were left absent and that they downplayed the significance assigned to certain variables while highlighting some previously under-written ones. This is hardly surprising as datasets change and as variables are selected or ignored and constantly redefined. In addition to the fragility of the civil war definition based on a threshold of an absolute number, a basic conceptual error is inevitable because of a hasty lumping together of all incidents of civil war. Their model states that 'In the 1950s many low-income countries were still colonies and colonialism suppressed the possibility of civil war' (ibid., pp. 94–95); however, this is a gross understatement. Let us consider the following cases to see the embedded misconceptualization in the lumping together of all civil wars with a 100-plus death toll.

How can the case of civil wars in the ex-Portuguese colonies (Angola, Mozambique, Guinea Bissau and Cape Verde) be considered anything but an outcome of primitive colonialism (or 'shopkeepers colonialism' as nicknamed by FRELIMO) that did not leave behind any traceable, let alone viable, institutions save a tiny population of the educated? Colonialism suppressed civil wars but laid the foundation for its immediate onset. Even when the colonial administration was compelled to develop civil services, functional to its extractive cost-effective indirect role, in the case of Northern Sudan such administration was hardly capable of suppressing civil war. Civil war started in 1955 before the last battalion of the British army left the country in 1956. Indeed it is a gross understatement to suggest that 'While colonial legacy presumably effects the risk of conflict to some degree, the connection appears to be weaker than the influence of economic performance' (ibid., p. 66).

How can we call the conflicts in Angola and Mozambique 'civil wars' while their quasi-inter-state features overwhelmingly exceed that of their internal causes? Both countries were part of the South African Apartheid regime's destabilization strategy in the region.

Civil wars in countries endowed by non-renewable, mostly lootable[5] natural resources (Angola, Sierra Leone, Zaire-DRC, and Congo) can hardly be seen as independent of the external role of the powerful interests of multinational corporations. This is not merely a case of corruption or transparency. Not one country is divorced from the historical context of a semi-Portuguese colonialism or, in the case of Congo, Belgian colonialism. In that sense, the civil wars in these countries appear to be very much characterized by the 'ripple' effect of the fight between powerful international actors.

One obvious way out of the serious conceptual limitations of the failed state thesis is the static notion embedded in such a discourse. Once state collapse was seen as a process as in the works of Mitchell (1991), Migdal (1988) and Azarya and Chazan (1987). Raeymaekers (2005), stressing the need to go beyond the state collapse thesis, views state collapse not 'so much as an end of the state or breakdown, but rather as a culmination point in the continuous struggle between various forces in society, to control the three core functions that are generally connected to state performance' (ibid., p. 9). These three functions are defined as the state capacity to provide security; its ability to extract and allocate economic resources; and representation of the population inhabiting a fixed territory (ibid., p. 9). But, beyond the critique focusing on the inherent limitations of these modelling exercises, their historical nature and total failure, in order to capture the dynamic processes leading to civil war and triggered by it a central question needs to be raised. The question is not different from Dudley Seers' (Seers, 1972) desperate question: What are we trying to measure? The answer was sufficiently spelled out in the document *Breaking the Conflict Trap* (Collier *et al.*, 2003). The report poses a central question: Why should the World Bank focus on civil wars? The answer is that civil war is development in reverse. Development can be an effective instrument for conflict prevention because civil war is not just a *problem for* but a *failure of* development. The three major findings are: (i) civil wars have highly adverse ripple effects that those who determine whether to start or end it do not take into account; (ii) civil wars differ massively according to a country's characteristics (i.e. economic, political and social); and (iii) feasible international action could substantially reduce the global incidence of war. For the sake of brevity, we will omit the ahistorical dimension of 'civil war as development in reverse' to accept fully the relevance and sequence of the questions. The major task is to prevent through 'right' and 'feasible' packages a reduced incidence of war and, by implication, to create the enabling conditions for 'development' or, in other words, a reconstruction package. This exercise leaves two unanswered questions:

- How can we prevent future incidents of civil wars by seeking to understand the variables that triggered them in the past unless we assume an absolutely static world? Civil wars are triggered by certain variables (i.e. economic, political and social) at a specific historical context, in a given socio-economic setting. But, once civil wars break, they trigger numerous processes that render the initial driving causes irrelevant. This we may call the first instance of an assumed '*tabula rasa*'. In other words what is needed is the reading of the 'now' not the 'before'.

- The second instance of a '*tabula rasa*' is where a fundamental shift takes place in the 'reverse development'. One must ask: how can we envision an alternative development or 'reconstruction' from reading the 'before' and not the 'now' – the emerging political, socio-economic terrains produced by the civil war itself? The longer the civil war, the more radically changed are such terrains. The new blueprints for reconstruction reject any notion of a transformative potential resulting from civil wars. In this respect, the 'breaking of the conflict trap' is consistent. By that we mean that 'Civil war is development in reverse for the countries directly affected in that it generates a huge cost to neighbors and internationally' (ibid., p. 120). This denies any categorical transformative potential and proves true that 'Modern civil war is not an investment in the future: It is not a catalyst for progress' (p. 120).

Towards an alternative reading of conflict and post-conflict situations

Why use the reading of civil wars and the processes that they trigger as an essential starting point? Simply because war itself produces a number of irreversibilities in the social, economic and political structures and institutions because of massive population flow. This massive population flow triggers changes in the structures of the immediate war zones as well as at the receiving ends. The constant production of irreversibilities as civil wars linger is the foundation of the transformative potential: new rural structures; new urbanities; skills lost and gained; changing family dynamics resulting from and shaped by increasing feminization of the labour processes; changes in the institutions and networks; and cultural changes through increased mobility involving losses and gains.

Furthermore, reconstruction is greatly shaped by the process through which the civil war ended and far less, if at all, by the initial conditions that triggered it. Licklider's study of the consequences of negotiated settlement in civil wars presents a very complex scenario and concludes suggesting an answer to his question: 'Why some negotiated settlements in identity wars "stick" and others do not and why victories are followed by mass murder and others aren't?' (Licklider, 1995, p. 687). Crammer (2004) provides a broader approach that transcends such narrow specifications: '... post-conflict and peace-building are not technical projects but are sharply political and largely determined by the coalition of interest groups that dominates the political process. Interestingly, the new blueprint repeatedly emphasizes that each post-conflict situation is distinctive and 'that the general principles are merely broadlines' (Collier *et al.*, 2003, p. 152).

Fearon's (2004, p. 275) work on the duration of civil wars provides a rare insight into the dynamics governing civil wars. Civil wars emerging from coups or revolutions tend to be short civil wars. By contrast 'sons of the soil' wars that typically involve land conflict between a peripheral ethnic minority and state-supported migrants of a dominant ethnic group are on average quite long lived.

In a more formal categorization, Fearon (2004) identified five types of civil wars and some of their characteristics: '(1) Civil wars arising out of coup attempts and popular revolutions are usually quite brief. (2) Anti-colonial wars have also been relatively brief. (3) Civil wars involving rural guerrilla bands typically operating near the state's borders have, with a few interesting exceptions, been remarkably difficult to end (one interesting class of exceptions are the wars arising out of the breakups of the Soviet Union and Yugoslavia, which have been relatively short-lived). (4) Among peripheral insurgencies cases involving 'sons of the soil' dynamics, land or natural resource conflicts between a peripheral ethnic minority and state-supported migrants of a dominant ethnic group, are on average quite long-lived and finally (5) Conflicts in which the rebel has access to funds from contraband such as opium, diamonds, or cocoa. (Ibid., p. 275)

The recent upsurge in civil war-related literature from a single discipline and/or case study of a particular war has certainly enriched our understanding of the various processes that were triggered by war, but as Sambanis (2002, p. 225) rightly noted: 'Political theories of civil war are especially relevant to the analysis of post-war peacebuilding. As economic theories find that the war onset and termination are quite different processes, analysts interested in post-conflict peace must try to understand both the root causes of conflict that drive and intensify conflict after its initiation. Many of these factors and processes are political, such as war-related hostility, institutional failure, loss of government legitimacy, and intensification of previously existing cleavages.

The centrality of civil wars' demographic dynamics

Here, I argue that the most unique feature of civil war is the way in which civil war brings about significant changes in the demographic dynamics of war-torn communities and in particular its civilian population.

The 'irrelevance' of the earlier post-war approaches may in part be explained by some, not so minor, differences between the intra-state wars and internal wars and in particular protracted social conflicts. There are, of course, some obvious similarities in terms of physical destruction, human cost (destruction of the physical productive infrastructure, social infrastructure and physical damage to agricultural lands which brings economic collapse to areas afflicted by war) and the resultant population displacement. Obviously, the site where war is taking place sets serious limitations to such similarities. In an underdeveloped economy as opposed to a developed one, the accumulated technical knowledge and human expertise render such similarities irrelevant.

Protracted social conflicts exhibit rather unique characteristics. Most of these characteristics are related to the relatively longer duration of war, greater involvement of people and institutions and, consequently, greater impact on the shaping of the post-war economy and society. One important manifestation of greater involvement of people in protracted social conflicts is reflected in the associated increase in civilian casualties. While in World War I only 5 percent of war casualities were among civilians, by World War II this percentage increased to 50 percent. By the 1990s, civilian casualities represent 80 percent of war casualities in civil wars (Green, 1999, p. 87). A recent work (Outram, 2002) on the demographic impact of early modern warfare, highlights the strength of links between seventeenth-century civil wars in Europe and current civil wars. On the magnitude of human-civilian losses, Outram wrote: 'The evidence for the demographic losses suffered in Germany was first compiled in 1940 by Gunther Franz, who reviewed a large number of local studies to arrive at his estimate that during the thirty years' war Germany lost 40% of its rural and about 33% of its urban population (Franz, 1979, p. 59), (ibid., p. 248).

A Protestant shoe-mender living in a village near Ulm in Bavaria narrates the events when Duke Bernard of Saxe-Weimar, then in the Swedish service, was fighting for the Protestant cause. In Herberle (1978 [1975], p. 31) cited by Outram (2002, p. 250):

> ... since we did not regard him as our enemy ... we had hidden nothing ... But Duke Bernhard's troops broke into our land and plundered us completely of horses, cattle, bread flour, salt, lard, cloth, linen, clothes and everything we possessed. They maltreated the people, shooting, stabbing and beating a number of people to death ... They set alight the village and burnt down five houses and five stables.

Furthermore, having established the case for the incomparable extensity of civil wars' casualties, compared to those of inter-state wars, a second crucial issue arises: are there conceptually meaningful differences between non-conflict-driven as opposed to war-conflict-driven experiences of displacement? We argue that both patterns are highly similar in spatial characteristics in terms of the direction of flows (within and outside the country) and the final destination at urban sites (shanties and slums) or in neighbouring countries or the global North. Given these similar spatial patterns in diasporic flows, are there meaningful differences that merit a different analytical framework in non-spatial aspects pertaining to the dynamics of such population flows and their political, social and economic ramifications? Earlier studies on failed modernization emphasized that excessive rural to urban migration was driven not by an expanding urban-based industrialization project but by unequal rural to urban exchange, failure to transform agriculture, unsustainable population growth and expectations of better opportunities for jobs and services. Such patterns of urbanization may be termed 'pseudo-urbanization' from a historical comparative perspective, but actually are ushering in a new type of urbanity. The term 'pseudo-urbanization' as well as other similar terms such as 'villagization and ruralization of urban space' are widely used within critiques of modernization discourse to convey an incomplete process. They may aptly fit the description of widely observed patterns of urbanities in largely poverty-stricken 'urban centres' or even in the discourse on relatively affluent rent-supported urbanities in the Middle East. Dismissal of the transformative potential of the so-called 'pseudo-urbanization' is carried to its extreme in Chabal and Daloz's (1999) description of 'African urbanity': 'Urban dwellers appear to replicate the type of informal and personalized social rapport which is a type of informal and personalized social rapport which is the "traditional" African life. City quarters tends to mirror regional and ethnic division. Welfare organizations and even traditional banking "tontines" thrive in part, of course, because they offer some form of (morally binding) social protection which no state institution could equal' (ibid., p. 30).[6] The basic problem with this notion is that it is too narrowly and too directly engaged with the immediacy of these urbanities and thus downplays the serious processes reshaping urban economies and gathering momentum for an alternative political socio-economic arrangement that might mark an alternative route to effective transformation. Todaro's (1969) pioneering work provides evidence of the invalidity of the explanation of rural to urban migration based on income differentials or short-term expectations: '... the decision to migrate should be presented on the basis of long term, more permanent income calculations ... Because expected incomes are defined in terms of both wages and employment probabilities, it is possible to have continued migration despite the existence of a sizable rate of urban unemployment' (1997, pp. 282–283). Taking Todaro's analysis beyond the limited notion of long-term income calculation, rural to urban migration needs to be seen as a process and indeed an irreversible one that perpetuates its momentum, albeit in diverse directions. Such a dynamic involves the creation of a new urban economy and new political and socio-economic dynamics. Ironically both successful and failed modernization projects accelerate the process but naturally with different outcomes and dynamics.

The massive, exodus-like forms of war- and conflict-led urbanization may share some common features with earlier forms of rural to urban migratory processes, but a close look at the salient features of the two migratory processes reveals some fundamental differences in all conceivable aspects in terms of type of survival strategies, demographics and characteristics of migrants, implications of migration to family structures and roles, potential for skills acquisition or loss, and erosion of old institutions and emergence of new ones.

Implications for the study of survival strategies among displaced families

Let us recall some of the main features of non-conflict-related migration (à la Todaro) that took place in the post-colonial state where migration was gradual and based on individual/household decisions: 'typically male-led and in most cases did not involve the migration of entire families; family reunion, when and if it took place, depended largely on rational calculations of the actual or perceived comparative advantages of such a reunion. Consequently, there is a limited occurrence of female-headed households in the receiving centres but a significant one in the sending areas. Substantial increases in the migration of women is related to more recent phases in post-colonial rural to urban migration and limited primarily to Latin America, Southeast Asia, and West Africa' (Todaro 1997, p. 279). 'In fact, women now constitute the majority of the migration stream in Latin America, largely as a result of its relatively advanced state of urbanization compared with other developing countries' (ibid., p. 279). Furthermore, in non-conflict-driven rural to urban migration a gradual development of skills is being shaped largely by the interaction of formal and informal sectors of the urban economy. Some predictable patterns of survival strategies can be identified as opposed to the typical unpredictabilities and discontinuities associated with survival strategies of war-driven population displacement (see Elnur *et al.*, 1996).

Turner (1968) provides the benchmark for such predicted trajectories in rural to urban migration. Drawing primarily upon his experience in and surveys from Lima, Peru, Turner describes three stages in the life cycle of an urban migrant. Each stage involves specific housing conditions, economic status, and location among a city's three concentric zones. As Conway (1985) notes, however, Turner's stages and their subsequent modifications should be thought of as ideal types rather than rigid categories. Turner also argued that a city's three concentric zones differ in definition and composition depending on which of the three sequential 'phases of urbanization' the city has reached.

By contrast, in war-related rural to urban migration one observes a complete departure from such predictable and orderly paths suggested by Turner. Instead, migration is abrupt with a total or significant loss of assets. In severe conditions, a majority of the population lost almost all of their assets at the site of the plight and en route to the final destination (Elnur *et al.*, 1996). Additionally, migration in this case involves the whole family, albeit mostly female-headed, with significant demographic changes as women, children and elderly are disproportionately represented as a result of the increasing feminization of the survival strategies. In other words, the feminization of survival is mostly a pre-displacement feature. In the initial phase of displacement, skill acquisition is gradual and is linked closely to the survival strategies being adapted. War-induced displacement involves a serious trade-off between skill acquisition and the urgency to ensure food security (securing immediate daily requirements) and therefore displaces and most often adopts survival strategies with a quick return. This means there is little or no scope for long-term skill acquisition. In addition, while child labour is usually associated with extreme destitution and family disintegration in non-war situations, child labour becomes a normal survival strategy under conditions of war-induced displacement. In the case of female-headed households, child labour seems to be a more dominant feature of the survival strategy. Male child labour seems to be disproportionately higher as female children assume more responsibilities for domestic work, compensating for the role of working mothers. In cases of both female and male child labour, a higher dropout from schools was observed in female-led households (ibid.).

War-driven population flows and the transformative potential: towards a conceptual framework

The rich theoretical discourses on the population flows–development nexus lend a great support for the notion of transformative potential unleashed by wars. De Hass's (2008) mapping of the frontiers of the migration–development nexus provides an excellent overview of the discourses over the last five decades from the 1950s–1960s optimisms, the 1970s–1980s pessimism laà the neo-Marxists-Structuralists to the subtle optimism of the 1990s based on the new readings provided by the new economics of the labour migration (NELM), migration system theory and transnational migration discourses. De Hass's (2004) extensive theory maps the frontiers of development–migration discourses from the 1950s optimism, 1970s and 1980s pessimism and back to what he termed the 'nuanced' optimism of the 1990s. De Hass, however, highlights the sheer heterogeneity of the accumulated empirical evidence of these studies and the inherent tendency to separate causes and impact of migration which he attributes to the lack of a single theoretical perspective on the migration–development nexus.

Three major contributions seem to dominate current discourses on the migration–development nexus and to a great extent shapes the paradigm shift in this crucial development-related area. These are: the new economics of labour migration (NELM); the migration systems theory; and the transnational perspective.

The starting premise of the NELM theorist is the critique of the basic foundation of the structuralists' pessimism based on a simplified remittance-use of studies that disregarded the community's wide impact of migration. Stark (1978, 1991) emphasized the need to shift emphasis from the individual to the family or the household as the initial basic unit for analysis. The transnational perspective (Castles and Miller, 2003; Faist, 2004; Vertovec, 1999) went further in this direction highlighting the impact of telecommunication revolution in enabling the migrants to foster links with sending communities at unprecedented intensity and hence enabling all forms of flows from financial remittances to ideational ones. Such a notion shares some common assumptions with the migration systems theory both in its early formulation based on rural–urban migration (Mubgunje, 1976), particularly in its emphasis on flows and counter flows of people, goods, services and information as well as its extension to international migration (Portes and Borocz, 1987; Kritz *et al.*, 1992), and the extension of such flows to include ideas and information in addition to goods and capital (as in Fawcett, 1989; Caces, 1992; Lee, 1996). The latter emphasized the tendency for spatially clustered flows where De Hass noted: 'In emigration countries, we often see that particular regions, villages, or ethnic (sub) groups tend to specialize in migration to particular areas, cities, or even city quarters, either within the same country or abroad' (De Hass, 2008, p. 22).

The three approaches are complementary and offer the genesis for a paradigm shift in the migration–development nexus as long as such a paradigm is not about a conclusive one-dimensional outcome. While much of the ground for extreme pessimism of the 1970s and 1980s has been challenged by some empirical results as well as processes triggered by the nature of technical change and globalization, some other equally important basis for that pessimism remains intact. The brain-drain, defined in a broader sense to include what Antonio Gramsci termed the organic intellectual, still holds largely particularly in the case of war-torn communities (Elnur, 2002). One serious problem hindering the coherent articulation of the alternative conceptual framework for analysing the development–migration nexus is the state of interdisciplinarity in making or borrowing from Lipton (1970) problems of transforming multi-disciplinarity into transdisciplinarity.

Going beyond structuralist pessimism and functionalist optimism, the transformation potential offers an alternative framework that leaves open the direction of such transformation. The direction of such transformation is shaped by a multiplicity of factors where both structures and agency matter within the spatial and historical specificity. The intensity and time-compressing nature of technical change tend to support the transformative potential thesis. The direction of such transformation, as was repeatedly stressed, is not readily deducible. In simple terms, migration–development nexuses are determined by both structures and actor perspectives.

New urbanities and new ruralities

An early contribution challenging the thesis of 'over-urbanization' and/or hyper-urbanization was made by Frankman (1971). Frankman suggested that rapid urbanization, even though not matched by similar growth in agricultural output, may still facilitate structural transformation in agriculture: 'I should merely like to suggest that migration from rural areas is not inconsistent with the eventual structural transformation of the agricultural sector. Historically, agricultural development and displacement of rural labour have been closely linked. The relative decline in rural population in Latin America may be a necessary prelude to the creation of an efficient agricultural sector' (ibid., p. 343). The notions of a single homogeneous urban space often associated with the rural to urban dichotomy and the assumption of a unilinear trajectory associated with urbanization have been challenged by several scholars (Bayat, 2002, 2003; Brockerhoff, 2000; Hall and Pfeiffer, 2000; Sassen, 2001; Yeung, 2000). Cohen identified six main features of such rapid urbanization: an unprecedented scale of change; an especially accelerated rate of change; that urbanization appears to have been partially decoupled from economic development; the nature and direction of urban change has become increasingly dependent on the global economy; an on-going convergence in urban and rural lifestyles; and, finally, urbanization is occurring under a broadly different set of demographic regimes (Cohen, 2004, p. 6). War typically accelerates and intensifies the rural influx into cities and urban spaces but most significantly accelerates the processes that produce multi-layered urbanities and ruralities. The question with both conceptual analytical relevance as well as policy dimension is how these new forms of urbanities, without supportive social and economic infrastructures, are going to shape the reconstruction of these communities or the construction of an alternative modernity project.

Wars bring new levels of intensity to the reshaping of the process of capital accumulation, new forms of urban economies, and also new dimensions to urban poverty dynamics. Thus, apart from new war-related forms of economic activities (legal or illegal), old routes of labour and commodity flows are disrupted and new areas created. In the process, new actors come to dominate the new flows. However, the most dramatic structural changes are those associated with the depopulation of rural areas. Despite observed variations, such depopulation can have devastating effects on rural communities as the young and able-bodied leave as combatants or migrants and, with the massive destruction of assets that accompanies war and flight, the incentive for a post-war voluntary return is almost completely eroded. Thus, rural to urban forced migration, under the conditions of war, is associated with higher levels of destitution and carries with it far-reaching implications for post-war repatriation and resettlement. This amounts to an almost complete erosion of incentives to return to rural settings – a return cannot be addressed unless new structures of incentives are created.

The potential for voluntary repatriation, whether urban to rural or rural to rural, is completely lost. Repopulation of rural areas becomes dependent upon a comprehensive package that compensates for lost assets, creating an attractive environment comparable to that of the urban setting, including its deprived shantytowns. Paradoxically, that is not only unattainable given the limited resources but also unforeseeable in the short and medium term.

Hence, post-war situations may pave the way for some deep-going trans-formations of the urban and the rural economy that were not attainable in the pre-war situation. For example, loss of assets may lead to a totally new comparative advantage, based on a new distribution of the population, completely changed consumption habits and lower population densities in rural areas. In some African cases, a shift away from communal ownership of land based on previous and discontinued mixed farming/pastoral activities may prove to be structurally inevitable. Equally, the massive population movement may render communal boundaries of land ownership obsolete. In other words, what has not been achieved by the failed modernization project seems to result from the radical changes brought about by war.

Still, the new dynamics of urban poverty, with their markedly high level of destitution, is effectively blocking the old paradigm of gradual, phased and sequential social mobility à la Turner. Post-war reconstruction and indeed the whole development package needs to be engaged with the new poverty dynamic and the urban economies of informality.

Disruption and continuity

'New urbanization' has to be seen in a different context whereby reproduction of the 'old' communal livelihood in an urban context, albeit in a ruralized shantytown, is not possible. This has further serious implications for the reconstruction of war-torn communities. Even in the event of a successful resettlement or repatriation, a reproduction of the old communal institutions which provided people's means of survival is nearly impossible. Thus, despite illusive similarities between rural areas and the ruralized shantytowns, the 'idealized' continuity and relevance of the indigenous traditions and institutions are seriously undermined. While traditions and institutions may keep their form and rituals remain intact, their functions and hence their relevance are radically changed. This inherent flexibility and adaptability of institutions and traditions is reflected in the diversity of coping mechanisms but also entails a reciprocal interactive relation.

The emancipatory impact of the feminization of the labour process within the household and in particular the feminization of bread-winning cannot be readily asserted or generalized. A number of studies (Xiushi, 1999; McClusky, 1991; Green, 1999) stress the double burden resulting from and the repressive nature of such a dual role. Yet such hasty readings of the impact of the emerging new dynamics may warrant a more careful reassessment and perhaps a reconsideration of the adequacy of analytical tools currently available. A focus on the immediacy of the impact rather than on the potential emancipatory processes is the first step towards producing such an alternative reading. A useful comparison might address the various ways in which changes in family dynamics resulting from population flows impact or trigger societal changes beyond the confines of household or nuclear families.

A departure from such a trend appears in recent works on women's role in post-conflict contexts. According to Manchanda (2001, p. 99) writing about South Asia, 'Conflict opens up intended and unintended spaces for empowering women, effecting structural social transformations and producing new social, economic and political transformations and producing new social, economic and political realities that redefine gender and cast hierarchies.' Referring to Turshen and Twagiramairiy's (1998) work, Meintjes *et al.* (2001, p. 9) draw attention to the need to assess the transformative potential of women's experiences to recognize the historical specificity of wars and the particularities of many groups of women within war-torn communities. However, such gains, concludes Manchanda (ibid., p. 121), 'generated from the trauma of loss are particularly ambivalent, and enabling cultural frameworks and solidarity networks are needed to legitimize them'. Such a need for enabling conditions is particularly crucial because of the reversed pressure, as Hale (2001, p. 139) noted in her study of Eritrean women: 'The pressure on former fighters to revert to traditional norms is a familiar pattern in liberation struggles. In post-war situations the men need the labour of women, but they need to channel into "appropriate" tasks for the common good, such as reconstruction, economic recovery and replenishing the population lost in war.'

One interesting site of such change relates to the reproduction of social classes. In all war-torn communities a phenomenal migration of the educated and middle class has taken place. In places like Sudan, Iraq and Palestine, such massive migration led to the reshaping of the processes reproductive of such classes. As noted in Elnur (2002), elites' reproduction trajectories were radically altered and, with the loss of the inter-generational transmission of knowledge and traditions, continuity and the potential for dynamism have also been lost. Such countries fell or are in the process of falling into a 'low equilibrium trap'. Sudan, Algeria, Iraq, Burundi, Rwanda and Afghanistan represent a wide range of initial conditions and development potential, and are just some illustrative examples. Studying changes in family dynamics offers a powerful lens through which many dimensions of societal change can be observed, particularly when such dynamic changes are inextricably intertwined with urbanization, transmigration and transnationalism. The focus on middle classes and educated elites is vital for considering their quasi model-role in the processes of reshaping societal change and its direction.

Conclusion

War, itself a complete departure from the linear progression of modernity, triggers multiple processes and transformative potentials that cannot be readily predictable. As was shown, war typically produces a number of irreversibilities that render the notion of retrieving old political and socio-economic formations obsolete. The processes perpetuated by massive rural to urban population flows produce new urbanities and ruralities. Concurrently, local, translocal and transnational diasporic experiences usher in new transformative potentials. The realization of such potentials will be the outcome of multiple renegotiations between the various actors involved in war, within various communities and within the household in increasingly diversified and multilayered spaces.

Once 'irreversibility' and 'irretrievability' are admitted, reconstruction becomes a process not only for addressing the structural root causes of protracted social conflict but also for redefining and reconstructing political and social institutions. A good example of the need to transcend the pre-war situation was given by Attas and Licklider (1999): '… it is misleading to talk about political "reconstruction" after civil war. Even if it could be done, there is no point in reconstructing the situation that produced war in the first place. Instead, the new leadership is faced with a problem of constructing a political unit which can transform conflict so that they can be routinely handled without large-scale conflict' (ibid., p. 51).

This serves as a pre-requisite for evolving mechanisms that ensure the equitable distribution of power and resources and for enhancing the participation of state and non-state actors in the process of consolidating peace and creating resources for trust building and for inter-community reconciliation. In this sense, protracted social conflict can be seen as an ultimate conclusion of a failed development model, not merely a 'failed state', and its resolution into a sustainable peace can be seen as essentially an alternative model for development. In other words, the post-war environment cannot be seen as peace, narrowly defined as a 'cessation of hostilities', but must rather be viewed as a transition to sustainable peace, broadly defined and based on a development model that addresses past structural causes of conflict. Additionally, in the post-war transition phase, we must provide sound political and social mechanisms for conflict deterrence and resolution; or, in fewer words, a sustainable development model based on sustainable social institutions and structures.

Part 2
The unmaking of Sudan

3   The failed modernity I

The early phase of the crisis (post-colonial to 1989)

This chapter and the following one focus on the processes that led to the unmaking of Sudan. The focus is on two periods of active state intervention in the economy and society which radically transformed the process of capital accumulation. This is not to deny a certain continuity in the post-colonial policies of the Sudanese state across the civilian–military divide, notably in preserving the lopsided development model, but rather to emphasize that the two authoritarian regimes of Nimeiri (1969–1985) and the NIF-dominated regime (1989–2004) stand out distinctively in the crisis-making process.[1] Both regimes, beyond the sheer relative time length (totalling 32 years over the 1969–2004 period), brought about irreversible structural transformations that undermined the relatively 'stable' and 'manageable', albeit stagnant, post-colonial structures of accumulation and social reproduction with its predictable and manageable flows of population, relatively sustainable mechanism of extraction of surplus and a great deal of stability in the relative efficiency of the state capacity despite regular civilian–military shifts in state control.

Hence, if Nimeiri's period of 1969–1985 is associated with crisis making, the Islamist-dominated regime of 1989–2004 triggered processes that brought the crisis to its ultimate conclusion. Chapter 2 maintains that the seeds of this crisis were sown largely in the 1970s. The main emphasis is on the role of the state and its relative autonomy because of its direct bearing on the central theme of this discussion. The chapter asserts that the accumulation crisis which became apparent in the late 1970s was fundamentally different from that of the early post-independence of the 1960s, with respect to its breadth, severity and the role of various actors in the process of capitalist accumulation (state, foreign and indigenous capitalism).

A comprehensive review of the 1960s accumulation crisis is beyond the scope of this chapter; it is important, however, to point out that the accumulation crisis in agriculture and the early exhaustion of the 'easy' phase of import substitution industrialization brought a contradictory dimension to the relationship between indigenous capital and foreign capital.[2] On the one hand, foreign trade and finance, a domain of foreign capital, were obvious targets for indigenous capital control. On the other hand, because of its relative weakness, partnership with foreign capital was indispensable in manufacturing. This contradictory nature of the relationship explains, to a great extent, the hesitant policies of the post-colonial state in the field of indigenization of finance and foreign trade activities. More importantly, it gives coherence and logic to post-1969 policy changes.

The period from 1960 onwards is especially different from the preceding post-independence years.[3] In particular, it marks the intensification of the struggle over the future path of development in the country. A disjunction in the political and socio-economic spheres with a complete change of emphasis and orientation occurred. External factors played a far more important role in the shaping of national policies and strategies. We may broadly divide the 1969–1983 period into three distinct blocks as follows:

(1) The 1969–1971 period

This brief period stands out as a very distinct phase because a new coalition of social forces came to play a decisive role in the economy and society. The polarization and intensification of the struggle within the new coalition over the future path of development was very pronounced. This struggle came to a dramatic conclusion following the defeat of the 19th July coup led by the left-wing (mostly members of the communist party) members of the 'Free Officers Organization' which had initiated the May 1969 coup d'etat.

(2) The 1972–1976 period

The period after 1972 witnessed a sharp departure from the declared 'socialist' oriented policies of the preceding period. This was a period of transition. On the one hand, it coincided with a process of political hegemony initiated by the military/civilian bureaucratic bourgeoisie (basically military but in fairly significant alliance with the civilian one), reorientation of the regime's policies and the adoption of its new socio-economic programme, the Interim Action Programme, promulgated in 1972. On the other hand, this process of reformulation and preparation of a more 'conducive' atmosphere (involving denationalization and de-confiscation, suppression of trade unions and introduction of new investment acts) was preparation for the next period, the 'open-door policy'.

(3) The 1976–1983 period

The emphasis of the post-1976 period was on the role played by foreign capital within the broad framework of a tripartite coalition. In examining the Sudanese version of the Egyptian 'infitah' policy, one must take into account the complex interaction of both internal and external forces which contributed to the policy in the first place, the impact of the 1973 oil price rise and the need for the recycling of OPEC surplus both regionally and internationally. In relation to the Sudan, conceptual frameworks such as the 'Afro-Arab Cooperation', 'Pan-Islamic Solidarity' and 'Pan-Arab Strategy' must also be considered. The latter is related directly to the food strategy of the major Arab oil exporters, in which the

Sudan figures as the most important partner in what was largely known as 'The Breadbasket Strategy'. From 1978, however, a new phase can be discerned within the open-door policy. The direct and indirect reshaping of the policies and plans were largely a result of pressures from multi-national donors and investors primarily through the IMF and the IBRD.

The chapter addresses only briefly the period of 1983–1989 as a period of crisis management through its three political phases: the end year of the authoritarian Nimeiri's regime, the transition to democracy of 1985–1986 and the short-lived third parliamentary democracy of 1986–1989. The shrinking state (declining extractable surplus, dwindling external support and strong pressures from IFIs and other donors) was merely pursuing a survival strategy that neither halted the crisis nor dramatically reshaped it.

The struggle over the future path of development 1969–1971

As noted earlier, the May 1969 coup initiated a new phase in the post-independence era. The declared 'Socialist Oriented' policies of the new political alliance were solidified in the Five Year Plan (FYP) (1970/71–/1974/75) adopted by the regime. The FYP was to a great extent a transitional stabilization programme emphasizing capacity utilization rather than new initiatives in commodity production and infrastructure. It advocated a selective, gradual de-linking of the economy from the world market through the diversification of external economic relations, reduction of import intensities throughout the economy, reduction of unnecessary consumption, an increase in the level of self-sufficiency in food and manufactured mass consumption goods and increased emphasis on internal resource mobilization through budgetary surpluses. Furthermore, the FYP aimed at increasing the provision of basic needs of material products and social services. The plan envisaged a 7.6 per cent annual growth rate of GDP, compared to the 4.9 per cent seen in the previous five years. Commodity production was planned to increase by 65 per cent, of which agriculture was to increase by 65 per cent, livestock by 75.5 per cent and manufacturing by 57.4 per cent (FYP, vol. 1).

The plan foresaw a substantial increase in the share of the state (together with cooperatives in the new planned expansion in commodity production). However, a few months after its adoption, the struggle for and against the FYP's implementation became the most important feature of the 1969–1971 period. This largely was due to the intensification of contradictions within the new political coalition. The FYP development model was gradually abandoned as new alliances started to emerge.

Nationalization/confiscation measures

In May 1970, successive measures of nationalization and government-imposed confiscation began. The measures affected all foreign and nationally owned private banks, export/import firms and a number of key manufacturing units.

Foreign-owned insurance companies were banned and only Sudanese-owned private insurance companies were allowed to work.

Except for the total control over the banking system, these measures did not follow any systematic pattern, neither in firm size (small hotels and restaurants to giant foreign trade companies, small workshops to large-scale manufacturing units), nor in terms of ownership (mainly naturalized Sudanese and foreign-owned enterprises were nationalized, few were not). Furthermore, few relatively large indigenous-owned enterprises were confiscated (e.g. Osman Salih Group) primarily due to political motivations.

It would be wrong, however, to conclude that the measures were limiting the growth of indigenous capital because of the manner in which they were implemented or because only a few indigenous entrepreneurs, albeit the largest ones, were affected. What matters is the overall impact on indigenous capital, not on a segment of it or a few of its members. Hence, when the measures are viewed from this perspective, one must conclude that the nationalization and confiscation measures realized substantial 'actual' and 'potential' indigenization. For the national bourgeoisie, save the few affected by the measures, there was a clear net gain giving them full control of the insurance industry over which they previously had held little power, allowing them to share with the state the formerly foreign-dominated foreign trade and eliminating their direct competitors in wholesale trade (i.e. the naturalized Sudanese). Furthermore, the measures were taken at the very time the dominant right wing and 'Nasserist' oriented majority of the revolutionary council were engaged in working out a formula for compromise with various segments of the national bourgeoisie and when the anti-left campaign of repression had already started.[4] The significance of these measures should also be seen in terms of enhancing the state's allocative capacity and/or state patronage. During the colonial period this was closely related to state's capacity to allocate land as in the case of religious leaders (in particular, the Ansar and Khatmiyyah and, to a lesser extent, Hindiyyah orders) and tribal leaders.[5] In the post-colonial economy the foreign trade and financial sectors were the commanding heights of the economy; the import and finance activities were almost exclusively controlled by foreign companies and expatriate communities, and export activities accommodated both indigenous and foreign business. Thus, state control over these activities enabled Nimeiri's regime to have direct access to resources in the immediate post-nationalization years and to shape and reshape the accumulation process, marginalizing or augmenting the fall and rise of various business activities.[6]

Studies on this period tend to overemphasize the negative impact of these measures on the private sectors (ILO, 1976; Nimeiri, 1976; Suliman, 1975). It is true that their arbitrary character, particularly that of the confiscation measures, greatly disturbed the business community. However, this should not overshadow the fact that these measures objectively opened new areas for the expansion and acceleration of the process of capital accumulation to the Sudanese bourgeoisie. Thus by its action, the state demonstrated an ability to realize the potential of effective indigenization of capital even beyond the extent of the most radical

'Sudanization' of the 1960s. Therefore, these measures did not contradict the regime's attempt to work out a formula for national compromise with the major segments of the Sudanese bourgeoisie. As shown earlier, the state actions resulted in net gains for indigenous capital as well as an expansion of its own sphere of accumulation through direct control over some enterprises and the banking system. These gains were predominantly at the expense of foreign capital. By enhancing its accumulative and locative capacity, the state had effectively strengthened its mediatory role among various segments of capital.

The consolidation of the leading role of the bureaucratic bourgeoisie

The 1972–1976 period

The defeat of the 19 July 1971 movement represents a decisive stage in the advent and consolidation of the leading role of the bureaucratic bourgeoisie in Sudan. A referendum establishing one-man rule was followed by the first congress of the only legal party, the Sudanese Socialist Union (SSU). The civil war in the South came to an end with the signing of the Addis Ababa Accord in 1972. Direct repression of the trade union movement was followed by new legislation curbing trade union activities and undermining their independence. However, at the propaganda level, the regime continued to advocate 'Socialism' in almost all basic documents. A leading public sector role was still stressed but with a different formulation that incorporated national and foreign private capital (Programme of Action, 1972, p. 3) and redefined respect to its investment pattern. In August 1973, the first batches of confiscated firms were restored to their owners (ACR, 1973/74, p. B113). Simultaneously, settlement was reached with a number of foreign firms affected by the nationalization measures but at much more generous terms than originally promised.

The alternative plan: programme for action and the AFYP

In November 1972, the newly established SSU adopted a new programme for social and economic development known as the Interim Action Programme. This programme was to redirect policy and replace the FYP. The overly broad and ambitious character of the programme can only be explained by its origin as a political programme of the newly established ruling party.

The programme was scaled down to an Amended Plan (AFYP) that replaced the FYP. The AFYP introduced new national priorities and envisaged a greater total investment (L.S. 666.2 million as compared to the L.S. 215 million of the FYP). This substantial increase in the planned investment reflected both the impact of national and international inflation but also the scale of intended investment. The AFYP, in this respect, bears no resemblance to the capacity utilization-oriented FYP. Sectoral allocations were sharply reversed; for example, transport and road building were assigned top priority rather than the FYP's emphasis on rail usage. Horizontal expansion in agriculture replaced intensification and capacity expansion replaced capacity utilization in agro-based industries. The AFYP reflected the over-promising nature of a political programme especially characteristic of the newly established 'One Party System' as well as the high expectations aroused by the positive response of Western and Arab donors to the dramatic political shift post-July 1971.

Furthermore, the most important departure from the FYP occurred with respect to the planned role of the public sector. The strong interventionist policy of the FYP was greatly diluted. The public sector's investment priority was shifted from directly productive sectors to the provision of infrastructure. This shift coincided with a gradual process of relaxation of state control over foreign trade in favour of greater shares for the private sector in imports and public/private sector joint ventures in exports (e.g. gum arabic, tea, coffee and oil seeds).

This shift from the FYP interventionist policies was simultaneously accompanied by the weakening of the planning machinery and its role. Thus in May 1973, the Ministry of Planning was reduced to a department among other measures aiming at the relaxation of the state's central supervision and control (see Abel-Wahab, 1976, p. 230).

Encouragement of investment legislation

A further step to restore 'business confidence' was taken in the area of investment legislation. In 1972, a new Act replaced the 1967 Industrial Investment Act. The new Act introduced priority-linked eligibility criteria for granting concessions. Projects utilizing local raw materials and located in rural areas, especially those of strategic importance, were given maximum concessions. In the area of foreign investment, the Act preserved the main features of its predecessors but introduced more precise and generally stronger guarantees against nationalization and recommended more favourable compensation should nationalization become inevitable.

In 1974, the Act was once more revised. The original five-year tax holiday was extended to ten, and the rural areas criterion was dropped. However, the most important change was the extension of concessions to non-manufacturing activities (i.e. tourism, transport and storage) and 'any other activity that may help to serve and develop the national economy as decided by the minister' (the Act, section 5, p. 2). This change in the incentive structure was said to be motivated by the desire to induce the private sector to maximize its investment activities in various sectors of the economy. It was not considered that such a change would likely result in the weakening of the state-capacity to channel private investment away from its traditional pattern (housing, commerce and finance).

Finally, this enormous package of plans, legislation, policy prescriptions and programmes not only signified an enhancement and consolidation of the leading role of the ascending bureaucratic bourgeoisie but also a retreat in favour of the private sector, composed of mainly merchant capital, in the active search for a formula to broaden its social bases of support. To them and to potential foreign investors, the state had created in a remarkably short period substantial concessions and created a more 'conductive investment climate' through the repression of trade union activities, weakening of planning machinery and shifting the state's investment emphasis from commodity-producing sectors to infrastructure.

The post-1976 period: the open-door policy and the tripartite coalition

Largely, the 1972–1976 period represented a transition to an open-door policy. The complicated process of the gradual 'liberalization' of the economy and the building up of a new political alliance eventually evolved into a fully fledged open-door policy. Under this policy, the major emphasis was on the role to be played by foreign capital within a broad framework of a tripartite coalition. The partners, represented through their capital, included the Sudanese state-, indigenous- and foreign-capital (mostly Arab). In examining the Sudanese version of the 'Infitah' (open-door policy), we have to take into consideration the interaction of external and internal factors. At the external level we recognize two phases:

- The first phase was closely linked to the impact of the 1973 oil price boom and the pattern of recycling Arab financial surplus internationally, regionally and most importantly in relation to the Sudan. The last was closely linked to the food security strategy of the major Arab oil-exporting countries.
- The second phase related to the direct and indirect re-orientation of the policies and plans as a result of pressures exerted by multinational donors and investors. From mid-1978 onward, the IMF policy package became the single most important external factor shaping policy formulation at the national level.

At the internal level, a great deal of preparation with regard to the 'conductive' atmosphere of the open-door policy had already taken place in the 1972–1976 period. However, further concessions for national and foreign private investors were made. These included:

- Abolition of the state monopoly over certain export/import activities. Extension of institutionalized concessions to investment in agriculture in 1976.
- Streamlining of incentives across sectors (the Unified Investment Act of 1980), which allowed the foreign and national private sectors to establish commercial banks.
- At the political level, 'reconciliation' allowed the regime to incorporate the most influential groups of the rightist opposition.

This open-door policy was further encouraged by the apparent preference for national organizations over regional ones. By 1980, of nine total Arab development organizations only four were regional. Fifty-four per cent of the $24 billion total authorized capital for national and regional finance organizations was provided to the five national organizations. Sixty per cent of the paid-up capital and their share in the total cumulative finance operations of all Arab regional and national development organizations amounted to $14,281 million, i.e. 62.4 per cent of the total (AMF, 1982, p. 68). However, in the same period (i.e. 1973–1980), Arab national and regional organizations contributed only 33.6 per cent to the total aid by Arab oil-exporting countries to LDCs. Therefore, aid from national development organizations amounting to approximately $37 billion represented 87 per cent of the total aid given by Arab oil-exporting countries to the LDCs during the 1973–1980 period. Thus, it is evident that direct national control – not regional – has been the most decisive element in aid distribution.

Furthermore, Saudi Arabia, Kuwait and the United Arab Emirates contributed 39 per cent, 24.3 per cent and 18 per cent, respectively, to the official aid from the Arab oil-exporting countries to the LDCs during the 1973–1980 period. Saudi Arabia surpassed Kuwait, which had been the single most important donor until then. Thereafter, aid from Arab oil-exporting countries in the post-1973 period was somewhat controlled nationally but dominated by only three countries and, given the Saudi political dominance over the Gulf Oil-sheikhdoms, controlled de facto by one country.

In the context of the food security strategy of the leading Arab exporting countries, the Sudan was seen as the country with the greatest potential. Post-1971 political changes, the geo-political importance of the country and its historical and cultural ties with the Arab peninsula, all argued for pursuing this 'breadbasket strategy'. The strategy was elaborated in two long-term plans: first, the Basic Programme for Agricultural Development (1976–1985) and, second, the Food Investment Programme (see AFESD, 1976).

The breadbasket strategy

The Basic Programme for Agricultural Development (1976–1985) drawn up by the Arab Fund for Economic and Social Development (AFESD) was by far the most comprehensive formulation of food security strategy. The document advocated an 'Integrated Programme Approach' as opposed to the 'Project-by-Project' method because of the need to incorporate and ensure a functioning infrastructure and supporting services (AFESD, 1976, p. 2).

The first ten years of the programme envisioned an increase in production ranging between 100 per cent to 150 per cent for most major crops and livestock commodities, with the exception of sugar (700 per cent increase) and wheat (500 per cent increase). This would make possible a three-fold increase in the volume of oil seed and its products and Arabic gum exports, and a ten-fold increase in the volume of maize and meat exports. Exports of raw cotton were expected to be maintained at the base year level (i.e. 1972/73) while 20 per cent of the total lint production was to be exported as yarn and textiles (ibid. pp. 6–7). Realization of these targets was expected to enable the Sudan to provide the Arab region with 42 per cent of its edible oil, 20 per cent of its sugar and 15 per cent of its wheat imports.

Table 3.1 The basic programme: investment composition in million US dollars

Category and sector	No. of projects		Total cost		per cent of total cost			
	Prog. BP^1	1st Plan FIP^2	Prog. BP	1st Plan FIP	Prog. BP	1st Plan FIP	BP	FIP
I: Commercially viable project:								
– Crops	9	6	385	170			17	22
– Livestock	9	5	240	100			10	13
– $ABIs^3$	11	4	355	90			16	11
– Transport	2	2	63	40			3	5
Sub-total	**31**	**17**	**1043**	**400**			**46**	**51**
II: Traditional agriculture:								
Crops/forestry	9	6	376	149			16	19
Livestock/fish.	10	4	169	22			8	3
Agro-industries	6	1	28	10			1	1
Sub-total	**25**	**11**	**573**	**181**			**25**	**23**
III: Infrastructure:								
Transport	23	17	411	111			18	15
Water resource/ Hydro-electric	6	1	122	5			5	1
Other indust.	5	5	78	58			3	7
Support	10	10	60	25			3	3
Sub-total	**44**	**33**	**671**	**199**			**29**	**26**
Total	**100**	**61**	**2287**	**780**			**100**	**100**

Source: The basic programme for agricultural development in the Democratic Republic of the Sudan 1976, The Resume.

Notes
1 BP = basic programme for agricultural development 1976–1985.
2 FIP = the first investment plan of BP 1976–1981.
3 Sugar industries are included in crops.

Thus, the programme aimed at a vast expansion of crop and livestock production and simultaneously an expansion of the agro-processing capacity in sugar, edible oil, textiles and animal fodder. This was to be attained by establishing 100 projects estimated to cost L.S. 2300 million at 1975 prices (i.e. US $6 billion), with the foreign exchange component representing 65 per cent of the total cost (ibid. p. 9).

Table 3.1 shows the distribution of the various projects of the programme as well as the estimated costs. The 100 proposed projects were classified into three major categories in the following manner:

1   Commercially viable projects: these are the projects which were considered suitable for joint ventures between the local and foreign private sectors, the Sudanese government and other Arab states. There are 31 projects in

this category with a share of 46 per cent of the total estimated cost of the programme.

2   Product-oriented and agro-industrial projects: the programme assumes, because of their lower return to investment, that they need concessional loans for their finance. They comprise 25 projects, a 25 per cent share of the total cost of the programme.

3   Supporting infrastructure and services: like the previous category, this requires concessional loans with a small element of grants. It includes a wide array of physical and institutional infrastructural adjustments (transports, water resources, grain storage, research, etc.). The 44 projects in this category were expected to absorb 29 per cent of the total estimated cost of the programme.

Most of the projects of the first plan were expected to be completed within the first six years, and on the fourth year of the first plan a second was to be formulated. This was to be composed of the on-going projects of the first plan and the rest of the programme projects.

The breadbasket strategy's frontal attack concentrated its wave of investment on four areas of material production:

1   Mechanized rain-fed farming as the main thrust for agricultural expansion with the aim of extending the area in which this is practised from under 12 million feddans to 71 million feddans.

2   A three-fold increase in the irrigation area which would raise total production to 9 million feddans.

3   Expansion of modern cattle husbandry through 'fattening centres'.

4   Simultaneous expansion of the ABIs to match the processing needs for the additional agricultural productions.

Thus, the breadbasket strategy preserved the continuity of the post-colonial development strategy based on the horizontal expansion of agriculture with top priority assigned to export-oriented products, particularly in the central and eastern regions. It did not advocate a transformation of 'traditional' agriculture, but it penetrated it through dispersed patches of the market economy (rain-fed mechanized farming) and through the modernization of livestock production (modern fattening centres and more efficient marketing). In effect, it was based on the accelerated expansion of large-scale capitalist farms in crop production. Livestock production was neglected except for marketing.

The basic assumption of the breadbasket strategy was the availability of huge untapped, potentially cultivable land in the neighbourhood of 200 million feddans (i.e. 76 million hectares) and an extremely favourable man-to-land ratio. However, serious technical, economic, ecological and social limitations to this estimated potential have been raised (FAO, 1973; Farah, 1983; Ali, 1982; Kiss, 1977; O'Brien, 1984).[7]

Expansion in manufacturing was tightly linked to downstream processing. It did not address itself to the problems of structural deficiencies of the manufacturing sector nor to its integration with the rest of the economy. The strategy's major thrust was to maximize agricultural exports (mainly food) directed to the Arab countries, thus consolidating the traditional position of the Sudan in the international division in labour and in the Arab region with 'an increasing risk of the Sudan of becoming a secondary periphery' (Osterdiekhoff, 1983, p. 25).

The Six Year Plan (SYP): 1977/78–1982/83

The Six Year Plan reflected the major aspects of the breadbasket strategy. The SYP was formulated as the first phase of a long-term plan (the 18-year perspective plan for 1977/78–1994/95). The particular features of the long-term macro-economic projection established by the document were:

> A sustained economic growth of 8.5 per cent that concentrates on food production, expanding industrial capacity in import substitution and agricultural export processing.

> 'An unprecedented reliance on massive capital funding in recognition of the crucial role of external capital in accelerating the economy's rate of growth'.
> (SYP, 1977, p. 25)

> Regional integration and transformation of the 'traditional' sector.

> An open and outward looking economy policy, whereby Sudan would benefit from Arab and non-Arab external capital and appropriate production technology and contribute a much higher level of primary and processed goods and agricultural commodities needed by Arab capital-exporting countries and the world at large.
> (SYP, 1977, vol. 1. p. 25)

With its target for annual growth rate of 8.5 per cent of the GDP over the 18 years and 7.5 per cent during its first phase of six years, the planned sector growth rates and the anticipated structural changes in the economy are shown in Table 3.2.

Major policy changes

Apart from the SYP, the second major accommodation at the national level for the breadbasket strategy was in the area of investment legislation. In direct response to its prerequisites, a new Act for the development and promotion of agricultural investment was declared in 1976. The main aim of this Act was to encourage 'national and foreign capital to invest in the field of agriculture for realization of the objectives of agricultural development' (The 1976 Act, p. 145). These objectives were identified as self-sufficiency, export orientation, diversification, equitable development among the country's regions and qualitative integration between crop and animal production. The Act provided incentives similar to others in manufacturing, economic services etc., in tax holidays, exemption from customs duties on machinery and equipment, reduced rates for power and transport,

Table 3.2 Planned growth rates and structural changes

Sector	% contributed to GDP (base year)[1]	% contributed to GDP 1982–1983	Annual growth rate	% contributed to GDP 1994–1995	Annual growth rate
Agriculture	39	37	6.5	33.0	7.1
Manufacturing	9	10	9.5	15.5	11.4
Public utilities	1	1	8.0	2.2	11.3
Construction	4	5	9.0	7.4	11.4
Transportation	6	6	7.5	8.5	10.4
Commerce/finance and real estate	24	24	8.0	24.4	8.3
Government and other services	11	11	7.5	9.0	7.0
GDP at market price	100	100	7.5	100.0	8.5

Source: SYP vol. I, pp. 27, 32 and 35.

Note

1 Actual 1976/77 data were not available – the plan maintained the structural relationship of 1974/75.

protection of local agricultural products and identical clauses on foreign investment rights and duties. Additionally, it provided a 25-year grant of land, subject to renewal, and preferential facilities linked to the location of the project.

By issuing the agricultural Act of 1976, the state completed a process of streamlining incentives and privileges across the different sectors of the economy. In 1980, the various investment Acts were replaced by a single investment Act (The Encouragement of Investment Act), which eliminated the disparities in the incentives provided by various investment Acts. Before 1973, only the manufacturing sector enjoyed institutionalized incentives, then the Encouragement of Investment Act expanded incentives to economic services. It encouraged investment in agriculture, animal production, mining, industry, transport, tourism, storage and housing fields and any other economic milieus prescribed by the Ministerial Committee (Section 5, article (i), The Act, 1980, p. 86).

Several motives seem to have stimulated the 1980 changes in investment legislation:

- The drive to accelerate the inflow of foreign investment, particularly Arab investment, at a time when expectations were again high following the second oil price boom of 1979 and in response to the recommendations of the Sudan–US Business Council.
- To match the Sudan's investment legislation with the Unified Inter-Arab Investment Convention signed earlier by the Sudan. The convention established the Kuwait-based, 'Inter-Arab Investment Guarantee Corporation' as a guarantor of Arab investment at the regional level. The 1980 investment Act provided special arrangements for the settlement of investment disputes concerning 'Arab' capital.

- Finally, motives arising from the fierce competition between Arab capital-importing countries cannot be underestimated. The Sudan has to compete with countries like Egypt, Tunisia and Morocco with far more conducive conditions for attracting foreign investment. This is perhaps why the Sudanese legislator was 'overgenerous' in the provision of incentives and privileges (see for example Egyptian Law No. 43 of 1974 concerning investment of Arab and foreign funds in Gillespie, 1984, pp. 167–189, and other responses in Ajami, 1979, pp. 96–141, on the Arab response to foreign investment).[8]

The streamlining of incentive structures across various sectors of the economy, which started in 1973, was finally completed by the 1980 Act. Given this, it can be argued that the pattern of foreign and national private-sector investment would be decided by the free play of market forces. This certainly weakened the planners' capacity to influence investment patterns for foreign and national capital, except for that of Arab vis-à-vis non-Arab.[9]

Following the adoption of the 1980 investment Act, foreign and Sudanese joint venture banks were allowed to operate in the country. Thus in January 1980, three Islamic joint venture banks opened. These were funded mostly with Saudi capital. Five more Islamic banks were licensed by 1982, together with six subsidiaries of foreign ones. The monopoly of the Sudan Oil Seed Company (a private/public joint venture company) over exports was repealed by 1980. Private oil seed exporters were allowed to compete with the company. Foreign capital was allowed again into the previously Sudanized insurance industry. These measures together with the streamlining of incentives across sectors amount to a deliberate policy of weakening the state's capacity to channel national and foreign private investment and the state's capacity to accumulate (in banking and foreign trade in particular).

This policy illustrates a desire to maximize the inflow of foreign capital and to stimulate greater participation by the national private sectors. Additionally, it is a reflection of the accommodation processes characteristic of the different and often conflicting interests of the partners in the tripartite coalition.

The economy: an overview

On the basis of national account data, growth rates and subsequent percentage shares of various sectors in gross domestic product are given in Table 3.3. It should be noted that, in the absence of a suitable GDP deflator, the formula suggested by the Department of Statistics for constructing a deflator using available price indices was followed.

While services and some branches of secondary production exhibited relatively high growth rates, primary production growth can only be characterized by stagnation and decline. The average growth rate of agriculture over the 1970–1983 period was one third that of the population (3.2 per cent) and GDP (3.2 per cent) growth rates.

Table 3.3 Growth rate and percentage share of various sectors 1970/71–1982/83 (GDP constant 1970–1971 factor cost)

	Compound growth rates		% share in GDP				
	1970/71 1978/79	1978/79 1982/83	1970/71 1982/83	1970/71	1970/71	1978/79	1982/83
1) Agriculture	1.2	0.03	1.1	44.3	37.6	34.4
2) Mining	−6.0	13.1	0.0	0.3	0.1	0.2
3) Manufacturing	2.5	5.0	3.3	7.6	7.0	7.7
4) Construction	6.2	6.1	6.2	3.5	4.3	4.9
5) Public utilities	−2.3	9.2	1.4	2.5	1.6	2.0
6) Transport/Storage	9.3	−2.8	5.1	7.6	11.7	9.5
7) Commerce	8.4	5.7	7.4	13.7	19.5	22.2
8) Banking, insurance and finance	6.4	4.1	5.5	5.6	6.1	6.5
9) Public admin and defence	−0.1	3.4	−1.0	13.1	9.8	10.2
10) Dom. services	−6.5	2.0	−5.9	7.5	2.5	2.5
11) GDP at factor cost	3.6	2.3	3.2	100.0	100.0	100.0

Source: Department of Statistics – national account section, based on Appendix 6.1 and the note on GDP accounts and estimation of the GDP deflator.

Notes
Based on estimate (see Elnur, 1998); Separate account for this sector, available from 1972/73 only figures do not add to 100 due to rounding.

Policy formulation-related bottlenecks accounted for a large number of the disparate growth rates of various sub-sectors of the economy. The clearest case was that of public utilities, especially electricity, which declined rapidly during 1970/71–1978/79. The high growth rate of the transport and storage sub-sectors was a result of the policy shift from an emphasis on the railway's capacity for rehabilitation (FYP) to road-building in the amended plan (AFYP).

However, the emphasis on capacity expansion in both commodity and non-commodity production sectors was common across sectors in post-1970 policies. Invariably, this led to slow or negative growth rates in sub-sectors because of under-investment in the existing production capacities at the beginning of the 1970s.

The performance of the agricultural sector: 1970–1983

The performance of the largest sector of the economy, agriculture, is better understood in relation to its heterogeneous structure. The agricultural sector can be divided into three sub-sectors: irrigated, mechanized farming and traditional-subsistence. Except for the traditional forms of *sagia* (ox-driven water-wheel) and basin irrigation, whose importance was declining rapidly, the whole irrigation sector was and is dominated by the state. Both mechanized (i.e. gravity and pump irrigation) and flood irrigated schemes were organized as partnerships between the government and tenant farmers. Along with the dramatic change in the agrarian policy in the early 1970s, the state's role had been reduced to the performance 'pioneering' functions that supplemented rather than competed with private capital (Adam, 1983, p. 62). By the early 1980s, the private sector controlled over 92 per cent of the mechanized farming area.

The performance of the sub-sectors of agriculture are presented in Table 3.3 and Appendix II. Three distinct periods in relation to growth patterns of output, cropped areas and yields can be identified. Each period corresponds to a certain set of policies emphasizing horizontal or vertical expansion, relative neglect of or importance given to a particular sub-sector, weather-related factors, and the long-term impact of the differential growth rates of various sub-sectors on the performance of the sector as a whole. The three distinct periods are:

- The 1965–1973 period: Irrigated agriculture witnessed impressive growth rates in cropped area, output and overall yield. Dramatic increases in yield reflected the policy emphasis on intensification and diversification particularly with regard to the major irrigated scheme, the Gezira. There was less emphasis on the expansion of mechanized rain-fed agriculture. This and other weather-related factors and low-intensity cultivation practices were considered to have contributed to the declining yield of commercial mechanized farming.
- The 1974–1981 period: This period coincided roughly with the 'breadbasket strategy' and tripartite partnership of the open-door policies. Emphasis, as mentioned earlier, was on horizontal expansion in both irrigated and mechanized rain-fed agriculture (Chapter 4). However, horizontal expansion in irrigated agriculture was simultaneously accompanied by a policy of disinvestment in the already existing schemes. Inevitably, this led to stagnation in output and yield in the major irrigated schemes particularly in the Gezira. Inadequate provision for depreciation of both infrastructure and machinery meant that no improvement in the incentive structure could yield positive results without basic rehabilitation of the whole irrigation system, transport and agriculture machinery.

This decline in cropped area was accompanied by a severe decline in yield with negative growth rates for all crops except for some minor products (e.g. medium and short staple cotton and irrigated groundnuts).

The decline in yield from mechanized rain-fed agriculture was even more dramatic for its major product, sorghum. The increase in sorghum output was made possible through vigorous horizontal expansion in cropped area. Official statistics show that the rain-fed mechanized cropped area more than doubled during the 1970s (from 2.1 million feddan in 1970 to 5.4 million feddan in 1983). As shown in Table 3.4, the dramatic increase in the total area of sorghum crops was not matched by a proportionate increase in output because of the sharp decline in yield.

Table 3.4 Sudan: sources of change; in agricultural output, 1971/83 average annual per cent change in output

Crop	Total	Area effects	Yield effects
All Sudan			
Cotton	−13.9	−12.1	−1.8
Long staple	−30.9	−16.8	−14.1
Medium staple	16.2	13.3	2.9
Short staple	0.8	−2.3	3.1
Groundnuts	13.5	18.2	−4.7
Irrigated	5.1	3.3	1.8
Rain-fed	8.5	12.5	−4.0
Sesame	−13.1	−6.1	−7.0
Wheat	1.4	0.7	0.7
Sorghum	43.2	77.3	−33.9
Irrigated	−3.1	−2.0	−1.1
Rain-fed of which:	46.3	74.4	−28.1
Mechanized (1974–83)	33.9	62.4	−21.3
Traditional (1974–83)	12.7	21.8	−9.1
Rice	0.5	0.5	−0.0
Gezira only			
Cotton (LS)	−19.8	−10.0	−9.8
Cotton (MS)	6.7	6.6	0.1
Groundnuts	4.8	0.0	4.5
Sorghum	−1.6	0.9	−2.5
Wheat	6.7	4.2	2.5

Sources: MNFP (Annual Economic Survey, several issues) and IBRD, 1985.

The only rain-fed crops which showed positive yield trends during the period were minor products of the sub-sector (i.e. short staple cotton and millet).

- The post-1981 period coincided with the rehabilitation programme for irrigated agriculture, which led to a substantial growth in yield. However, output remained short of reaching the pre-1973 level for the principal product of irrigated agriculture, cotton. In rain-fed agriculture, the yields of sorghum, millet and groundnuts declined sharply while sesame recovered slightly but not enough to offset the long-term decline in its yield.

To sum up, the overall performance of the agricultural sector during the 1970s was one of stagnation and decline.

The root causes of the crisis in primary production

A considerable number of studies on the performance of the agriculture sector were undertaken during the 1970s and early 1980s by donor agencies, relevant government institutions and independent researchers. Broadly speaking they can be classified into two categories. The first was concerned with rehabilitation and/or maximization of the export capacity of the economy and had the underlying assumption that the perfection of market operation would ultimately bring the desired long-term effects. The second group of studies concerned itself with the crisis in primary production which it associated with the existing pattern of specialization and development strategies since independence.

The findings of the first group of studies (Nashashibi, 1979; Sigma One Corporation, 1982; MNFP, 1982; Sattar, 1982) can be summarized as follows. Whereas gross-nominal income rose dramatically, real individual crop incomes declined for cotton, wheat and sesame, and rose for sorghum and groundnuts. Consequently, shifts in crop mix took place in both irrigated and rain-fed agriculture. In irrigated agriculture, this shift was not fully realized because of the limitations imposed by the tenancy arrangement. As Faki notes of the situation, 'If, however, the tenant were completely free to decide, he would grow no cotton and would increase the production of wheat and sorghum instead' (1982, p. 159).

Data on the output of rain-fed traditional agriculture clearly reflects the shift in crop-mix. The area and output of groundnuts in traditional rain-fed agriculture almost tripled in the 1970–1983 period (Appendix 6.2) but the increase in staple foods (sorghum and millet) was less impressive, indicating the rate of change in traditional agriculture from food production for the internal market to cash crop production.

A number of studies further confirm the bias against small producers in irrigated and rain-fed agriculture written into the incentive structures. In general, little credit is available through formal institutions. As Ahmed points out, 'What little credit there is, is available at far higher effective rates for smaller, inexperienced borrowers than medium and large borrowers' (1980, p. 164). Borrowers in the traditional sector and small borrowers in irrigated agriculture have had to rely on informal credit systems, known as '*sheil*', from private money lenders. In the Gezira, effective interest rates on informal credit in the range of 115–230 per cent have been reported (Ahmed, undated). In the Kordofan region in the mid-1970s, the *sheil* system depressed the producer prices to one-sixth of the crop market price (HTS, 1977, p. 66) and consequently profits of 300–400 per cent, were pocketed by *sheil* moneylenders.

This stands in sharp contrast to the situation in large-scale mechanized farming where the farmer benefited from inexpensive credit provided for both machines and working capital. Since the early 1960s external donors, including IBRD, USAID and IFC, directed their finance to mechanized farming. A recent study has shown that 87 per cent of the agricultural credit provided by the state-owned Agricultural Bank of Sudan went to rain-fed mechanized farmers (Gelabi and Elshafie, 1986, p. 26). This bias was further accentuated by the exclusion of the traditional sector from the programme of institutions serving agriculture such as research, extension and marketing (Adam, 1986).

Several surveys of the cost of production of major crops were carried out in the 1976–1982 period. The main findings justified the present pattern of specialization in the agriculture sector. With the exception of rice, nearly all export crops had a clear comparative advantage. Given the prevailing low yields in irrigated agriculture, rain-fed crops, both traditional and modern, had a comparative advantage over irrigated agriculture. These studies showed that the relative advantage varied inversely with the level of use of imported inputs. This is highest in irrigated agriculture, which uses machinery, fertilizer, pesticide and herbicide, and less in mechanized agriculture, which only uses machinery and is non-existent in traditional farming. In absolute terms, international value-added per feddan varies over a wide spectrum. The irrigated crops, with the exception of wheat, produced higher international value-added per feddan than the rain-fed crops, though the former require a much higher initial investment and subsequent inputs. In other words, the high import intensity of irrigated agriculture is more than compensated for by higher international value-added per feddan.

The problem with the first group of studies does not lie with their findings: the distortions in the price system, neglect of and bias against the small producers across the incentive structure, etc. In fact, some of these findings demonstrate the need for deeper investigation into the roots of the agricultural sector crisis and the long-term implications of any policy adjustment. Two examples serve as a clear indicator of the limitations of this approach in exploring the roots and the way out of the agricultural crisis:

> Prices are distorted and the whole incentive structure is biased against the small producer in the 'traditional' sector. Several detailed studies on the marketing of agriculture products in the 'traditional' sector concluded that government price policies and/or transport problems are only minor factors in explaining the difference between producer prices and export/market prices.

The major problem arises from the imperfection of the markets characterized by the unequal position of sellers and buyers (Low, 1967; El Bashir and Idris, 1983; Behsai, 1976). Oesterdiekhof's (1969) study provided a detailed analysis of the mechanism through which marketing of the products took place at three different levels: primary (village level), secondary (regional) and tertiary (export centres). The first two levels were dominated by traders, whose structure was characterized by oligopoly on the demand side and competitive conditions on the supply side. At the third level, joint private/public companies function to guarantee the minimum price. 'Under these conditions, the system of government minimum prices did not work effectively. Rather, these prices protected small traders selling on primary and secondary markets, but for the producer they were maximum prices in fact'. A similar conclusion was reached by Behs, who asserts: 'It is meaningless to talk of mining agricultural productivity when the conditions of productivity and marketing are as described. The producers do not get the necessary incentives via price increase' (ibid., p. 268).

Seasonal shortages of labour at peak periods in irrigated agriculture have been pointed out as one of the major problems. The ILO-sponsored study in 1976 stated that there was no evidence of an overall shortage of unskilled labour in the country. The study concluded that, given the high mobility of the rural migrant labour and well-functioning labour markets, problems of seasonal shortage of labour could be resolved with the provision of adequate facilities and incentives. However, a World Bank study (1983) admitted that, with the enormous expansion during the 1976–1983 period of areas under various irrigated schemes often in close proximity to each other, the labour shortage became even more acute.

The debate on labour shortage in irrigated agriculture was confined to two alternatives: reduction of the demand for wage labourer through further mechanization (favoured by management) or more efficient management of the supply and demand of wage labourers (favoured by the World Bank). Neither the short nor the long-term implications of this high wage-labour mobility nor the expansion of this pattern of migrant-labour-dependent agriculture to other 'labour supplying' sub-sectors of agriculture was considered.

The limitations of the agricultural development strategy

The second group of studies emphasized the historical and long-term implications of stagnation and decline in primary production. These studies questioned the rationale, assumptions and long-term viability of the 1970s agricultural development strategy, which did not differ from the pre-1970 strategies (of both colonial and post-colonial Sudan). The strategy emphasized the horizontal expansion of cropping with the aim of maximizing the agricultural sector's net exports irrespective of the long-term economic, sectoral, regional and social impacts. The starting point in these studies was the impact of such a strategy on the heterogeneous structure of the agriculture sector and, in particular, on peasant agriculture.

The limits on this strategy of modernization were set by the interaction of socio-economic and ecological factors. A substantial number of studies from the 1970s provide a wealth of evidence in this respect. In the early 1970s, there was still considerable room for the expansion of capitalist and peasant agriculture before the point was reached at which they came into significant direct competition (ibid., p. 10). Once that point was reached, a process of cause and effect was set in motion. The increasing displacement of peasant and nomadic pastoralists resulted in increasing pressures to maximize returns.

Many pastoralists were displaced from their pastures by the rapid expansion of mechanized farming during the 1960s and 1970s. In many cases, herds declined below the ecologically determined minimum sizes necessary for subsistence, and consequently pastoralists were forced to supplement their income through wage labour (O'Brien, 1984, p. 12). Thus, centuries-old patterns of crop rotation and livestock raising were changed or abandoned altogether, resulting in several ecological damages. Over-grazing, over-cultivation, deforestation and the lowering of water tables due to increased water use accelerated the process of desertification and consequently led to further pressures on land cultivation and grazing areas (Sorbo, 1977; Ali, 1982; D'Souza and Shoham, 1985).

Macro level indicators further support the findings of these studies. Desertification on the national level was estimated to be at an average of 6.5 kilometres per annum during the 1970s. Dramatic changes took place in the structure and competition of the workforce in agriculture. The total number of people engaged in agricultural production (traditional and modern) increased from 2.9 million in 1970 to 4.2 million in 1983, representing a decrease in the percentage of the total labour force from 70 per cent to 65.5 per cent. In 1983, it was estimated that 70.6 per cent of the total labour force were seasonal labourers, 24.2 per cent, in traditional rain-fed agriculture and 1.1 per cent in rain-fed mechanized agriculture. The displacement process is further reflected in the changes in the nomadic pastoralist population which declined from 4.2 million in 1965 to 2.1 million in 1983. Nomadic pastoralists were responsible for 95 per cent of total livestock production. Data indicates that only ten thousand people are today engaged in 'modern' sector animal production activities (Abd-elgabar *et al.*, 1986). Most of them are in the rapidly growing poultry and dairy industry, with some in the few fattening centres for cattle and sheep. In sharp contrast to the decline in the pastoralist population, the livestock population almost doubled between 1970 and 1983 mainly as a consequence of improved vaccination services. However, in 1981 it was already estimated that there were 27.8 million animal units, implying substantial over-grazing (Ali, 1982, pp. 72–92). The potential for the maximization of exports through horizontal expansion of irrigated and rain-fed mechanized farming was soon exhausted by both socio-economic and natural limitations.

'Traditional' (pre-capitalist) formations were destroyed, wage-labourers replaced the self-sufficient peasants and those who remained became cash-crop producers. However, contrary to the historical pattern, the new capitalist farmer could neither increase the yield nor sustain output growth. In other words, the traditional, shifting agriculture of the peasantry was replaced by a 'tractorized' shifting agriculture lacking both the traditional pattern of rotation that had for centuries preserved the ecological balance or at least minimized the damage through the use of modern inputs such as fertilizers and herbicides.

The yield of mechanized farms declined sharply after the fifth year. The old farm, a minimum of around 1,000 feddans, had to be left and a lease obtained for a new farm. Throughout the 1970s, mechanized rain-fed agriculture expanded annually at an average of 400,000 feddans. Perhaps there was still some room for further horizontal expansion of mechanized rain-fed and traditional agriculture to compensate for the declining yield or to increase output. However, this could have been done only at immense political, social, economical and ecological costs. Even in the short term, any further squeeze on the pastures could prove economically disastrous given the relative share of livestock in total primary production (34.1 per cent) and in exports (12 per cent) in the 1980–1983 period.

The implication of the crisis in primary production

In an economy where primary production contributes to 36 per cent of the GDP, employs 65 per cent of the working population, constitutes 95 per cent of exports and where much of the activity in manufacturing, commerce and transport is concerned with the processing, transportation and distribution of primary products, the negative impact of stagnation and decline in primary production on the economy is self-evident. There is a need, however, to highlight certain aspects particularly crucial to the industrialization process, such as profitability of manufacturing capital. Increasing productivity in agriculture is held to be essential to the reduction of reproduction costs of labour in urban areas. Thus the decline in agricultural productivity during the 1970s was likely to lead to an increase in the prices of major items in the consumption basket of the workers and hence to a decline in the profitability in non-agricultural activities because of higher labour cost. However, the impact of the stagnation and decline in agriculture was not fully reflected in the reproduction cost of labour because of two major external factors:

- Increasing imports and subsidization of foodstuffs. The most important example is wheat flour, which effectively replaced sorghum as a staple food for the urban population. Because of subsidies, the price relation between the two was dramatically reversed.
- Remittances from Sudanese nationals working in the oil-producing countries who were estimated at between 0.3 and 0.6 million persons.

These two external factors had a moderating effect on the rate of increase in labour cost in urban areas until the late 1970s. From then on, this could not be sustained because of the declining capacity to import and decreasing export and external financial inflows – with a consequently reduced capacity of the state to sustain subsidies.

Supply of raw material for the manufacturing sector

The negative impact of the decline and stagnation of agriculture on predominantly agro-based manufacturing activities needs no further emphasis. However, this negative impact cannot be generalized because of differences in the conditions of supply and demand for various primary products and consequently on various branches of the ABIs.

Supply of labour

During the 1970s, with the increasing displacement of traditional peasants and pastoralists, there was concurrently an increasing rate of urbanization (6.2 per cent as opposed to 4.1 per cent during the 1960s). Thus, given the relatively small size of the manufacturing sector, such a conclusion should be balanced by some other factors:

- The impact of the 'boom' in the non-commodity-producing sectors.
- The impact of emigration to neighbouring oil-producing countries.

- The composition of rural–urban migration in terms of skill-intensities on the supply side and the degree of skill-intensities of various branches of the ABIs on the demand side.

In these three crucial aspects, the dynamics of interaction between primary production and manufacturing has been influenced by factors external to the economy and the commodity-producing sectors.

Managing crisis with a weak state: 1983–1989

This period comprises two politically distinct phases: 1) the final years and 2) the parliamentary regime (1986–1989) that followed the popular uprising that brought down the second authoritarian period. With the deepening of the crisis in commodity-producing sectors and mounting debts during the 1970s, the drying up of external sources of support and the resumption of the civil war in Southern Sudan, there was practically no room for manoeuvring policy options. Both sub-periods were essentially characterized by a quickly shrinking state. The financial crisis of the state is well illustrated in Table 3.5. As shown in the table, the percentage share of the government revenue in GDP continued to decline while total expenditure was maintained at an unsustainable level that represented more than double the revenue. Such a relatively high level of expenditure was maintained through excessive borrowing internally, unfavourable terms of external borrowing and an extremely high unsustainable level of inflation.

The situation has been further complicated by the fact that the state's relative autonomy and its capacity to transcend the immediate and direct interest of the various segments of capital controlling it have been severely curtailed. Several factors have contributed to limit the state's capacity to accumulate and allocate extractable surplus. The state's financial crisis and liberalization policies have severely limited state control over banking and financial institutions, rendering the state's mediatory role far less important in the accumulation process and finally

Table 3.5 The shrinking state: government budget as per cent of gross domestic product

Year	Total revenue	Total expenditure
1981/82	12.7	21.2
1982/83	13.3	19.1
1983/84	12.5	21.3
1984/85	9.7	24.7
1985/86	8.7	20.4
1986/87	9.2	20.6
1987/88	10.0	23.8
1988/89	8.6	22.1
1989/90	8.1	18.3

shrinking the state share of surplus generated in directly productive activities because of privatization and relative inefficiency.

During this crisis management period, it was clear that the restoration of profitability in the commodity-producing sector was central to the way out of the crisis and would entail harsh structural adjustments to address past distortions. Short-term adjustment policies should incorporate long-term objectives aiming at reorientation of both the agricultural and industrial sectors' policies as well as addressing imbalances in infrastructure, training and human resource development. Policy measures directly related to the restructuring of the economy involved changes in the incentive structure and active but efficient state intervention aiming at fostering linkages between manufacturing and agriculture in a way that promoted more dependence on domestic resources, efficient operation of production capacities, elimination of biases in the incentive structure against small-/medium-scale enterprises and some measures of positive discrimination aiming at encouraging rural-oriented, skill-intensive and basic-needs-oriented production activities.

However, such options did not seem available even when a new coalition of social forces came to power following the overthrow of the Nimeiri dictatorship and the restoration of a democratic system. The potential for an alternative model for development or a way out of the crisis, beyond some short-term measures, is both complex and analytically problematic because of two major reasons. First, the possibility of such potential lies more in the political than the economic sphere. Second, such a possibility, besides being determined by the likely balance of forces internally, will also greatly depend on the particular nature and outcome of the interaction between national and international variables.

The situation has been further complicated by the fact that the relative autonomy of the state, and its capacity to transcend the immediate and direct interest of the various segments of capital controlling it, has been severely curtailed. Several factors limited the state's capacity to accumulate and allocate investable surplus. The state's financial crisis and liberalization policies have severely hindered its attempt to control banking and financial institutions, rendering their mediatory role far less important in the accumulation process. Finally, privatization and inefficiency have diminished the state's share of surplus generated in directly productive activities. As was explained earlier in this chapter, the agricultural development strategy adopted by Nimeiri's regime particularly following the 'open door' policies and the tripartite coalition of the breadbasket strategy laid the foundation for undermining the structural foundation of the rural economy. Mid-1980 Sahelian drought could not be averted and accommodated within the still functioning rural economy, as was the case in the 1970s drought. Rather, the mid-1980s led to fierce competition over resources, in particular in Western Sudan (Darfur), in response to population pressures, multiplying livestock as a consequence of the strategy selective intervention (improved veterinary services and watering centres) in a fragile eco-system. From the mid-1980s onwards, the crisis in the rural economy with its diversified patterns (traditional agriculture and livestock, mechanized, rain-fed, as well as irrigated, agriculture) became a dominant feature of the economy. From the mid-1980s onwards, Sudan's economic survival was based on 'reaping' the remittances of labour export rather than commodity exports. Except for livestock exports which effectively replaced cotton (the symbol of colonial and post-colonial modernity in agriculture), agricultural products of both modern and traditional agriculture (largely oilseeds) stagnated or declined. These important shifts in the composition of the country's exports as well as the state sources of extractable surplus, albeit not necessarily produced within the economy, are more than symbolic. It highlighted at the same time the full dimensions of the process of erosion of the structural foundation of post-independence Sudan's economy and state.

Essentially, there were very few options for a successful resolution to this crisis. One option involved the maintenance of the contemporary structure of capitalist accumulation and exploitation. During the transition to civilian parliamentary democracy, the delicate balance of forces between the popular mass movement and those representing the interests of dominant segments of the Sudanese bourgeoisie did not allow an outright policy in support of such an option. However, the hesitant policy of the ruling coalition was soon replaced by an outright swing to the right. A policy of maintaining the existing right-leaning structure of accumulation took the upper hand. This was signified by the incorporation of the fundamentalist front, the Muslim Brotherhood, and pro-Nimeiri elements, which included an important section of the military bureaucracy in the ruling coalition. Naturally, such an option cannot be sustained without extreme repression of wages, continuation of the existing or higher level of surplus extraction from the low/shrinking base of commodity production and naturally leading to a further aggravated income disparity between and within regions even if a higher level of external financial support could be secured.

The other option of pursuing policies aiming at the restoration of profitability in the commodity-producing sector was not viable as it conflicted with the interests of the powerful financial capital of the nouveau rich, who were dominating the new coalition and were well entrenched in the social fabric of the three ruling parties. It was obvious that pursuing policies that preserved the existing accumulation structure would pose the greatest danger to hard-won democratic rights and was certainly a recipe for continuous civil war, triggering other serious conflicts in the Sudan. The weak coalition of post-Nimeiri government was not capable of pursuing such policies involving harsh repressive measures. The route for the end of the third democracy was paved.

It was concluded that Nimeiri's regime, particularly during the 1969–1982 period[10] which we coined the 'crisis-making period', laid the structural foundation for the unmaking of post-independence Sudan: triggering a new round of South–North war; laying the foundation for the structural crisis of the vast traditional sector and its most dramatic manifestation (Darfur); marginalizing modern agriculture; and shifting dependence from external borrowing to 'human capital export'. The implications of these multiple crises as discussed in the following chapter were most prominently reflected in the creation of multiple hotbeds of conflicts in the increasingly non-sustainable vast traditional economy; loss of post-independence gains in human capital formation; the erosions of the fragile basis of modern production; and the weakening of the state capacity to administer the economy. The Islamist ascendancy as elaborated in Chapter 4 was driven by the outcomes of this crisis-making phase, and the consolidation and sustainability of the Islamist control over the economy and society was only possible through bringing such a crisis to its ultimate conclusion: the unmaking of post-independence Sudan.

4 The failed modernity II

The crony capitalism of political Islam (1989–2004)

Introduction

This is the second major chapter looking at the unmaking of post-colonial Sudan. In Chapter 3 we concluded that the Islamist ascendancy was, by and large, a product of the crisis-making process of Nimeiri's regime and was further facilitated by its outcome. This chapter traces back the Islamists; ascendancy to power from the mid-1970s onwards. It examines both internal as well as external factors that enabled such an ascendancy. The chapter examines various strategies employed by the NIF, a narrowly based political movement, to consolidate its power through measures aiming at complete monopoly over violence, social and economic structures including privatization of the state; hegemony over the accumulation process that crowded out the old elite's and consolidated the ascending Islamist elite's leading position; fragmentation of the social basis of actual and potential contending forces through re-tribalization; and ethnicization of conflicts in marginalized territories. The chapter addresses the impact of increasing international isolation of the regime and how this isolation exacerbated the process of stagnation and shrinkage of the economy and state, leading to further repression of wages, increased outflows of skills and capital, proliferation of conflict perpetuated by deepening of the crisis in the economy and society and the NIF's own policies of divide and rule. As stressed earlier, while the previous phase of crisis making was responsible for the erosion of the structural foundation of the post-colonial economy and state, this phase witnessed the ultimate conclusion of this crisis.[1]

Turabi came to power at a time when the economy was in a state of fundamental disarray. Sudan was in debt heavily from the previous authoritarian regime of Nimeiri (1969–1985). The short-lived democracy failed to restore the declining profitability of the commodity-producing sector and was exacerbated by negative, at best reluctant, responses from external donors on the eve of the end of the cold war.[2] State capacity to manage the economy was seriously eroded by harsher conditions imposed by the IFIs. Finance from external sources began to disappear while the potential for a negotiated peace in the aftermath of the civil war was continuously sabotaged by the Islamists and finally aborted altogether by the *coup d'etat* of 30 June 1989. Furthermore, the grand strategy of turning Sudan into a 'Bread Basket for the World', or, in its modest version, 'Bread Basket of the Arab World', was seriously undermined by misconceived implementation plans, squandering of resources and corruption and mismanagement, leading, as elaborated in the previous chapter, to the undermining of the structural foundation of both the modern and traditional economies. These reduced Sudan to a 'Skills Basket of the Arab World'. Then, following the two oil hikes of 1973 and 1979, Sudan's major source of income became exported labour, with remittances amounting to 1.7 billion or more than three-fold total exports. As was explained in the previous chapter, the ascension of the Islamists was essentially built upon the out- and inflow of the three components of the new labour-export economy (i.e. labour outflows, remittances and back flows of financial surpluses generated by the higher oil prices) as well as the excessive rural–urban migration resulting from the erosion of the structural foundation of the traditional rural economy.

Islamists' ascendancy strategies

In his book on Islamic movement, Turabi (1991) outlined with great detail the development trajectories of Islamic ascendancy, strategies and cumulative build-up of the Islamist power bases. The periodicity he used is equally indicative as it corresponds to a major shift in the ascendancy strategies. In this interesting reading of the history of the Islamic movement, he identifies seven periods (ibid., pp. 23–36):

- The 1949–1955 pre-independence formation years with the twin influences of the Egyptian-based Islamic brotherhood and the parallel build-up of the Islamic student movement within the Sudan. Turabi's narration of this period grossly minimizes the role of the founding Sudanese students in Egypt as well as the Egyptian brotherhood movement.[3]
- The 1956–1959 early post-independence years which witnessed a more visible presence of the movement.
- The 1959–1964 period when the movement followed a two-tier strategy of open student advocacy while non-student activities were carried out under the disguise of cultural activities.
- The 1964–1969 period when the movement came to the open, forging alliances with traditional political forces, advocating an Islamic constitution and confronting the communist movement, its historical rival in the student movement. The confrontation with the communist movement culminated with a successful build-up of a broad coalition of traditional forces, banning of the communist party and dismissal of its representative from parliament.
- The 1969–1977 period corresponding to the early phase of Nimeiri's regime which witnessed open opposition and confrontation with the regime and forging of a stronger alliance with the major traditional parties (Umma and Democratic Unionist parties).
- The 1977–1987 period following reconciliation with Nimeiri's regime and the strategy of economic empowerment of the movement.

- Finally, the 1984–1987 post-Nimeiri era of the building up of broader alliances incorporating both Sufi Islam and traditional communal leaderships.

Why the emphasizes on Turabi's theorization of the Islamist ascendancy? Simply because Turabi's theorization was central to the Islamic movement's ascendancy in two crucial aspects that rendered him a strategic thinker. Turabi's own ascendancy as the indisputable leader of the Islamic movement dates back to the April 1969 party congress. According to Ali (1996), the April congress witnessed a vertical division between two dimensionally opposed factions: the old founding cadres still favouring a less direct political engagement and more focus on advocacy (Da'wa) and Turabi's faction calling for wide and aggressive involvement in the political arena (see ibid., pp. 283–285). Turabi emerged victorious from this ideological battle and most of the old guard opted for an independent platform (the Muslim Brotherhood). In this respect the post-1964 era can be described as the era of both Turabi and the movement ascendancy. Turabi's ascendance as the indisputable leader of the Islamic movement followed a radical change in movement dates back to the April 1969 congress. The congress adopted Turabi's line of aggressive, direct involvement in the political as opposed to the traditional approach based on spiritual and the moral education and gradual build-up of the movement (see Ali, 1996, pp. 283–285). This, as Mahmoud (2001) observed, marked a radical change in the Brethren movement: '… the *Ikhwan* movement turned into a dynamic and vociferous movement, distancing itself from the parent Egyptian movement, building alliances and reaching out beyond its narrow student power base (ibid., p. 76). The key dimensions to that strategic transformative thinking were the twin concepts of *Tamkeen* (literally, 'empowerment') and *Figh Eldarura* (literally, 'theology of necessity'). The empowerment, *Tamkeen*, was translated into economic as well as political empowerment of the movement and its members, while the theology of necessity, *Figh Eldarura*, provided an ideological justification for a wide room of manoeuvre for the Islamist movement forging alliances, collaboration or even cooperation with a wide range of allies or with the enemy himself as defined by the dominant discourses of the movement. The two concepts were the cornerstone of Turabi's strategic thinking because they enabled the crucial breakthroughs that made the Islamist ascendancy possible. First, *Tamkeen* was crucial in allowing the Islamic movement access to material resources in a predominantly 'Sufi' society, including the movement itself in its early formative years, that despise material wealth and symbols, Turabi acknowledged was not an easy task even within the movement. At its start, the movement kept a distance from economic activities. It was a purely intellectual and cultural movement with a great deal of Puritanism. It was driven by young people with no access to wealth or clerks with limited income and with no connection to the spheres of production in both the traditional and modern sectors (ibid., p. 172). 'The new circumstances that faced the movement, following the political repression in the 1970s, and the purge of its supporters from the civil service, forced its members to seek income generating activities in the commercial sector. As their numbers multiplied, I started to enlighten them about the religious stand in this unusual field ... while the temptation of this new experience might be prohibitive, yet it proceeded well and the number of activists working in business multiplied' (ibid., p. 174).

This new transformation became

> a new method of promoting the movement and its empowerment. Such orientation is not a new one. All minorities that faced political repression moved into business. It is known among Muslim minorities that faced political repression is some African and Asian countries and in the case of Jews in the West. (ibid., p. 174)

Second, *Figh Eldarura* provided the movement with unlimited flexibility in forging alliances and cooperation within and outside the country in the simple terms of no permanent enemies or friends but permanent interests à la Churchill. The flexibility of *Figh Eldarura* was certainly instrumental in paving the way for Islamist-traditional Islam sect partnerships; Turabi and his followers viewed the traditionalist, whether Khatimyya or Mahadist adherents, as a reactionary dynastic who could not be entrusted with leading a modern Islamic state. However, when it comes to moderate Islam sharing the same constituency with the movement, such tolerance and flexibility evaporates. This was typically the case of the uncompromising and brutal response to moderate Islam represented by the Republican brotherhood. Furthermore, it was this extreme flexibility of the theology of necessity (*Figh Eldarura*) that paved the way for forging alliances and simultaneously infiltrating the ranks of Sufi sects, *Ullama* (Islamic official clerics) and finally the state apparatus itself during Nimeiri's national reconciliation era (1977–1985). It was this infiltration, particularly of the military and security apparatus of the regime, that gave the NIF a tremendous advantage over all other contending forces. This was openly admitted by Turabi himself (ibid., p. 199)[4] and was acknowledged by a number of recent writings (Sidahmed and Sidahmed, 2005; Galander, 2005), but very little has been written on the alliance between the pro-Nimeiri group known as the *Maiost* (an Arabic word referring to the month of May in which the coup took place) and the NIF. Such alliance, I will maintain, was instrumental in enabling the NIF ascendancy, takeover and later the consolidation of its power. The fact that these two strategic concepts were successfully used by his disciples against him in the power struggle within the movement does not in any sense undermine the fact that he conceptually engineered the breakthroughs of the Islamic ascendancy. In other words it is a typical case of when magic turned on the magician.

The political economic foundation of the Islamist ascendancy

The Islamists in Sudan encountered many challenges: a strong secular educational system; a vibrant and influential urban space with well-established traditions of political organization and trade unionism; and a flexible, accommodative and moderate Sufi Islam. Such an environment was certainly not conducive for the growth of militant Islam nor was the traditional rural sector with its communal, rural and village lifestyle using Turabi's terms (Turabi, 1991, p. 148). The Islamists' political empowerment strategy was shrewd and successfully built on the multi-directional utilization of the rural–urban nexus. The strategy cultivated several links and tools: the educated elites of these communities; social services provided by the movement; and infiltration of the tribal, village and Sufi sect leaderships through their educated offspring. Thus, the rural–urban links were not left to normal flows but were subjected to a planned process of acceleration.

The context within which this ascendancy took place is extremely important and provided crucially enabling conditions. The erosion of the structural foundation of the vast traditional sector, the stagnation and decline in modern sectors and the economic and politically driven exodus of the country's human capital through migration to the neighbouring oil-producing countries, all being consequences of the 1980s crisis, reshaped the political, economic and social terrain of post-independence Sudan and are central to the understanding of the factors that facilitated the Islamist ascendancy to power in the late 1980s. The central agent in this reshaping was the massive population flows out of the ailing traditional sector into urban centres mostly in riverain Sudan coupled with the educated elite, professional and skilled worker movement out of the urban space into the new labour markets outside the country. A new urban political and social space was created with the erosion of the structural foundation of the undermined earlier forms of organization of habitat, institutions governing inter and intra-community relations. Where such erosion was coupled with man-made and natural crises, overwhelmingly ecological, fierce competition over resources laid the foundation for prolonged conflicts and new allegiances and alliances. Traditional and modern; urban and rural; religious and secular; and tribal leaders and trade unionists all lost out. The massive rural influx and the stagnant modern economy meant that informal economic activities became the norm, marginalizing the once well-bounded and vibrant, albeit small, organized sector.[5]

The ascendancy of the Islamist movement from the rural areas and in particular Darfur was based on a strategy to compensate for the relatively weaker presence among urban educated elites and to overcome the influential northern urban elites. Quoting Ghazi Salah al din, a leading Islamist, referring to Turabi's strategy, 'He learned from history the Mahdi had faced the elite of northern Sudan who rejected and ridiculed Mahdism. So he turned to the West and stormed the Nile from Kordofan and Darfur' (cited in Flint and De Waal, 2005 p. 20). But beyond the general notion of learning from the Mahdi strategy, the movement had its own effective mechanisms. Thus, as noted by Abbasher (1991), 'During the 1970s there was a large number of Brethren supporters who had become teachers in Western Sudan and consequently there has been a major support for the movement there. When these students went to universities in Khartoum, they came to dominate student politics' (ibid., pp. 15–16). There is another important support for such a line of reasoning for the Islamist ascendancy based on swamping the riverain urban elite by the rural population. Severe droughts of the 1980s, and subsequent conflicts over resources in Western Sudan, resulted in massive rural–urban migration from

Western Sudan during the 1980s. The Islamists, during the parliamentary elections of the third democracy (1986–1989), out-stripped the riverain elite in their one-time stronghold. In the 1986 election the Islamists emerged as the third most popular party in riverain Sudan, largely relying on the votes of newcomers to the urban setting.[6]

Sources of Islamic economic ascendancy

El-Affendi (1991) reveals that the first Islamic Bank (financed by Prince Mohamed al-Faisal and a group of Arab and Sudanese businessmen) in 1978 tended to support the Islamic movement in employment and by preferring to provide 'loans and other advances to customers who could be supporters' (ibid., p. 117). Given that, it was far less significant who owned major shares in the Bank. El-Affendi notes further that 'the truth is that the Faisal Islamic Bank (the symbol of Ikhwan economic power) is 60 per cent owned by Arab businessmen from the Gulf and 40 per cent Sudanese businessmen, few of whom are Ikhwan' (ibid., p. 117). This is irrelevant based on what is being argued.

The Islamic banking system and in particular Faisal Islamic Bank was the single most powerful tool for the ascendancy of the Islamist economic elites, institutions and political activities and for the crowding out of non-Islamist traditional businesses, particularly in internal and external trade. While El-Affendi is right in stating that 'Islamic banking was a political liability to Ikhwan in at least one sense. It created a revolution of expectations by allowing the evolution of a totally new class of businessmen who became rich almost overnight' (ibid., p. 116), he also suggested that this negative aspect should not, however, discount the deep impact which the credit revolution had on shifting the balance of power within society. The Islamic banking movement revolutionized access to credit, and wrested the virtual monopoly of this vital sector from privileged groups (many of whom were of foreign extraction). Before the 1970s, few even among the top government employees had current accounts, let alone knowledge about the many service opportunities the banking system offered the Ikhwan who managed to place themselves in a strategic position to try to influence and utilize this revolution (ibid., p. 116).

This statement provides a negative reading of the political economy of the Sudan in several respects. First, during his Nasserite phase of the 1970s, Numeiri's nationalization and confiscation measures virtually eliminated foreign domination – El-Affendi calls this foreign extraction. This paved the way for the ascendancy of the lower strata of Sudan's business class concurrently with the emergence and ascendancy of new groups of businessmen closely associated with the state.

Second, the banking system, particularly the specialized agricultural and industrial banks with strong state support, was instrumental and played a major role in augmenting the nascent 'national' strata of the business class in agriculture and in the manufacturing industry during the 1960s and 1970s, well before the emergence of the Islamic banking system.

Third, the control of the Islamic banking institutions essentially manipulated access to credit and accelerated the demise of certain factions of capital that were already greatly weakened by Nimeiri's regime. This encouraged the ascendancy of certain factions of capital (namely pro-Islamist business establishment) which were accompanied by a clear and well-articulated agenda of infiltrating the traditional structure of the central riverain elite and affecting cross-political patronage that was functional to the various tactics and strategies of the Islamist movement.

Following the national reconciliation with Nimeiri's regime in 1977/78, the Islamist movement secured a number of privileges for the Faisal Islamic Bank (FIB). These included exemptions from taxes (for assets, profits, salaries, gratuities and pensions), protection from confiscation and nationalization and complete freedom in transferring foreign exchange deposits (Shaaeldin and Brown, 1985). Given these generous concessions and tax holidays, the FIB earned a profit of 35 per cent for investors in 1981, rising to 35 per cent by 1983 (Khalid, 1986, p. 369). The FIB effectively crowded out established commercial entities which did not enjoy similar concessions. During the 1978–84 period, the FIB allocated 90 per cent of their investments to external trade, internal trade and services (El-Battahani, 1996, p. 14).

The second important source of Islamic economic ascendancy and empowerment was the Islamic relief organizations.[7] The plethora of Islamic relief organizations established by the movement was instrumental in both politically oriented and purely philanthropic funds from the oil-producing 'sheikhdoms'. This was further facilitated by networks of Islamic professionals who migrated to the oil-producing countries following the oil price hikes of 1973 and 1979. The Cold War and the Afghanistan War provided the rising Islamists with effective political empowerment. By the time of the overthrow of the authoritarian regime of Nimeiri, with which the Islamists allied until just short of their last days, hundreds of their cadres, particularly in the mass media, were US trained (Elnur, 2002). The combined effect of the internal and external empowerment of the Islamist movement was dramatically leading to a reshaping of the political and economic terrains.

The full control over the state apparatus, resources and the political and technical cleansing of the state personnel, but also the complete erosion of the long-inherited traditions of accountability, procedures and bureaucratic hierarchy, makes the NIF regime the most distinctive authoritarian regime in the history of post-colonial Sudan. Once the NIF controlled the state, economic empowerment was brought to its ultimate dimensions. The boundaries between public, private and party were completely blurred. The hanging of a carefully selected group of three innocent young people in 1990 looks like a Greek tragedy, but it ushered the start of a well-orchestrated process of using the state as the major tool for economic empowerment. The horrifying act of state terrorism was carefully planned to intimidate the rival factions of the elite. This was followed by the 1991 Bank Act which effectively under state control put the entire liquid money in the hands of the government, driving most of the old elite out of business or practically vetoing any activity by them. In the drive to erode the capacity of the old elite and assisting the rising Islamic one, the new privatized state was not short of any means, from the sale of public enterprises, import/export licences tax exemptions, to undeclared bids for selling state and owned land and real estate.

The aggressive Islamist strategy was remarkably successful in replacing old elites or marginalizing them so that 'lower and middle strata of urban entrepreneurs expanded considerably to the extent that at least one-third of the 4000 firms and commercial establishments registered during 1984–1994 were owned by the Islamist and sympathizers' (El Battahani, 1996, p. 17).

Pan-Islamism and ascendancy

The 'pan-Islamism' of Turabi has enjoyed wide support from the Islamist movements from Algeria to Asia and became a major source of conflict within the NIF leadership. The tension and trade-off between a strategy based on the consolidation of the loosely founded Islamist regime and the heavy burden of supporting fellow 'Islamists' in neighbouring countries is too obvious. After June 1989, a two-tier strategy was pursued simultaneously with a manageable level of contradiction and friction within the NIF joint civilian–military leadership. Turabi concentrated on his grand 'pan-Islamist' scheme driven by high expectations of an imminent breakthrough in Egypt, Algeria, Tunisia and Yemen and, to a lesser degree, a stronger presence in the Somali and Eritrean political scenes. Turabi's focus was the 'Islamic Popular Conference', which was founded and led in 1990. This umbrella organization, modelled after 'communist' national fronts, brought together remnants of leftist and pan-Arab movements (including Nasserites and Baathists) in addition to fundamentalist Islamist groups.

El-Bashir and the majority of the NIF leadership were focused on the immediate tasks of consolidating the power of the fragile Islamist state: transforming the state institutions including the civil service, armed forces and security structures into tight party-controlled organs. According to the original plan, by 2005 the popular defence forces (PDF) would replace the armed forces and the popular police were to replace the regular police. The NIF would monopolize the civil service and would control all sovereign and constitutional positions. In actuality, they completed a large part of those transformations by 1997. With the harsh crackdown on non-Islamist politics and the 'reign of terror' that took place in 1991 and 1992 and the complete monopoly over the mass media, the NIF succeeded in destroying the civil society that was emerging from the previous period of parliamentary democracy (1985–1989), during which a wide range of perspectives from political, social, economic and religious organizations were expressed. However, maintaining such a manageable level of tensions stemming from a two-tier strategy proved to be difficult. Khartoum's siding with the loser, Iraq, against Kuwait in the Gulf War (largely a result of the pan-Islamist strategy) resulted in international and regional isolation with tremendous cost to an increasingly labour-exporting economy.

International isolation, the deteriorating economic situation and the intensification of civil war all foresaw an end to the viability of the two-tier strategy.

It became glaringly obvious that the adventurous policy of exporting the 'Islamist Project' (internally referred to as the 'Civilization Project') could not go hand-in-hand with the vital needs for the external support of the ailing economy and the demanding civil war in the South. Tensions within the NIF ranks started to escalate between Turabi's faction, 'the historical leadership of the Islamist movement', and El-Bashir's faction. The failed attempt to assassinate President Mubarak of Egypt in 1995 highlighted the 'beginning-of-the-end' of the Sudanese version of the Iranian dual leadership. In December 2000 President El-Bashir took the lead and ended 'the duality'. The move was followed by a major departure from the pan-Islamist project.

It should be noted, however, that the pan-Islamist movement led by Turabi was not devoid of economic aspects. It was accompanied by a well-orchestrated campaign to attract Islamic investment into the country, ranging from 'Zakat' transfers from pro-movement financial tycoons in the oil-exporting countries, to Islamic financial institutions and direct investment and cultivation of pro-Islamic elements as far as Malaysia. As revealed by recent economic revelations in the Sudan, the results of Turabi's project were disappointing. Despite exaggerated estimates, Bin Laden's total investment in the Sudan totalled a mere $170 million. Other direct investments by sympathetic 'Sheikhs' were less impressive. The recent closure in Khartoum of many small-scale pastry shops, sweet shops and bakeries owned by Arab Islamists shows that the expected gains from pan-Islamist solidarity were negligible.

Moreover, it would be a gross under-estimation to judge the economic returns of pan-Islamism on account of its limited direct investment. Islamist ascendancy was closely linked to its success in capturing the windfall resources of Islamic charitable aid. There were two major Islamic institutions which helped facilitate this trend. The first of these two institutions was the Islamic *da'wa* (the call to faith). The Islamic African Relief Agency (IARA) was established as a branch of *da'wa*. The history of Islamic charity in Sudan goes back to the 1960s, with the establishment of the African Islamic Centre funded by the Gulf countries in 1967. Benthall and Bellion-Jourdan (2003) described its mission as being 'designed to mould African elites to the Westernized or Christianized elites' (ibid., p. 113). The organization survived with some interruption from the galloping phases of the Numeiri regime's ideological leanings. *Da'wa Islamia* (Islamic Call) was established on the recommendation of the Islamic *Da'wa* conference that took place in Khartoum in 1980, with the aim of propagating Islamic ideals in Africa. In May 1980 a head office was established in Khartoum with the predominant support from the oil-producing countries. While not originally NIF controlled, the Islamists succeeded in outmanoeuvring the other contending major parties with strong Islamic orientation (both the Umma and DUP). In an interview with Benthall and Bellion-Jourdan, Sadiq al-Mahdi acknowledged such success: '[The Islamists] succeeded in grasping the resources of rich Muslims from Saudi-Arabia and Kuwait ... who considered it their duty to work for the Islamization of the Sudan's non-Muslims. The NIF appealed to them as follows, "If you put your resources in our hands, we will be able to convert non-Muslims of Sudan, and indeed Africa" ' (ibid., p. 120). 'That was the pretext ... for grasping resources which they proceeded to use for another purpose. By politicising these agencies, they involved them in the political confrontation, at the risk of weakening them and putting their future in doubt', (ibid., p. 120). Since mid-1983, the African Islamic Centre has played a major role in NIF penetration into the armed forces. Under the guise of religious awareness training courses, a number of army officers were recruited. 'The Military security was certainly aware of these activities but it itself was already infiltrated by pro-Islamist elements' (Mirghani, 2002, p. 239).

In the critical early years of Islamist rule, links between Islamist Iran, Islamist financial institutions and the 'old' comradeship with the Iranian and later the Iraqi Baathist provided vital support for the military operations in the South (weapons and training). Furthermore, the returns on Bin Laden's investment in the Sudan were immeasurable if we take into account the services provided by the official state apparatus including its diplomatic services. Over half of the 1990s, the Sudan served as a haven for Muslim militants. Recent accounts of such services (*The Guardian*, 17 October 2001) show how Bin Laden was able to extend Al-Qaida assistance to Islamists in diverse places as Saudi Arabia, Algeria, Syria, Chechnya, Turkey, Eritrea, Tajikistan, the Philippines and Lebanon.

An unfinished power struggle

The December 1999 measures taken by President El-Bashir included the sacking of pro-Turabi ministers and liquidation of his pan-Islamist organization, the 'Islamic Popular Conference', with the formation of two Islamic parties, the ruling 'National Congress Party' and Turabi's opposition party 'Popular National Congress', ending the dual leadership dilemma. El-Bashir's wing was a clear winner among the top leadership of the NIF, but the power struggle was merely temporarily resolved.[8] For a small party like the NIF, taking over the state apparatus meant that the entire membership was directly involved in the power structure (civil services, military and para-military organizations) including its PDF and the party vanguard units of the Dababeen (literally means tankers or highly charged Fedayeen type).

The rapprochement between the American administration and the Sudanese government following the traumatic 11 September events took many observers by surprise, but certainly not the keen observers of Sudanese affairs. The confusion was largely a result of the Sudanese Islamist groups maintaining two parallel discourses since coming to power in 1989. One discourse expressed a very militant anti-American sentiment and was used for internal mobilization. The 'Mojahhedeen' and 'Dababeen' (literally, 'tankers') and the PDF still chant anti-American songs promising the demise of American hegemony. Externally, a radically different image was portrayed according to the audience.

The mastermind of such a double discourse was not President El-Bashir but his adviser, Turabi, who justified his Machiavellian shifts by nicknaming his projects '*Figh Eldarura*' (literally, 'theology of necessity'), as was discussed earlier in this chapter. It was Turabi who engineered the hand-over of 'Carlos the Jackal' to France, carefully working his way through the corridors of French–African diplomatics.

Such policies continued all through the vicissitudes of American–Sudanese political relations. As early as 1992, the Sudanese government was carefully planning the normalization of its Western relations, commissioning two public relations offices in Washington and London and hiring American and British experts to handle counter lobbies.

The ability to comprehend and to influence the American political terrain should not be a surprise coming from a party with long-standing relations with the American establishment and whose most influential cadres were trained in the USA during much of the 1975–1990 period. It has now been revealed that the handing-over of Bin Laden to the American authorities was seriously considered by the NIF government as early as 1996. A similar deal was worked out with Egypt, while the handing-over of Libyan Islamists was undertaken with almost absolute clandestinity. Since then, the various rifts within the Islamic groups have become deeper and cross-accusations on the responsibility for the Libyan deal only recently have been aired publicly.

Post-September scenarios

Post-September events and political actions taken by the regime highlight the difficulties in maintaining two dramatically opposed levels of discourse (i.e. an external moderate and quasi-sectarian foreign policy and an internal discourse retaining the 'civilizing project' or at least its slogans). Such a challenge cannot be underestimated and can be costly for a minority regime whose only claim to legitimacy is the adherence to Islam and Islamic solidarity. Turabi, the original engineer of this dual policy, took no chances in staging a counter-campaign against such treason. Free from the direct burdens of 'responsible' foreign policies, Turabi's party was quick to condemn collaboration with the USA. In a statement issued on 26 October 2001, the Popular National Congress of Turabi condemned in unequivocal terms the surrender to the Americans, 'the sell-out of Islam', the hand-over of the suspects and the disclosure of their bank accounts. Ironically, Turabi's position brought him closer to the fragmented Northern opposition parties across the political spectrum. For example, the Communist party (statement on 24 October 2001), while condemning the senseless killing of civilians and taking a position that reflected the prevailing mood of deep distrust in American policy in the Middle East, condemned the killing of civilians in Afghanistan and called for a greater role for the UN in dealing with international terrorism. A similar position was taken by the leading Umma party and the Democratic Unionists (DUP). In other words, the tragic events of 11 September left clear marks on the political scene in Sudan and contributed to the process of accelerating the dissolution and realignments of the political arena. Faced with its own crisis of inherent dangers in maintaining dual discourses, the ruling Islamist faction of El-Bashir tried to diffuse the imminent danger of leaning on an unidentifiable mix of military support. Yet a pre-requisite for the success of such an option is the broadening of its power base to incorporate 'moderate' Islamist traditional parties of the Umma and DUP, or a section of them. This was an attractive option, as it could reduce the relative weight of a narrow fundamentalist support. The attempt to pursue such an option met with very limited success as it relied more on 'divide and rule' instead of genuine reconciliation with the various contending forces.

State privatization

The NIF's economic policies during the 1990s were by and large dictated by political survival agendas. The failed attempt at reconstruction that marked the early stage of the new regime consolidation, as was shown earlier, was soon replaced by policies emphasizing the maximization of surplus extraction, rather than the direct expansion and control over the process of surplus generation. The declining share of the modern agriculture and manufacturing sectors and the emergence of the traditional sector, particularly livestock, as a major surplus generator made the new macroeconomic stability policies conducive to the state's capacity to siphon the surplus. With negligible investment, the state was able to reap huge returns from taxing trade in this vast underutilized wealth. The quasi-floating exchange rate and removal of restrictions on holdings, as well as direct measures mentioned earlier aiming at maximizing the inflow of remittances and savings of migrant labour, all served to increase the visibility of inflow and its taxation.

The economic empowerment drive of the NIF's regime aimed at broadening and strengthening its grip of the commanding heights of the economy and was also perpetuated and legitimized by the liberalization policies. As discussed earlier, the control over Islamic banking was the major and initial tool for economic empowerment of the Islamic movement through multiple forms of preferential finance. Before the liberalization policies, direct looting of public funds and widespread corruption involving the use of public funds dominated. The well-documented corruption and illicit acquisition of state revenue became widely known following the rift within the NIF leadership in 1999. However, before such corrupt practices, the report of the Auditor General to the People's Assembly indicated that, in the period from October 1996 to the end of September 1997, 273 million Dinars were embezzled (155 million Dinars from states and 76 million Dinars from federal government). Out of this only 44 million Dinars were retrieved (cited in Ibrahim, 2003, p. 156). In the same report, the Auditor General indicated that, of the public funds illicitly squandered by the federal administration, 47 per cent was in the form of unauthorized expenditure, 34 per cent through illegal appropriation, 15 per cent through wasteful expenditure, 3 per cent forgery and 1 per cent outright theft (ibid., p. 157). Another widely publicized case of corruption was the misappropriation of public funds that was provided for building the so-called 'Western Salvation Road' linking the capital to Darfur. It was through this project that the pro-Turabi Minister Dr Ali El Haj (the second-ranked man in the Turabi faction) became well known following the rift in the Islamist movement. His response was to accuse the government of not being transparent about oil revenues (ibid., p. 174). After a saga of accusations and counter-accusations between the two factions of the NIF, President El-Bashir ordered the case closed. Addressing a rally upon the completion of the first phase of the road in July 2002, the President openly accused the former Western Road committee, led by Dr Ali El Haj, by then deputy leader of Turabi's faction PCP, of appropriating public funds that were collected from the impoverished population of the region, leaving him for God's judgment in heaven (ibid., p. 175).

The other important factor of state privatization and the ruling party's economic empowerment was import tax exemption for Islamic NGOs. The mushrooming of Islamic relief organizations led by NIF cadres during the 1990s was instrumental in financing the party, first, through Zakat and sympathizer funds from abroad and, second, through windfall profits accruing from the local sale of custom-exempted goods. The drain of such unjustifiable exemptions was huge. In 1996 the Minister of Finance complained that exemption had reached unsuitable levels, claiming half of the expected revenue. As a consequence of such policies revenue mobilization lagged behind both inflation and GDP growth. Total federal revenues deteriorated from 11.4 of GDP during 1981–1985 to 8.0 during 1996–2000 (World Bank, 2003, p. 44). The same report noted that, before a tax reform was launched in 1998, 'the revenue system was a complex web of a number of different taxes, tax exemptions, and tax brackets, which spawned loopholes. Lack of enforcement encouraged abuse of tax exemptions. The tax base eroded partly as a consequence of the weakening economy with falling trade and profits, and partly as a response of failures of the tax system to adjust the value of traded goods and tax brackets to multiple fixed exchange rates' (ibid., p. 49).

This process of empowerment was brought to its ultimate conclusion by the NIF takeover of the state apparatus. Tracing back the 'empowerment' trajectory before June 1989, Abdel Gadir (2006) concluded: 'The Salvation revolution was the era that witnessed a complete fusion between the Islamist empowered businessmen and the state'. This involved also a process of 'elite recycling between state apparatus and Islamic economic enterprises'. In his words, 'Who was the director of Baraka Islamic Bank became the minister of finance; and who was the director of Faisal Islamic Insurance Company became the minister of energy ....' The Sudan economy became their private property as they became the new ruling elite.[9]

All these forms of economic empowerment and restructuring of the economic and social bases of accumulation were occurring simultaneously with a process of formal privatization of the economy. The divestment process which started in the early 1990s, with the passage of the public sector Enterprises Disposition Bill of 1990, was formally inaugurated with the passage of the Privatization of the State Cooperation Act in 1999. The methods of privatization as shown in Table 4.1 varied including direct sales to the private sector, partnership, lease, management contract, free transfer to state governments, employee associations and NGOs, creation of holding companies, debt swap arrangements, and liquidation.

Table 4.1 Privatized companies

Instrument	Industry & Energy	Agriculture	Tourism & Transport	Miscellaneous	Total
Sale	10	2	3	4	19
Partnership	1	1	–	–	2
Leasing	–	–	1	–	1
Joint ventures	–	–	1	3	4
Restructured	–	3	–	3	6
Liquidation	2	2	–	–	4
Transferred to public sector	11	10	7	8	36
Total	24	18	12	18	72

Source: Technical Committee for the Disposition of Public Enterprise.

The privatization drive was, by and large, a transfer of federal assets to individual states. Only 20 enterprises have so far been sold to the private sector. The World Bank (2003) notes that,

> in addition to the uncertainties created by the war, implementation of the program has been constrained by: compensation costs of affected workers; limited market of buyers; resistance from managers; and lack of direct institutional base and dearth of technical expertise to prepare and manage transactions. The main criticism of the privatization program inside Sudan relates to the transfer of enterprises to state governments. Increased transparency and publicity about the disposition or transfers of public enterprises would have been welcomed. (ibid., p. 59)

Generally, the privatization programme failed to build momentum, and planned high-profile sales of key assets such as the National Electricity Company and Sudan Airways failed to materialize (EIU, 2003, p. 33). By 2005, Sudan Airways was effectively liquidated but the actual transaction to the foreign or local private sector has not yet taken place as this book goes to press. Assessing the overall performance of the privatization drive, the *Economist* annual country profile (2003, pp. 33–34) notes:

> Overall, however, the pace has been slow, reflecting a range of factors, not least of which has been the skills shortage among senior officials charged with overseeing what has often been a highly complex process of defining and valuing SOE assets. The valuation process has also been undermined by the large losses run by most state companies for many years. These have led to the accumulation of substantial debts, many of which are owed to public-sector financing agencies or commercial banks that were required to extend credit to them.

However, when examining the drive for the empowerment of the NIF, privatization does not come across as an effective tool. Previously public-sector companies were re-registered under the 1925 Companies Law, effectively relegating such enterprises to the private domain of the emerging official/business class of the Islamist movement. The ousted 'godfather' of the NIF was clueless as to how this new complex web of interests within the Islamist movement caused his downfall. Questions such as 'Why did the majority side with President El-Bashir within NIF?' were answered in a straightforward manner:

> The state expanded tremendously. It now incorporates companies, corporations, states and governments, the federal system was greatly enlarged, governments mushroomed and the corporation and companies that belong to the state more than in any socialist system in the world. It became difficult to forgo power and wealth. (Ibrahim, 2004, pp. 292–293)

The Auditor General (AD) reports for the years 2001–2005 revealed an unprecedented degree of opacity and unaccountability. Using public funds to support a one-party system is not unique to Sudan – certainly not in the surrounding region. The total lack, however, of boundaries between the NIF organs and its individual members on the one hand and state, civilian and military apparatuses on the other is indeed unprecedented in post-independence Sudan. A few examples from these reports will clarify the point:

- During 2004, proceeds from sales of public enterprises following nationalization were not reported anywhere. In the same report the total unreported receipts were estimated at 12.2 billion Dinars while the privatization committee in charge appropriated some 8.7 billion Dinars for itself.
- All bids and contracts with foreign and local business were not verified or reported to the General Auditor's office as regulation postulates.
- The 2004/5 report by the AD disclosed that a number of final accounts by state enterprises, provinces and states were factious and were meant to meet formally the presidential decree which introduced an incentive for closing accounts in time.
- In 2004, the total amount of illegal dealing in the three publicly owned commercial banks amounted to 373.3 billion Dinars.
- The AD report for 2004/5 revealed that, in one government unit, the director approved 42 financial incentives for himself and 40 for his financial manager 'for doing their normal job-specified tasks' (AD report 2004/5, *Alayaam Daily*, 23 May 2006).

The Islamist self-sufficiency project

Following an aggressive post-coup consolidation involving extreme repression, mass-arrest and purge from the state civilian and military machinery, the Islamists launched their vague populist project, known commonly as the 'civilization project'. In essence, the project was advocating self-sufficiency in food production and manufacturing. The dominant themes of mobilization became 'we shall eat what we produce ... we shall wear what we manufacture'.[10] The drive to self-reliance was dictated largely by international isolation and a severe deficit in the balance of payments, as both exports and remittances declined because of rocketing inflation and the persistent conditions that led to the erosion of profitability in the commodity-producing sectors. Emphasis in the self-reliance strategy was placed on changing the cropping pattern in irrigated agriculture, replacing cotton and other cash crops by wheat, banning imported sugar and enforcing lower rations for subsidized prices and a parallel free market for the sale of sugar and other basic commodities.

The pragmatism of the programme aimed at restoring profitability in the commodity-producing sector was undermined by the ideological symbols of the 'Islamic Project'. While Shari'a laws were seen as the umbrella of the Islamist state, Islamic banking was its major and perhaps only political Islam-driven institution with direct bearing on the economy. In the Sudanese version of Islamic Banking (IB), the most common Islamic financial instruments in use include the following:

Murabaha: a buy and resell contract. The bank purchases goods ordered by the client and resells them to the customer at a higher price (markup), usually on a deferred payment basis. This is IB's most favoured mechanism of financing. In effect, the yield from such contracts was consistently much higher than the 'non-Islamic' conventional interest-bearing financial contracts. IB is allowed to have a maximum 30 per cent of Murabaha contracts.

Musharaka: a partnership contract wherein the bank and the client share a project and its profits. Ownership corresponds to partnership in terms of financing, while losses are shared according to a specific ownership formula and profits are shared according to a pre-determined ratio.

Mudaraba: a form of partnership between the bank and client. As opposed to Musharaka, the client does not provide capital and management profits are shared according to a contract. Losses are the bank's responsibility.

Salam: a new formula designed for agricultural finance operations. According to this formula the bank purchases in advance the future output of agriculture at an agreed price.[11]

Other less important forms of Islamic financing include the more controversial 'Qard Hassan', literally 'free loan'. According to this formula IB advances a loan to a client provided that the repayment is made in foreign currency. Given the three-digit inflation prevailing in 1990 (averaging 106.4 per cent in the 1991–1995 period; World Bank, 2003, p. 44), IB used this formula as a safeguard against local currency erosion, but its impact on clients was devastating. Other forms include 'Ijara', which is a contract under which borrowers lease their assets to a third party subdivided into 'Mugara' for agricultural land as a crop-sharing contract; 'Mugawala' as a contract of hire of labour; 'Istisna'a' which is a contract of sale, used mainly for industrial finance, whereby a seller commits to produce a specific commodity at the request of the buyer; and, finally, 'Musaqu'a', which is a partnership and resale contract whereby banks buy goods and resell them with a markup.

All four major forms of Islamic Banking were ill suited for the commodity-producing sectors and in particular primary production. While Musharaka, the main mode of Islamic finance, is hardly applicable to agriculture, the main sector of the economy, other forms have their serious limitations. Musharaka partnership in management between banks and clients is equally unmanageable particularly with regard to medium and small agricultural projects. To address such serious limitations, the 'Salam' formula was introduced as a potentially suitable remedy for agricultural financing. 'Salam' proved to be nothing more than the exploitative traditional '*sheil*' system. In the non-formal '*sheil*' system rich village traders lend to farmers at the beginning of the planting season while output is sold to the trader at a pre-determined price. The impact of the 'Salam' formula was disastrous because of extremely low prices offered while the actual cost of production was escalating. Hundreds of farmers who failed to meet IB's 'Salam' contracts ended up in jail (Ali, 2004, p. 217). In effect, IB's lending policies and other government taxation and pricing policies, as well as erratic import policies, led to further deterioration in the commodity-producing sectors.

While the declared objectives of the 'Islamic Project' was self-sufficiency in food, the agricultural sector as a whole suffered from underinvestment, leading to deterioration in its basic infrastructure. This has been evidenced by a marked decline in the irrigated agricultural area under cultivation. 'Declining credit provision to the agricultural sector has also undermined growth, as the large number of non-performing loans to private agricultural enterprises have discouraged the commercial bank from providing new credit' (*The Economist*, 2003, p. 38).

The manufacturing sector showed poor growth throughout most of the 1990s, constrained by shortages in investment, trained personnel, raw materials, and foreign exchange for the import of essential intermediate inputs. These problems led to chronically low capacity utilization rates. In 1997, for example, the Ministry of Industry estimated that average capacity utilization for textile companies was just 10 per cent, despite the ready local supply of high quality cotton (ibid., p. 45).

Sugar refining was the most prominent exception in the manufacturing industry during the 1990s. The sugar industry throughout the 1990s maintained a positive growth and, by 2001, Sudan became a sugar exporter as production rose to 775,000 tons per year. In addition to its marked deficiency in providing suitable formulas for lending to the under-financed commodity-producing sectors, IB suffered from other major structural problems. The IMF's evaluation of commercial banking in the Sudan (Kireyev, 2001) identified the following institutional deficiencies: the excessive role of the central bank has discouraged the interbank market, competition and market discipline; high credit risks and the lack of competition among banks contribute to the high cost of borrowing; the weak private deposit base because of institutional and historical reasons; a central bank that is largely cut-off from the international financial system; and under-capitalization. In 1991, the government imposed limits on deposit withdrawal which seriously undermined people's trust in the banking system. Despite a later reversal of such a policy, the share of investment deposits never retained its pre-1991 level. The annual Economist Report (EIU) rightly noted that the shift to the Islamic system, the upheaval of the post-coup period and extensive political interference in the banks' operations compounded the pre-existing frailties of the banking sector, generated by years of neglect and the demands of a war. Bad debts grew as proportion of total loans, profitability fell, and the banks' capital bases were eroded. Intermediation also fell, with bank credit to the private sector falling in real (and even nominal) terms throughout most of the early and mid-1990s (EIU, 2003, p. 47).

In addition to disinvestment in the agricultural sector and lack of finance internally, the terms of trade for Sudan's traditional exports deteriorated over the 1990–2001 period. The prices of cotton and sorghum fell at an average annual rate of 11.3 and 3 per cent respectively. The prices of groundnuts and sesame also declined (World Bank, 2003, p. 27). Thus, despite the growth of exports in the late 1990s as Northern and Central Sudan enjoyed relatively drought-free conditions, the prices of Sudanese key traditional exports experienced a downward trend between 1996 and 2001. During this period the price of sorghum declined at an average annual rate of 2.2 per cent while the price of cotton fell 10 per cent per year on average. A combination of under-investment in irrigated agriculture, lack of finance for the whole sector and unfavourable international prices led to a dramatic structural shift in the agricultural sector. Traditional agriculture and livestock became the dominant sources of growth for primary production and export, as shown in Table 4.2.

In the war-torn Southern Sudan, agriculture is characterized by subsistence farming, shifting cultivation, intercropping, rotation and the raising of livestock. Even before the start of the civil war in 1983, Southern Sudan was not self-sufficient in cereal production. The 1998 drought had a devastating effect on crop production. A survey by the FAO and the World Food Programme (WFP) shows that smallholder crop production in Southern Sudan declined sharply in 1998 because of serious drought (FAO/WFP, 2002). Since then, production has

Table 4.2 Relative growth of sub-sectors of agriculture during the 1990s

Sub-sector	Average annual growth rate during the 1990s
1. Rain-fed traditional agriculture	24%
2. Livestock	10%
3. Irrigated crop	7.9%
4. Semi-mechanized crop	2.9%

Source: World Bank, 2003.

Table 4.3 Cereal production in Southern Sudan (1997/98–2000/01)

Region	Production ('000t)				Yields (tons/ha)			
	97/98	98/99	99/00	00/01	97/98	98/99	99/00	00/01
Traditional Production	477	162	321	370	1.05	0.38	0.69	0.57
Upper Nile	91	45	85	83	0.60	0.34	0.71	0.65
Equatoria	218	71	166	175	1.47	0.37	0.87	0.70
Bahr El Ghazal	168	46	70	112	1.10	0.49	0.44	0.41

Source: FAO/WFP Crop and Food Supply Assessment, January 2002.

Table 4.4 Growth rates of major crops across all farming systems (1971/72–1999/2000)

Crops	1971/72– 1980/81 Output	1981/82– 1990/91 Output	Output	1987/88– 1999/00[a] Area	Yield
Cotton	−8.8	−6.4	−7.21 (3.07)	−4.63 (2.09)	−2.64 (2.85)
Groundnuts	6.4	−11.4	12.26 (3.18)	11.31 (3.24)	0.48 (0.29)
Gum Arabic	–	–	2.68 (0.61)	–	–
Millet	0.4	−10.4	11.74 (2.81)	7.01 (2.31)	4.16 (1.81)
Sesame	−3.5	−4.1	7.25 (2.39)	7.40 (2.87)	0.09 (0.05)
Sorghum	3.7	−3.5	4.69 (1.45)	3.46 (1.69)	4.52 (2.40)
Sunflower	–	−23.2	−10.17 (2.75)	−14.73 (5.26)	4.52 (2.40)
Wheat	4.1	14.9	0.55 (0.13)	−2.86 (0.81)	2.40 (1.60)

Source: Ali Abdel Gadir Ali, 'Economic Growth and Growth Prospects in Sudan', Background Paper for the CEM, mimeo, April 2002.
Note: Growth rates calculated using least square fit of semilog function to the base. Numbers in parenthesis are statistics that indicate the degree of statistical confidence in the growth rates; if above 2, statistics usually indicate 95 per cent confidence.

increased but yields are still much below the pre-drought harvest, as indicated in Table 4.3.

A 2002 survey of livestock marketing suggested that the number of cattle, estimated at 5.8 million per head, with similar numbers of sheep and goats, has been increasing for several years in Southern Sudan as a result of improvement in animal health care and weather.

The outcome of the NIF's short-lived populist project of self-sufficiency during the 1990–1995 period was disastrous. Emphasis was on wheat production at the expense of cotton with its established comparative advantage. As shown in Table 4.4, the agricultural sector which was already at a low point in 1984/1985, coinciding with the end of the severe drought of 1983–1985, continued its decline. The growth rates induced by a strong incentive package attracted many farmers. Consequently, 'the area of wheat increased sharply in 1990/1991, but then declined steadily because of disappointing profits. Yields for wheat improved only slightly and the production of irrigated wheat declined considerably' (World Bank, 2003, p. 89). Cotton never recovered from the 1990–1992 government-enforced shift to wheat. Overall, the profitability in irrigated agriculture continued its downward trend despite the government abandoning its efforts to administratively increase grain production as part of the self-reliance strategy.

The era of economic survival policies

The NIF's economic policies during the 1990s were by and large dictated by its political survival agenda. The early post-coup attempt at restoring the profitability of the commodity-producing sector of the economy was soon given up in favour of a quick yielding strategy. The increasing international isolation of the regime following the Gulf War and the drying up of external sources of finance coupled with the escalation of the cost of civil war internally dictated the direction of economic policies. The obvious targets in the Sudan were two major sources of surplus generation: first, the traditional sector – particularly livestock – which became the major export earner among commodity exports and, second, remittances from Sudanese Working Abroad (SNWA) which since the mid-1980s became the Sudan's major export (representing almost two-fold of the total export earnings). The increasing role as a labour exporter in the 1990s was further reinforced by the massive migration of educated elites resulting from economic hardship and a large-scale political purge from the state apparatus as the NIF started its state privatization programme. Following the mid-1980s informed estimate, by the mid-1990s remittances must have reached four- to five-fold total earnings from exports.

The severity of the economic crisis by the mid-1990s is well reflected in Table 4.5. Sudan's exports and external transfers continued to decline while inflation remained at three digits.

Attempts at achieving direct control over the flow of remittances and channelling all foreign currency transactions largely failed. Despite the summary hanging of three citizens accused of hoarding foreign currency and the 1991 measures of freezing deposits in commercial banks and setting a very low ceiling for withdrawal

Table 4.5 Balance of payments, 1982–1995 (US $ millions)

Item	1982–1985	1986–1990	1991–1995
Trade of goods (net)	−188.5	−417.4	−543.8
Exports	531.0	478.4	424.2
Imports	−1138.6	−912.4	−1000.4
Current transfers (net)	251.8	341.7	117.5
Inflation	32.1	43.3	106.4

Sources: IMF Balance of Payment yearbook, Central Bureau of Statistics, Government of Sudan, World Bank 2003.

from deposits, the growing gap between official and parallel exchange rates reached its peak between 1989 and 1991, averaging over 150 per cent before going down to an average of 50 per cent over the 1991–1995 period. The combination of aggressive monetary control, deteriorating economic conditions and escalation of political repression led to actual decline in remittances and widely observed capital flight to neighbouring countries. It was estimated that capital flight to Egypt alone was around two billion dollars by the mid-1990s, mostly in the form of real estate and manufacturing activities (Elmahadi, 1997). An additional reaction to the conditions prevailing in Khartoum was that Cairo, rather than Khartoum, became the destination for Sudanese summer vacations. This further reduced the inflow of remittances into the economy. The introduction of higher taxation rates on income and high charges on various administration services provided to expatriate Sudanese reached such a high level that many Sudanese nationals working abroad found it more rational to minimize the number of visits home.

By the mid-1990s, the state, measured as a share of GDP, shrank to the lowest level since independence. As shown in Figure 4.1, state revenue and expenditure were slightly above 5 per cent of GDP by 1994.

In the mid-1990s, the Sudanese economy reflected fully the economic costs of civil war: immediate and substantial decline of output and the larger repercussions on physical, human and social capital with all the effects of conflict suggested by Collier (1999) manifesting their negative impact on the economy. Military destruction reduced the capital stock, government expenditure was diverted to the military, disruption raised the cost of transactions and lowered the cost of opportunistic behaviour so that social capital started to break down, people spent their money haphazardly and, because investment opportunities were unusually poor and risky, agents shifted their portfolios abroad. These have implications for the composition of economic activity as, accordingly, the GDP growth rate is typically 2.2 percentage points per year lower than in a time of peace. Capital-intensive activities typically suffer disproportionately. Thus, analysing the economic consequences and causes of civil war is central to understanding

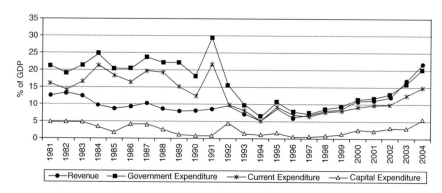

Figure 4.1 Government revenue and spending (% of GDP).
Source: Sudan Ministry of Finance and National Economy.

the growth and development process in the Sudan. Estimates of the possible costs incurred by the Sudan during just four years (1989/90–1993/94) and due to just two of the above channels – (i) the intensity of the war, which is assumed to lead to political instability, erosion of the state and civil society instruments, and the consequent decline in property rights and the enforcement of contracts; and (ii) the diversion of the limited human, financial and physical resources to military ends – suggest that the Sudan investment ration ended up as less than one-third of its potential level under normal conditions, leading to a reduction in the growth of real national output per person by 2 percentage points annually (JAM, 2005, p. 80).

The era of savage stabilization

Faced with the deepening of the economic crisis, state shrinkage and civil war intensification, the Islamist regime sharply reversed its policy of state control and self-sufficiency. Since the mid-1990s, the regime has engaged in sweeping macroeconomic stability and liberalization policies. The ruthless implementation of the Sudanese version of macroeconomic stability and liberalization programmes needs to be seen in light of the fact that, while state capacity to extract surplus or allocate it was seriously undermined, its defence and security needs were mounting. Failing to appropriate migrant remittances through administrative means, the macroeconomic stabilization policies, leading to almost a free-floating exchange rate, were the only available means to capturing the increase in remittances. Ironically, the three-digit inflation of the first half of the 1990s which triggered a new emigration phase was at the same time instrumental in increasing the flow of remittances particularly for unaccompanied migrants as the cost of living increased exponentially. This was further aggravated by the removal of subsidies for consumer goods and increasing cost of education and health as the state spending on both services dwindled down to its lowest level since independence (see Table 4.6).

Several ad hoc measures were introduced to encourage the flow of migrant remittances and savings abroad into the economy. The measures included establishment of a high yielding government bond that secured the purchase of badly needed arms and the establishment of arms industries which eased the pressure of sanctions. Other measures included the widespread sales of

Table 4.6 Gini coefficients for wage labourers in urban and rural areas (1967/1968–1996)

	1967/68	1978/80	1990	1996
Rural	0.34	0.51	0.69	0.65
Urban	0.41	0.42	0.56	0.72
Total	0.41	0.50	0.61	0.74

Source: Ibrahim Ahmed Ibrahim, Abdalla M. Elobodi and Mustafa Y Holi, 'Poverty, Employment and Policy Making in Sudan', Draft, November 2001.

government land for residence, commercial activities and farming. However, these measures, particularly the high rate bonds, effectively crowded the commodity-producing sector from the credit market. Borrowing by business at these extremely high interest rates led to widespread default rates. Thus by 1998/99 non-performing loans amounted to 18–19 per cent of total credit, leading to further weakening of the already inadequate capitalization of the commercial banks in the Sudan (Kireyev, 2001, p. 9). The increasing inability of the Sudanese financial system to credit private sector companies reflected its prolonged deficiencies. Kireyev reveals that these deficiencies reflect the deep-rooted problems of the Sudanese economy – it remains heavily skewed towards agriculture, with immature industrial and service sectors, confidence in banks is remarkably low, and external financing is virtually non-existent. The decline in credit was also due to the inefficiency of the banking business's structural inadequacies (lack of mechanisms for agricultural financing, outdated financial laws, design shortcomings in consortium financing), as well as the need to observe religious rules unavoidable under the Shari'a (ibid., p. 19).

The social costs of the government's stabilization drive were huge. It is true that the government succeeded in bringing inflation down to a single-digit level by 1997. With no access to external funding and escalating war, productive sectors and services were the prime losers. The World Bank (2003) notes that, 'between 1992 and 1998, expenditures were cut by more than 50 per cent relative to gross domestic product (GDP), causing considerable reductions in social services and infrastructure development' (ibid., p. i). Despite the lack of a comprehensive household survey since 1978, several studies (Ali, 1985, 1992; Ali and Elbadwi, 2003) do show an increasing disparity between and within states and regions, between urban and rural areas, between war-affected areas and between men and women. With the rural to urban exodus that resulted from civil war, drought and eroded traditional means of subsistence, urban poverty acquired new dynamics and reached unprecedented levels of destitution (Elnur, 2003). Middle-income and low-income groups were severely squeezed (World Bank, 2003, p. vii). Table 4.6 shows the results of four surveys undertaken in 1967/68, 1978/80, 1990 and 1996 which reflect the World Bank's findings that 'inequality in income has been much higher in urban than in rural areas' (ibid., p. 31).

Remittances and the deepening of disparities

The exodus of Sudan's best trained professionals and middle-income groups to oil-producing countries and diasporas in the global north, besides its significant drain on human capital, has accelerated inequalities within the urban sector. Fageer *et al*'s (2002) study of wage differentials noted that such exodus sharply increased the wage differential through the effect on the dispersion of wages. In order to retain well-educated staff, employers had to offer higher wages to the remaining professionals. Labour survey data in the 1990s suggest widening inequality in formal salaries. The top 10 per cent acquired 51.6 per cent of all earnings in 1990, and 64.3 per cent in 1996. At the same time, the poorest docile had become poorer. The lowest-income group's share decreased from 28.3 per cent in 1990 to 21.9 per cent in 1996.

While estimates of 70–90 per cent of Sudan's population living below the poverty line may be subject to some serious criticism in the absence of a reliable household survey and because of wider observed underestimation of income in less comprehensive surveys, the sharp increase in poverty during the 1990s is evident nevertheless. Indeed, remittances from migrant labour augmented declining incomes. However, given the fact that the overwhelming majority of migrants are from Northern Sudan and riverain Sudan meant that the severe deterioration of household income was halted or reduced by additional income from remittances. A number of studies at regional and sub-regional levels indicated the importance of this additional income support (see, for example, Gelal Eldin, 1985; Elnur, 2002). Such positive impact of migrant remittances applies to both rural and urban riverain Sudan. Migrant savings continue to have a positive impact on urban employment, yet the skewed distribution of remittances meant that the regional disparity between central riverain Sudan and the rest of the country further exacerbated. The already excessive educational disparities between the centre and the rest of Sudan were reproduced via migration into income disparities.

While the implications of the deepening of poverty and regional disparities are pervasive, the medium and long-term implications of disinvestment on health and education may prove irreparable. As shown in Table 4.7, spending on education decreased to less than 1 per cent from a high of 4.8 per cent of GDP. Post-independence gains of expanded competitive educational systems that made possible Sudan's emergence as a predominantly labour-exporting economy were almost completely cancelled out. The pattern of expansion favouring higher education against a narrow-based general school system that failed to accommodate half of the children of schooling age was disastrous. A shift from elitist education to mass education at the university level as part of the so-called 'revolution of higher education' was a leap on feeble legs. With meagre resources made available for education and the exodus of trained faculty to neighbouring oil-producing countries, the expansion resulted in a sharp decline in quality. The planned 'Arabization' of the higher education, deteriorating infrastructure

Table 4.7 The drastic cuts on public spending on education: 1970–2000

	1970	*1980*	*1985*	*1990*	*1995*	*2000*
Education as a % of budget	12.6	9.1	15.0	8	10.5	7.8
As a % of GDP	3.9	4.8	4.0	1.3	0.8	1.1
Enrolment Primary	38	50	50	50	53.1	58.5
Secondary	7.4	16	19.9	22.2	27.9	30
Tertiary	1.1	1.7	1.9	3.4	7.7	9*

Sources: Elnur (1998); World Bank (2003) for 2000.
Note: Private universities accounted for 14.7 per cent of those enrolled in tertiary education.

and the simultaneous establishment of 27 public universities in less than three years brought about a disaster in Sudanese higher education. Old centres of excellence were largely eroded through huge losses of experienced staff and under-funding. The dwindling resources made available for higher education did not allow post-graduate training. Thus the combination of the trained staff exodus and lower quality local graduate education meant effectively that intra-generational transmissions of knowledge and academic traditions were blocked. With the advent of the post-1995 liberalization, another important change in educated elite reproduction trajectories took place. A parallel private schooling from pre-school to universities emerged. This new emerging integrated system catered to the relatively affluent population and became the new path to excellence at the primary level, 4 per cent at the secondary level and 14.7 per cent at the university level.

Gross enrolment rates disguise considerable regional variations. The enrolment rates of primary (basic) education were around 80 per cent in the northern Khartoum, Gezira and Nile states; they are below 20 per cent in the government-controlled areas of Southern Sudan and much lower in SPLA-held areas (UNICEF, 2001; World Bank, 2003). Strong urban biases in terms of access to and quality of education and in the gender balance is vastly closing in urban areas; however, the disparities between rural and urban settings are serious. Much higher gender imbalances persist in Southern Sudan (GoS and UN, 2004). At the university level, female students outnumbered males. From 1990/1991 to 2000/2001, enrolment at university level grew on average by 16 per cent per annum, with the result that by the end of the 1990s female students outnumbered males (World Bank, 2003, p. 136). However, it seems that this phenomenon may reflect some cultural preferences wherein parents prefer to educate females at home universities rather than abroad. For example, out of over 6,000 Sudanese students in the private universities in Egypt, male students represent 80 per cent. (Based on data from the three largest private universities in Egypt.) Similar percentages are believed to be the case for Sudanese university students in India, Malaysia and Syria where there are large concentrations of Sudanese studying abroad.

Expenditure on health averaged less than 1 per cent (i.e. 0.08 per cent) of GDP during 1998–2000 for the Sudan, compared to an average of 3.1 per cent during the 1980s and 3.5 during the 1960s–1980. Similar to education, but at a much higher rate, post-independence achievements in primary health care, disease control and practically all aspects of health services were almost completely wiped out. The state-sponsored stabilization and liberalization policies amounted to the state's complete withdrawal from health services. The World Bank assessment report (2003) concluded that 'it is therefore not surprising that, following the decline in public health services, many of Sudan's health indicators are among the lowest in sub-Saharan Africa' (ibid., p. 109). In addition to a serious increase in the mortality of children under five years of age, malaria is the most serious health problem. 'An estimated 7–7.5 million cases of malaria occur annually. It accounts for 21 per cent of all diseases seen at outpatients in health facilities throughout Sudan, ranging from 14 to 25 per cent according to location. Malaria is also a major cause of child mortality'. 'Next to malaria, but much less important in terms of incidence, are tuberculosis, meningitis, typhoid fever, schistosomiasis, and leishmaniasis, for which people are treated at inpatient hospitals' (GAPS, 2003, p. 4). The direct economic cost of the widespread malaria is immense. The World Health Organization's Commission on Macroeconomics and Health (CMH) led by Jeffery Sachs 'spelled out the immense returns to health. The CMH illustrates the economic return to health by calculating the number of life years lost through preventable deaths, taking account of the lower productivity through illness and disability ("disability-adjusted life years" or DALYs). The cost of DALY is estimated at three times average national income'. Applying this to the case of malaria in sub-Saharan Africa the cost of malaria is no less than 17.4 per cent. 'Accordingly countries with endemic malaria have a GNP per capita about 75 per cent lower than countries without' (cited in de Waal, 2001).

Politicization of ethnicity

Darfur is a good example of how a complex story of competition over resources can be transferred through political agency into an all-out ethnic conflict. The political manipulation of ethnicity during the third democracy (1986–1989) was brought to its conclusion by the NIF during its ascendancy to power and then again whilst settling accounts between its two factions following the 1999 split. In addition to the erosion of its structural foundation, the use of traditional communal leadership to consolidate the NIF's power and to settle disputes between Islamist factions completed the process of rendering these structures entirely dysfunctional. In his excellent study of the links between local government and the social fabric in Darfur, El Zein (2003) described how the NIF regime introduced a parallel system to the traditional communal leadership structure. The so-called '*Shura* Councils' (literally Advisory Councils) gradually replaced the traditional leadership. The Shura Council, intended for rural communities, was soon established in urban centres where communal allegiances had been in decline. El Zein notes: 'The *Shura* leaders where no longer confined to the maintenance of peace and order as the major tasks of the traditional communal leadership. Instead *Shura* leaders presented themselves as missionary spiritual leaders: Leading prayers; advising people in religious matters; mobilizing people for the holy *Jihad* war in Southern Sudan and they themselves became warlords' (ibid., p. 13).

This is yet another example of a minority regime, weakly supported by its populace, attempting to use or to regenerate tribal and ethnic associations in order to extend its outreach. Jabar's (2000) work on the detribalization and retribalization of Iraq over the 1968–1986 period draws similar conclusions. He coined such processes as '*Etatist* Tribalism' as distinct from 'Social Tribalism', whereby the state surrenders some of its authority to tribal and lineage networks. The re-emergence of social tribalism within an urban setting usually denotes the increasing isolation of the regime.

Conclusion

As opposed to the previous period of the 1970s which witnessed the laying of the structural foundation of the crisis in the economy and society of the Sudan, NIF rule brought this crisis to its conclusion. Measures aiming at consolidating power through privatization of the state and manipulation of tribal and ethnic differences ended up with an almost complete state collapse. The Islamist-dominated regime of 1989–2004 triggered processes that brought the crisis to its ultimate conclusion of the fragmentation of the state and the disintegration of old routes of societal reproduction through repressive and chaotic management of the process of capitalist accumulation. Ironically the same process that enabled the Islamist ascendancy, i.e. political and economic empowerment, triggered a process of sharp differentiation within the ranks of the movement elites that was not concluded by the formal split of 1999. Furthermore, over two decades of relentless *Jihad* advocacy produced far more militant Islamist groups that now enjoy the support of the disgruntled youth. The ascendancy of *Ansar Elsuna*, a Sudanese closer version of Wahhabi Islam, as the most powerful Islamic group of university students is an example. The proliferation of other uncontrollable *Jihadist* groups is yet another manifestation of the crisis of the Islamist movement.[12] The Islamic movement which ascended to power as a highly organized and united block is no longer there. The movement was reduced to a small, albeit powerful, clique that controlled the state apparatus and in particular its military and security sections. The oil export started in 1999 came at a time of political, economic and military exhaustion, marking the decline rather than the ascendancy of the NIF. Its implications for war intensification and peace negotiations are discussed in the next part.

Part 3
Re-negotiating a Sudan

5   Sudan's war-produced economy and society

The case for transformative potential

> It is hardly possible to overrate the value, in the present low state of human improvement, of placing human beings in contact with persons dissimilar to themselves, and with modes of thought and action unlike those which they are familiar ... such communication has always been, and is peculiarly in the present age, one of the primary sources of progress.
>
> John Stewart Mill

Introduction: the case of transformative potential

Earlier on in Chapters 3 and 4 it was shown how the active agency of the state through strategies, action and inaction undermined the structural foundation of the post-colonial economy and society. Man-made and natural calamities (drought) intensified such a process. As a result state capacity to manage and control flows in the economy and society were equally eroded. The post-Islamist ascendancy brought the crisis to its conclusion as the state relative autonomy was completely undermined. The state itself became a faction, albeit the largest, among the contending factions. In simple terms, this chapter states that war is not a natural calamity and as such changes produced by war are irreversible. It further suggests that understanding these changes from war is central to the understanding of potential challenges to post-war reconstruction both in terms of governance and sustainable economic and social rebuilding of war-torn communities. Understanding the changes triggered by both internal and external population flows that result from prolonged civil conflicts represents the single most important challenge to a successful reconstruction and peace-building effort at the end of war. As it was argued and concluded in Chapter 2, an alternative conceptual framework for analysing war-produced communities is needed. Such an alternative needs to go beyond the static notion of retrieving the pre-war situation. The framework elaborated before in Chapter 2 suggested that war and other forms of conflict that affect stable and secure human habitats trigger processes that result in the constant production of 'irreversibilities'.

This chapter, using Sudan's war-torn communities as an example, shows how intensified and accelerated massive population flows produce new urbanities, ruralities and local to translocal and transnational diasporic experiences that pose serious challenges to any notion of retrieving a pre-war situation. Data and analysis of the war-displaced population in Greater Khartoum are based on extensive fieldwork that was carried out during the 1990 to 1993 period (DPSG files,[1] Elnur *et al.*, 1993, 1994, and follow-up visits in 2000 and 2002). This fieldwork provided a rich and indispensable understanding of the processes shaping the livelihood of the displaced populations, the urban space and its economy. The chapter concludes that war, itself a complete departure from the unilinear path of modernity, triggers multiple processes and transformative potentials that cannot be readily predictable. Furthermore, this chapter suggests that the nexus between development and post-war reconstruction lies precisely in the ability to capture such transformative potential. As explained in Chapter 2 such transformative potentials are not readily attainable and their direction (progressive or regressive) is not evident. The context of post-war policies, whether conducive or not for harnessing such potential, is a central issue.

The wars of displacement

The massive population displacement resulting from the second civil war in Southern Sudan (1983–2005), and the ongoing humanitarian crisis in Darfur that peaked in 2003 onwards, is a result of a significant change in the nature of wars and conflict in the two most war-torn regions. People, their land and their assets became the target of contending forces. The objective varied: recruiting; denying the opportunity to recruit; looting assets; determining potential threats; or simply denying 'others' the potential for establishing an orderly populated zone.[2] The dynamics of such a policy was shaped and reshaped by the changing balance of power between the contending forces, ecological changes and more visible direct interest (e.g. oil exploration or transport). Invariably, the impact on targeted communities was huge, leading to significant changes in the 'home' and 'receiving' ends of migratory flows as well as the forced migrants', composition, assets and institution. By the time of the signing of the Comprehensive Peace Agreement in 2005, roughly 80 per cent or so of the Southern population were no longer in their usual habitat (the overwhelming majority for over two decades). With the ongoing Darfur crisis the figure in 2007 stands at roughly 50 per cent of the population.

The history of massive forced population displacement in Sudan in the last two and a half decades resulting from civil wars, drought, famine, intertribal disputes and the gradual erosion of the foundations of the nation state is a poignant manifestation of the overall political and socio-economic crisis in the Sudan. The Sudan became independent in January 1956. Since then the country has been ravaged by prolonged civil wars. The first civil war in Southern Sudan carried on for 17 years (1955–1972). This ended with the Addis Ababa 1972 peace agreement, but the peace lasted for only a decade, and a second, far more violent and larger-scale civil war erupted again in 1983. By mid-2006, almost one-fifth of the Sudan's total population of 36 million were either internally or externally displaced. Roughly 10 per cent of the total forced migrants were externally displaced. The casualties, human losses and displacement of civilian population were enormous, but the pattern, sequence and direct causes of displacement in the two civil wars were significantly different.

The most salient consequence of the civil wars that has plagued the Sudan over the past two decades is depopulation. This has resulted in the loss of approximately two-thirds of Southern Sudan's population (4 million internally displaced persons (IDPs) in the North and transnational areas between the North and South and 5 million as refugees). Within the South, the remaining two million are mostly not residing in the indigenous home communities. One study describes the 'combined effect of militia attacks, bombing raids and mass eviction of ten exacerbated during periods of drought, is to create a state of chronic insecurity and poverty, particularly among rural communities in the South towards transition zone between North and South, and another further north of the capital, Khartoum' (IRIN, December 1999, web special).

The early 1970s estimate of the first civil war was that up to 25 per cent of Southern Sudan's population was displaced (one million; Mills, 1977). However, following the UN-sponsored repatriation and resettlement operation in 1974 some estimated that the number displaced by war could be as high as 2–2.5 million, suggesting that almost half of the population was displaced (Akol, 1986, p. 146; Mills, 1977 and 1982). Such estimates were difficult to substantiate. Total external refugees did not exceed 219,400 (Repatriation and Settlement Committee, 1974, cited in Akol, 1986) with another 800,000 internally displaced, supporting the generally accepted figure of around one million displaced persons in total or roughly 20 per cent of Southern Sudan population.

The displacement resulting from the civil war of 1983 is far greater. Southern displaced persons were estimated to be more than two million (half of them resettled in Greater Khartoum) by March 1989 (Burr, 1990, p. 18). Out of these, the UNHCR reported 333,000 Sudanese refugees in four camps in Ethiopia in January 1989. Such figures amount to almost half of the Southern Sudan's total population of five million, according to the 1983 census. By 1992, 4.5 million people were estimated to be internally displaced. Considering the post-1992 war-induced migration to neighbouring Ethiopia, there is no doubt that more than half of Southern Sudan's population is currently displaced.

Furthermore, drought and famine during the mid-1980s led to the displacement of hundreds of thousands of nomads from Kordofan and Darfur, who mostly headed towards Greater Khartoum. When the more recent escalation of the conflict in Darfur is taken into consideration, the scale of such unprecedented displacement must be entirely magnified. Despite its shorter duration, the Darfur conflict, which started in the early 1990s, led to the displacement of more than half of its population of six million: 1.8 million IDPs, 200,000 in refugee camps in Chad, and an estimated one million in Northern Sudan and abroad (UNHCR, 2006; IDMC, 2006; Assal, 2006).[3]

Another more interesting aspect is the overlapping and interlocking nature of variables pertaining to displacement (for example, drought, famine, sudden eruption of epidemic, inter- and intra-tribal conflict). During the 1980s and since, these variables were and have been bolstering one another. For example, the 1984 drought and famine in Western Sudan coincided with the intensification of the civil war in Southern Sudan. Drought in Western Sudan during the 1985 to 1987 period resulted in animal deaths which led to raids and massive attacks between the Rizeigat, Misseriya and Dinka tribes. This crisis culminated in the notorious Eldein massacres of April 1987 (see Ushari and Baldo, 1987). Thousands of Dinka women, children and elderly fled the North. Some communities were almost completely displaced: 'nearly 70 per cent of all Mgok Dinka agriculturists were displaced by war and Misseriya Arab herders took possession of their vacated lands in their absence' (p. 39). One of the least displaced populations is in Eastern Sudan where a population of around 1.6 million (UN, 18 November 2003, vol. 11, p. 42) includes 60,000 IDPs and the largest population of Eritrean refugees: 'Kassala is a catchments area for IDPs, refugees and migrants' (ibid., p. 32). The Nile State is considered a heaven for IDPs from neighbouring states and hosts 153,000 war and drought-drawn IDPs as well as 20,700 IDPs from the Nuba Mountains (Global IDPs, p. 6). Effectively, this means that IDPs represent 17.3 per cent of the original home of riverain Sudanese whose population has been depleted by both internal and external migration.

Almost half of the 50 per cent population, who are still in the Nuba Mountains, are themselves internally displaced: 'original inhabitants in the hills who now have three to ten times the original population living around them and sharing the same limited resources, and people who no longer have access to their traditional land and livelihood, e.g. the returnees of Shuwa in Saada *Payam*' (UNRHCR, Nuba SPLM, 30 June 2003, pp. 4–5).

A different hosting urban space

Simone (1994) provides a description of Khartoum, a city whose population has tripled in less than three decades (from two million to seven million) as the result of famine (1984), devastating war (1982 and onwards) and war-related famine and disruptions. Simone provides an apt description of the war-induced urbanity: 'the orderliness and tranquility of Khartoum is gone, it has become a wild, uncontrollable city full of crimes, thieves, drunkards, whores, hustlers, homeless, shills and terrorists, which all the various security organs and religious police are hard pressed to "tame"' (Simone, 1994, p. 118). It is within the context of such new 'urbanities' and 'ruralities', with boundaries completely blurred, that questions relating to the implications of new urbanities emerging out of the wreckages of old modernity and the new economic, social and political structures and processes should be directed.

In addition to war-led rural to urban migration being significantly different from the earlier post-colonial mode (in terms of initial conditions, demographic characteristics and pace), the urban host space also is significantly different from that of the earlier post-colonial one. The urban space, as a centre for expanding quasi-egalitarian social services, has been greatly reshaped by the 'premature' shrinkage of state-sponsored welfare regimes. In the case of the Sudan, the aggressive post-1989 application of structural adjustment policies, privatization and trade liberalization meant that the old route to urban mobility à la Turner has been effectively blocked. The government's spending on social services, in particular on health and education, was less than half of its 1989 percentage share of a shrinking national income with a significant shift away from spending on basic education in favour of higher education (Elnur, 1999, pp. 318–319). By the 1990s, public expenditure on health slipped down to less than 1 per cent of GDP (0.7 per cent) representing only 20.9 per cent of total per capita expenditure on health care (AHD Report, 2002). Public expenditure on education decreased from approximately 5 per cent in the 1970s and 3.3 per cent in the 1980s to an all-time record low representing a mere 1.4 per cent. (ibid., Elnur, 1999). Trade liberalization, privatization and ensuing deindustrialization ultimately resulted in a shrinking of the urban formal sector. Informality became the order of urban growth, bringing in new institutions and new agents. While the Sudan case, with its uniquely long history of civil war, may represent an extreme example, the LDCs' retreat from the earlier commitment to welfare is universal. The past three decades have shown that an accelerated expansion of urbanization is neither linked to state capacity, to service urban expansion, nor to overall output growth. Accelerated urban growth as shown in Table 5.1 is associated with both positive and negative growth and with both shrinking and sustained welfare.

Displacement and survival

A study of survival strategies in internally displaced communities in Sudan (Elnur *et al.*, 1993) suggests that the sequence of events, which led to the displacement in the first place, is critical in determining the options that are open to households to ensure their survival. Furthermore, it was found that the particular strategies selected by a household can be expected to vary according to the sequence of events which caused the displacement, people's acquisition of assets, the traditional source of household livelihood, the proximity to urban centres, the

Table 5.1 The pace of urbanization: a comparative perspective urbanization (percentage of total population)

Country/Region	1980	1990	2000	2005	Slum dwellers as per cent of total urban population
Sudan	20.0	26.0	37.0	40.8	40.0*
North Africa	44.6	48.8	52.2	58.1	71.9
SSA	21.1	26.3	33.2	38.2	30.7

Sources: World Global Report on Human Settlement, 2002, and UN-Habitat Global Urban Observatory data, World Urbanization Prospects: The 2005 Revision Population Database.

Note: Based on projected average growth rates of the previous decade.

duration of stay in urban centres, and professional skills and social barriers (such as knowledge of Arabic). At the initial phase of displacement, several significant drawbacks to the survival strategies adopted are that they do not allow for skill acquisition or income-generating activities and that they have a negative impact on children's education because child labour is an essential part of such strategies (ibid., p. 55).

A common conclusion to several studies on survival strategies is that households tend to combine different activities simultaneously or to allocate the labour of family members to different economic activities, taking advantage of wage and accessory benefit differentials (Kibreab, 1990; Elnur *et al.*, 1993; Yath, 1993). In such studies, there is general agreement that the majority of the displaced in Greater Khartoum were from the Southern region, which reveals that the particular patterns of behaviour concerning survival and work choices might be linked to specific traditional practices. Likewise, the cause of resettlement may have a more salient effect on survival patterns causing a similarity in the practices among populations. A study conducted by the Sudan Council of Churches (SCC) on causes of displacement showed that 63 per cent were displaced for reasons of insecurity. Of these, 41 per cent were from the Upper Nile region, 27 per cent from Bahr-el-Ghazal, 14 per cent from Kordofan, 10 per cent from Darfur, 5 per cent from Equatoria, and 4 per cent from south of the Blue Nile province. These populations overwhelmingly were displaced by war or, as one study shows, over 80 per cent were displaced in the period *following* the resurgence of the civil war in 1983 (NPC, 1992, p. 19).

By 2003, the composition of IDPs changed significantly with the influx of those fleeing from Darfur. A survey conducted by CARE and IOM in partnership with the government of Sudan revealed that almost 39 per cent of IDPs were from Southern Sudan; the largest portion, being Dinka (25.4 per cent), followed by Nuer (2.3 per cent), Bari (4 per cent), Fertit (3.2 per cent) and Nuer (2.3 per cent) (CARE and IOM, 2006). Additionally, populations from the Nuba Mountains composed 20.6 per cent of IDPs, Arab ethnic groups 14 per cent, Darfurians 13.1 per cent, and Funj of the southern Blue Nile province amounted to 2 per cent. Nearly half of the IDPs in Khartoum (47 per cent) left their place of origin during the 1980s and 25.9 per cent during the 1990s. Thus, the IDPs', sequence of arrival and changing composition reflects clearly not only the intensity of various conflicts but also its ethnic composition. More detailed data on the arrival sequence and composition reveals further commonalities in terms of the dimensions of loss incurred by various ethnic and regional groups.

Camps, shanty towns and IDPs

Scholarship on forced migration and in particular internally displaced populations typically focuses on the most visible and accessible site of IDPs, the camp. This inevitably leads to the misreading of the political and socio-economic dimensions and the dynamics of displacement because of two major sources of bias: first, the focus on immediacy and visibility and, second, the negligence of non-camp

IDPs, who in many cases represent the majority. Within the context of studying prolonged conflict, neither the initial conditions of displacement nor the site-tied camp IDPs give a proper reading of the dynamics at work. Non-camp IDPs may be characterized by all together disparate processes and dynamics. The story of Sudan's IDP story presents a salient demonstration of the misleading readings due to an analysis based on initial conditions and a camp-bias in studies of IDPs.

By the mid-1990s only 20 per cent of the displaced population in Greater Khartoum were living in officially designated camps. A more accurate measure of the permanent communities in these camps notes a much smaller population. As early as 1993 we noted that IDPs maintained both residence in official camps and urban residence (often squatter residences) as complementary survival strategies. As the focus of NGOs and donor communities is often on the visible IDP sites, the residents' registration in these areas entitled them to various humanitarian assistance packages, such as food distribution (DPSG files).

Skills acquisition and transformations: the case of the construction industry

While the immediate post-displacement survival strategies did not allow for any significant skill acquisition, the same is not true with the passage of time.[4] Across ethnic boundaries, skills gradually diffused among the different networks that formed. Such an interesting diffusion, although neither unique to Sudan nor to skill diffusion processes, was clearly manifested in a number of newly acquired skills and crafts among various ethnic groups.

The construction industry is a good example of how the passage of time factors into skill acquisition among war-displaced IDPs. The industry itself is predominantly characterized by small firms, a high level of informality and typically easy entry conditions. However, the most important feature of the industry is the plethora of skills that are generated and required within the industry. These include brick-laying, blasting, metalworking, carpentry, painting, electricity and water piping, among others. The industry is strictly hierarchical. This means that on-the-job learning is the dominant mode of skill acquisition and thus the mechanism of ascending the hierarchy. Until the mid-1970s, the skilled ranks of the industry were dominated by riverain Sudanese – but with strong ethnic or location-based structures because the industry expanded through informal networks. The unskilled labourers were typically recent rural migrants. However, the two oil price hikes of 1973 and 1979 radically altered both the ethnic composition and the growth of the industry. The excessive demand for skilled and unskilled labour for the booming construction industry in the neighbouring Arab oil-producing countries almost completely wiped out the riverain Sudanese. Skilled and unskilled workers in the Gulf countries were typically earning 7–10 times higher than their average wages in the Sudan. Naturally, the migration regime favoured Arabic-speaking Muslim workers. Given the high proportion of skilled emigrants, Mustafa (1983) is right in observing that 'the urban market, in fact, is rapidly being depleted of its skilled manpower, its intellectually trained administrative stratum, and even some if its healthiest and most-experienced farmers' (ibid., p. 281).

By the mid-1980s, remittances from Sudanese workers were estimated to be around 1.7 billion US dollars, an average of 43 per cent of the estimated income of Sudanese emigrants in 1983 (Galal el Din, 1985). Most studies estimate that official transfers represented less than 20 per cent of total remittances and that 80 per cent went through unofficial channels. I found previously that 'private transfers from Sudanese working abroad continued to be channelled mostly in kind and mostly in the form of consumer durables and luxury consumption goods … The bulk of investment by migrants went into construction' (Elnur, 1988). Thus the construction boom in oil-producing countries wiped out the skills in the construction industry but simultaneously fuelled a construction boom in the Sudan.

Both these factors in the emigration of construction workers and the subsequent boom led to some radical changes in the ethnic composition of the construction industry. As noted earlier, language was the dominant entry barrier for many jobs during the early phase of population displacement. However, in the construction industry, old migrants from the same ethnic group were instrumental in facilitating jobs which provided them with a marginal premium as labour sub-contractors. By the mid-1990s, the industry became a major employer of IDPs. Within its rank two major ethnic groups were dominant: the Nuer as bricklayers and plasterers and Nuba Mountain IDPs as metalworkers. The rest of the construction-related skills were more mixed ethnically but predominantly composed of IDPs (Elnur, 2002, and fieldwork notes).

The construction industry, as one of the largest employers of displaced persons, was an important site for skill acquisition. Brick laying, plastering and more sophisticated techniques became increasingly associated with the Nuer, the second largest ethnic group in Southern Sudan. This agro-pastoralist ethnic group dominated the entire hierarchy of the cement plastering industry. Therefore, skill mobility took place within the same ethnic group. A similar story can be told about the metal-working and carpentry industries. These sectors were largely dominated by war-displacees from the Nuba Mountains who ascended the skill-ladder of this sub-speciality. In both cases, the process of skill acquisition and rapid ascendancy was accelerated by the vacuum and shortages resulting from the massive population exodus especially among Northern Sudanese to the oil-producing Middle Eastern countries.

In conclusion, the construction industry constitutes the largest employer of IDPs and the most vibrant sector of the economy and provides strong evidence that both skill acquisition and social mobility are functions of time within the displacement cycle. This of course has some serious implications for the previously assumed temporality of the displacement process. While the plight of the normal rural to urban migrants seems to diverge greatly from the miserable initial conditions of IDPs, the passage of time tends to blur such differences. This indeed undermines some of the typical assumptions about 'voluntary' repatriation and ultimately the assumed paths to the reconstruction of war-torn communities.

Education: access and achievements

As early as Elnur *et al.* (1993) it was noted that IDPs who moved to Greater Khartoum enjoyed better access to education despite child labour and the widely prevalent street children phenomenon. Recent studies among IDPs confirm these early observations. A UN survey of IDP camps in Khartoum observes: 'in Khartoum camps 42.5 per cent of IDP children are enrolled in schools, while in North Kordofan the average enrolment rate is 8.2 per cent' (UN, 30 November). This needs further qualification:

> Only 18 per cent of IDPs live in camps, the remaining 82 per cent live in squatter and other residential areas where they have better access to schooling (average school attendance in Greater Khartoum is around 88 per cent).
>
> A more detailed analysis shows that a 'significant percentage of IDPs were below school age (18.2 per cent are between 0 and 4 years old). Between 0–5 years old, 11 per cent are in preschool and 83 per cent have yet to start any education. Between 6–18 years old 67.6 per cent have attended primary, 5.9 secondary and only 0.2 per cent university. Whereas 20 per cent of this group have had no education. Between 26–50 years old 25 per cent have been in primary, 12.7 per cent secondary schooling and 4.2 per cent university. In all age groups, less than 1 per cent has had vocational or technical training. Over 50 years old, 11.3 per cent have attended only primary education, less than 10 per cent attended either secondary or university education and 65.5 per cent of IDPs have received no education at all' (CARE/IOM, 28 February 2003, p. 14). In other words, among those over 50 years old who fled the war, 21.3 per cent had an education, for some university, and among those born in displacement (6–18 years old) 73.7 per cent attended schools up to university. Much lower enrolment rates for the primary cycle of education (8 years) were reported in both government controlled areas (54 per cent) in 2000/01 and SPLM/A controlled areas (30 per cent) in 2001/02.
>
> (CARE, IOM, 28 February 2003, pp. 143–144)

In this respect, Mark Duffield's statement, 'given that a whole generation has been lost to education in South Sudan, peace will probably see its incorporation as an annex of cheap labour resources for Northern-controlled project and enterprises' (Duffield, 2001, p. 255), is a gross underestimation of Southern Sudan's achievements despite the horrors of war. Yet, the differential access to education between IDPs, refugees and those who remained behind in the South highlights certain challenges to the reconstruction process particularly in relation to voluntary repatriation and for integration in the event of successful voluntary repatriation. As Klugman and Kallaur (2005) concluded, the return of skilled and educated Southerners is far from assured (ibid., p. 17). The IOM (2006 IDPs', intention survey) had recorded 40 per cent of the displaced persons wishing to stay in the areas of displacement because of the availability of employment opportunities in these areas.[5]

Arabization: some aspects of cultural changes

Fleeing North has led largely to the Arabization of the IDPs. Initially, learning Arabic was an important survival strategy which helped to make available job opportunities for IDPs (Elnur *et al.*, 1993). However, the whole second generation of IDPs[6] and those who came as children began to speak Arabic during their schooling and in everyday social interaction with the other Arabic-speaking residents of the camps and squatter communities. It is thus that Arabic became the dominant lingua franca for at least two-thirds of the population of Southern Sudanese who fled northward.

Integration into the labour market was the most important factor in the process of Arabization of Southern IDPs. As early as the mid-1980s, knowledge of the Arabic language was crucial for individuals to attain access to the widening survival strategies available, including a wide range of jobs in the informal sector. Thus, rather than 'policies of acculturation and Islamization or cultural suppression' (Duffield, 2001, p. 211), integration into the labour market was the primary driving force behind Arabization. The learning of Arabic as the most important entry point to a successful integration into the labour market was not in any sense driven by the National Islamic Front's 'Arabization and Islamization' movement as alleged by a number of soldiers, human rights activists and development practitioners.

A large survey undertaken by CARE International and the National Population Committee (see Table 5.2) in 1992 showed a remarkable ascendancy of Arabic

Table 5.2 Al-Salam and Al-Jebel population by other language and sex

Other language	Male	Female	Total
Arabic	18,246	16,953	35,199
	51.84	48.16	100.00
	64.11	62.55	63.35
English	910	830	1,740
	52.28	47.72	100.00
	3.20	3.06	3.13
Other	5,535	5,369	10,904
	50.76	49.24	100.00
	19.45	19.81	19.63
No Other Language	3,050	3,217	6,267
	48.66	51.34	100.00
	10.72	11.87	11.28
Not Stated	719	733	1,452
	49.54	50.46	100.00
	2.53	2.70	2.61
Total	**28,459**	**27,103**	**55,562**
	51.22	**48.78**	**100.00**
	100.00	**100.00**	**100.00**

Source: Commission of Displaced, CARE International Sudan and National Population Committee (1992): 'The registration system, socio-economic and democratic characteristics of Al-Salam, Omdurman and Jebel Awlia displaced camps', final report, December 1992.

among the displaced Southern population. Assuming that most of the population speaks a tribal dialect as a mother tongue, the most dominant second language in the camps is Arabic. Some 63.3 per cent of the total population of the two camps noted that Arabic is their common language of communication (lingua franca). The most dominant first language is Dinka with its different dialects, according to geographical representation. In Al-Salam, the prevalence of Arabic is 62.4 per cent and in Al-Jebel it is 65.1 per cent. Those who speak other languages, excluding English, total approximately 19.6 per cent of the population, or up to 21.2 per cent in Al-Salam and 16.8 per cent in Al-Jebel.

However, 'Arabization', should not at any level be associated with any reconciliation with Islam. In fact during our fieldwork we witnessed a phenomenal protest of Christianity. Thus, during the first phase (1990) of fieldwork among Southern IDPs in Greater Khartoum, less than 30 per cent of the displaced population claimed adherence to Christianity. In the second phase in 1993, following the forced relocation of IDPs away from Khartoum town centre to the outskirts (Jebel Awlia and the western desert area of Omdurman), almost 80 per cent identified themselves with Christianity. In addition to the political response to the harsh relocation policies, respondents were also clear about such preferences. Both Islamic '*Igatha*' *Relief* and *Sudan Council of Churches*-related relief agencies were actively present in the camps. However, the services provided by Church-related agencies were much superior to that of the Islamic Relief. While the Church Relief agencies were providing a better education, Islamic Relief schools were much inferior, emphasizing preaching of Islam rather than basic literacy and numeracy. Interviews with parents and students confirmed this. Respondents noted that, while in general the quality of education is poor due to lack of teaching resources and trained teachers, Church-sponsored schools faired far better. In addition, Church-sponsored schools provided a free meal that reduced the considerable drop outs of children because of extreme poverty (DPSG Files).

Illiteracy

For those of school age (of whom 59 per cent are females and 41 per cent males) illiteracy is high, totalling about 60 per cent of the population in the two camps. In Al-Salam, the percentage of school-age (6 years) individuals who have no schooling is 66.9 per cent (of whom 43.4 per cent are males and 56.6 per cent are females). In Al-Jebel, 52.7 per cent are illiterate, total of 8,167 persons (of whom males comprise 38.7 per cent and females 61.9 per cent). Female illiteracy is higher in both camps and even higher in Al-Jebel. This is consistent with a higher female population there.

For the 6–24 age group, it was found that 55 per cent of them attend primary schools, 11 per cent junior secondary, 5 per cent higher secondary, 0.5 per cent university and above, while 29.2 per cent did not state. Of the total male population in this age group, 58.6 per cent attended primary, 11 per cent junior secondary, 5 per cent higher secondary and 0.5 per cent university, while 25.3 per cent did not state.

Table 5.3 Displaced population 6 years and over by literacy and sex

Literacy	Male	Female	Total
Illiterate	10,586	15,253	25,840
	40.97	59.03	100.00
	48.95	70.87	59.88
Literate	10,534	5,692	16,227
	64.92	35.08	100.00
	48.71	26.45	37.60
Not Stated	508	576	1,084
	46.84	53.16	100.00
	2.35	2.68	2.51
Total	**21,628**	**21,522**	**43,151**
	50.12	**49.88**	**100.00**
	100.00	**100.00**	**100.00**

Source: Commission of Displaced, CARE International Sudan and National Population Committee (1992): 'The registration System, socio-economic and democratic characteristics of Al-Salam, Omdurman and Jebel Awlia displaced camps', final report, December 1992.

Table 5.4 Infomalization of the economy

Country/Region	1970s	1980s	1990s
Developed Economies	11.8	11.8	13.7
Africa	28.3	48.1	54.6
North Africa	23.0	18.8	34.0
SSA	**29.6**	**54.9**	**66.9**
Latin America	28.8	30.2	37.8
Asia	28.6	29.7	31.9
South Asia	33.4	35.3	43.7
Gulf	**13.0**	**6.4**	**4.8**
Sudan	33.3	–	53.7

Sources: CAWTAR (2001) and Elnur (2003).

Trade: petty and wholesale trade

With an increasing informalization of the urban economies (see Table 5.4), petty trade became a dominant feature of urban unemployment. The seemingly chaotic informal sector portrays interesting features of ethnic-based networks of trade and a highly differentiated and hierarchical structure. These informal networks of distribution effectively crowded out the traditional formal structures of wholesale trade and a substantial part of informal trade known as '*shanta trade*', literally 'travel bag trade'.

The case of Suq Libya (Libya Market) in the western part of Omdurman, in Greater Khartoum, is a case in point. As people flow out of Darfur, capital travels with them, and the vibrant Zaghawa entrepreneur elite who amassed fortunes through smuggling, trans-border trading and arms trading during the

1980s emerged as the 'sin qua non' commercial clan in Darfur. As they moved to Khartoum they established Suq Libya. By 2002, when I undertook fieldwork, the Zaghawa traders of Suq Libya effectively replaced the riverain wholesale traders of 'Suq Omdurman', which historically was the wholesale centre for the entire country. Old wholesale traders and importers of 'Suq Omdurman' were no longer visible as they rented their shops to groups of retailers and sub-wholesalers of Zaghawa origin. Within this informal market, 'ethnicity' and 'kinship' acted as social collateral for building up a chain-of-distribution hierarchy. The range of goods extended from sophisticated electronic products, to building materials, to 'shanty town' kitchen plastic utensils. The formal banking system was completely out of the picture. The state was only able to control the lower hierarchy, taxing the retail sellers who were the most visible. The big capital of the wholesalers and 'importers' was kept completely invisible as it did not deal with the banking system. However, this is also partially attributable to the undermining of confidence in the banking system following the 1992 confiscation and freeze of commercial bank accounts.

Petty trade and street vendor-related activities are typically widespread among both rural to urban migrants as well as IDPs. Among conflict-driven IDPs these activities are by and large dominated by the Dinka ethnic group. Non-food petty trade activities were almost exclusively male dominated. However, unlike the case of Zaghawa, ethnic-wide networks involving non-petty traders did not emerge. The only networks facilitating some sense of inter-ethnic community were those of the church and church-related NGOs. The thriving trade in second-hand clothes that gained prominence with the influx of IDPs in urban centres did not have ethnic-related networks. It followed largely the traditional pattern of multi-ethnic individual – distributor interaction in the market place.

In conclusion, involvement of IDPs in trade-related activities was widespread but not associated with mobility based on an enhanced concentration of capital, except in the case of the Zaghawa. In the latter, the concentration was largely associated with capital flight from Darfur and the effective utilization of ethnic-based networks to facilitate efficient retail-level distribution and consequently the crowding out of traditional northern wholesale traders.

Feminization of the labour process

Before and during the 1970s, rural to urban migration was mainly male-dominated and did not involve whole households. Since then, the situation has changed greatly due to the presence of females and whole families in the composition of forced migrants. The urban informal sector exhibited interesting features with a high level of female participation in the informal services, particularly food-related. Domestic services became increasingly the domain of female workers. Given this trend, the figures of the latest survey, that suggest a staggering 74.7 per cent unemployment rate (Care and IOM, 2004, p. 24), should be taken with extreme caution. The figure is based on the IDP camp populations, who represent less than 20 per cent of total IDPs. To a great extent, those remaining behind in camps were relatively less fortunate in terms and adaptability. In many IDP households, women are becoming increasingly heads of household, even if they are not widowed, separated or single parents. One obvious reason for this is that women have better access to jobs with high-sustained demand, such as domestic work and other income-generating activities such as brewing and the selling of food. A similar phenomenon was noted among Southern Sudanese transit migrants in Egypt (see Ahmed, 2003; Lado, 1986; Abu Baker, 1995; Al-Shamani, 2003; Nyoka, 1999). A recent study of IDPs (Assal, 2006) concluded: 'Women and youth are ones who carry the burden of putting food on the table. The youth go for work in the different neighbourhoods in Khartoum, stay for the whole week and return during the weekend. Women commute daily and get back in the evening to bring food and resume the next day' (ibid., p. 22). Thus interesting changes are affecting family dynamics, shown by the changing division of household labour and the increasing presence of women in the public sphere.

Institutions: not only did people undergo vast changes and transformation, so too did their institutions

Upon arrival to their new communities, IDPs re-established 'real' or 'quasi'-traditional institutions known as 'Sultan Committees' based on traditional tribal or ethnic leadership or on age hierarchy, to the extent that some camps were virtually 'elder' committees! Yet in the initial phase, these committees were functional to the community organization, solidarity, inter and intra-community dispute settlement and most prominently in negotiation with local authorities and donors. However, over time these committees underwent tremendous transformations as a result of several factors:

- Camps reflected a greater diversity in terms of ethnic and cultural composition that transcended the rural 'relative' homogeneity. Rather than reproduction of the rural home and origin community, a wider and more complex urban heterogeneity formed, akin to the new urbanity.
- The strict 're-imagined' traditional hierarchy based on tribal or ethic leadership or age soon gave way to wider representation based on education, access to donors and local authorities, and experience with urban realities. In subsequent visits to the camps (1993–1995), it became clear that the 'Sultan Committees', except for the name, had very little in common with their earlier manifestations.
- The old structure of ethnic representation was somehow maintained, but the new community leaders performed functions that were almost totally unrelated to earlier functions. Additionally, in many cases their duties transcended ethnic boundaries. In particular, the age hierarchy became almost irrelevant with the rise of a better-educated and more connected younger generation. In this respect the demographic transition taking place after over two decades of displacement left its marked influence in the reshaping of traditional inter-generational relations.[7]

- As IDPs kept moving out of camps and became increasingly integrated into 'normal' rural to urban migrant residences in 'shanty towns' and elsewhere, the 'Sultan Committees' virtually disappeared and were replaced by service provision committees, or what is commonly called 'community-based organizations' (CBOs).

While structurally becoming less functional in an urban setting, the traditional institutions and leadership positions were further undermined by a growing mistrust: '... many IDPs have lost trust in their tribal leaders, who they claim are bribed and serve as informers for authorities' (IRC, 2004, p. 8). 'In the North, some believe that the camps have become a sub-platform for the divide and rule policy wherein individual chiefs communicate directly with the GOS authorities, rather than via elected Popular Committee. The IDPs claim that, by turning tribal leaders in to "political agents", the traditional security network has been eroded, reaching a point where people in the same community no longer trust each other' (ibid., p. 8). This is certainly a common phenomenon in the rapidly growing urban centres. As noted by a recent study on the urbanization challenges in Africa, the powerful ties that used to secure social capital for migrant communities tends to shrink over time: '... the vigour of clan and ethnic solidarity tend to diminish' (UN-Habitat, 2005, p. 11).

New 'urbanities', new 'ruralities' and transformations

The socio-economic terrain produced by civil wars, conflicts and environmental crises provides a far more complex site of changes, potentials and 'irreversibilities' that defy any notion or relevance to the restoration of pre-war conditions. In two decades, more than two-thirds of Southern Sudan's population were forced to flee or leave their homes or habitual residence. Out of the 4.5 million IDPs and refugees, four million headed to Northern Sudan, producing a massive influx into urban areas as roughly 50 per cent of them became city dwellers. This amounted to the urbanization of over one-third of Southern Sudan's population, compared to an urban population of less than 10 per cent at the beginning of the second civil war in 1983. Beyond the most visible spatial reconfiguration of the population, a new highly complicated political, social, economic and cultural map emerged in both Northern and Southern Sudan that bears little if any relevance to the pre-war situation. Not only have serious transformations taken place, also new potentials for transformations are being created by the conflict. Such transformations – actual and potential – govern the dynamics of post-conflict reconstruction and form the structural basis of its challenges.

'Urbanity' itself, even if accompanied by poverty and poor living conditions, is transformative and produces irreversible changes in communities. Examining the changes among migrant pastoralists who were driven by droughts to the edge of the western part of Greater Khartoum, Salih (1985) found that the determinant material structures of the receiving urban centres and the market economy reshaped these communities in relatively little time. From natural grazing, the pastoralists became dependent on purchased fodder and water – 'they have thus become middlemen to market their produce ... pastoralists are incorporated into national and international economy through trading boards, livestock exporters and wholesale traders' (ibid., p. 18).

When rural IDPs are taken into consideration, this means that two-thirds of the Southern population were almost fully integrated into the Northern labour force. The integration of the rural IDPs into the agricultural labour force in the North coincided with the crisis of traditional (communal) land tenure and the tribal homeland system. The vast expansion of state-driven mechanized agriculture and the resultant environmentally damaging competition over limited natural resources, plus the increasing pressures of a rapidly growing human and animal population, were the underlying factors responsible for such a crisis. Such a situation accelerated the processes of differentiation that eroded the structural foundation of the traditional (pre-capitalist) rural economy, and a new political economy, of labour formation emerged. The loss of pastoralists' and small traditional producers' means to a livelihood was by and large based on migration to urban areas and beyond. The demand for agricultural labourers was filled predominantly by IDPs from Southern Sudan. Observing this phenomenon, Manger (2005) notes: 'The pastoralists have also adopted cultivation, the Baggara of grain and groundnut in Southern Darfur using Dinka labourers and grain and cotton in the Nuba Mountains using Nuer as labourers. Some rich Baggara were also interested in mechanized farming. The camel nomads have cultivated grain and groundnuts using labour from among themselves, as well as available labour from Arab and Fellata groups in the area' (ibid., p. 141). Thus the historical process of prolateralization, which implies a transformation of the independent subsistent producers into wage labourers (Ahmed, 1992; Ibrahim, 1993; Daly, 1993), seems to have been brought to some conclusion through the massive population displacement during the last two decades. The seasonal movement of labour, pursuing the dual function of subsistence farming and wage labour, ceased to function. Seasonal wage labourers moved physically to their wage-employment sites with no option of pursuing dual roles. A new economy was thus being produced by drought, environmental degradation (natural and man-made) and large-scale conflict-driven population displacement.

The brain drain

The history of the skills exodus out of the Sudan over the last three decades is an illustrative example of the disruptive effect of large-scale skills migration. In its African context, the Sudan example is extremely important given the country's initial relatively favourable conditions. By the time of its independence in 1956, the Sudan was well ahead of almost all countries south of the Sahara in terms of human capital endowment: a well-established educational system (albeit elitist); a relatively sizeable critical mass of well-trained professionals and technicians; a highly organized and functioning civil service that was once the pride of the British colonial administration; a smoothly functioning mechanism for the reproduction of educated elites; and an efficient incentive structure that ensured the retention of skills and their cumulative build-up.

Over the last three decades and through two distinct phases, the Sudan witnessed two waves of skills exodus that significantly eroded much of the post-independence gains in human capital formation. The first phase coincides with the economic hardship, mismanagement and political repression felt during Nimeiri regime, but more so by the attraction of much higher income levels in the oil-exporting countries of the Middle East. The second phase coincides with the advent of the Islamist government following the 25 June 1989 coup. The National Islamic Front (NIF) government employed effectively powerful policy tools that reshaped and redefined the political, social and economic frontiers of the educated elites, their livelihood and their role. These policies and the intensification of the war in Southern Sudan led to a massive exodus of educated and trained professionals and technicians. They were driven out by both direct political actions and economic hardships, radical changes in educational policies coupled with growing vertical differentiation in access to schooling, loss of training and employment opportunities, erosion of the material bases of the traditional educated elites and drastic changes in the institutional setup of both the state and society (Elnur, 2002). However, empirical evidence from migrant Sudanese communities demonstrates that the Sudanese diaspora does not only encompass the out-migration of Sudanese professionals, technicians and students, etc., but also a multiple process of emigration whereby a significant number of Sudanese expatriates do not return. Sudanese expatriates from the Gulf states emigrate to North America and Europe seeking citizenship, passports or using birth rights to acquire passports for their children.

It is also worth mentioning that the brain drain is particularly severe in the marginalized areas. In the case of Sudan, the war-torn Southern Sudan and Darfur, where there exists very narrow stocks of educated and skilled persons, were disproportionately affected by the brain drain, thus further exasperating Sudan's marginalization.

Conclusion

The two and a half decades of intensification of civil war, political conflict and environmental disasters resulted in dramatic changes in the ethnic composition and relative share of various provinces in the total Sudanese population. Notions such as the 'riverain Sudanese', 'Greater North', North–South and West versus North became irrelevant in terms of geographical and ethnic boundaries and physical sites. A situation akin to post-Stalin social engineering in the former USSR, involving forced re-meshing of nationalities and ethnic groups, emerged. It was shown that the massive re-shuffling of the population in the last three decades illustrates the dimensions of such blurring of geographic boundaries that used to mark ethnic groups and local communities. The new conflict-produced demography of the Sudan carries paradoxically both the potential for integration and further divisions despite closer proximity. Conflict-driven population displacement produces the first instance of a large-scale departure from the pre-war environment and, given historical experiences, a significant case of irreversibility.

These are very defining conditions for a war-triggered transformative potential:

- The transformative potential in civil war is a function of time. Thus, the longer the civil war's duration the greater is such transformative potential.
- The civil war-related transformative potential is a function of the proportion of the population forced into migration as a result of war and war-related violence and the destabilization policies of the contending forces.
- The transformative potential is closely related to the direction of involuntary migration. For example, rural to rural forced migration is likely to trigger less transformative processes than will rural to urban.
- The macro level study of involuntary migratory trends is unlikely to tell us much about the transformative processes taking place as a result of war-led displacement. Some of these transformative potentials are the result of changing dynamics and are related to new urbanities, new family structures, roles and division of labour, the erosion of old and emergence of new institutions and deeply transformed and redefined ethnic boundaries and identities. Failure to capture these changes is closely related to the assumption that urban squatters' homogeneity is most often masked by appalling levels of destitution.

All these are heavy costs of war but they represent elements of the tremendous challenges to a successful reconstruction.

The previous case studies suggest that far from the misery and inhumane scenes of initial displacement, which are absolutely true, dynamic processes of making and remaking communities are taking place. These involve better access to skill formation, build up of sophisticated and functioning networks, embryonic but vibrant entrepreneurship and a reshaping of gender roles within the family and the public sphere. Far from the homogeneous undifferentiated and helpless IDP communities functional to advocacy and humanitarian workers, we have vibrant communities that provide the initial readings for the aftermath of the civil war and its reconstruction. Some of these changes are irreversible due to repressive policies. The challenge of reconstruction is to capture the progressive potential of such a transformation and to maintain its momentum. Regression in gender roles and the emancipatory potential is plausible if repressive rather than enabling policy packages are supported, as was cited earlier, but overall neither the 'tabula rasa' nor 'absolute misery' and 'degradation' of human potential theories hold. This reading of the post-war political and socio-economic terrain is by no means a denial of the devastating impact of the prolonged civil war, but simply a better reading of the ongoing transformations and potential.

6 From Addis to Nivasha
War-Fatigue-driven peace agreement
Sources of fragility and challenges of governance

'I was clear about this War-Fatigue I fought for 20 years. I was not able to conquer neither they. So there is no alternative to negotiation.'

John Garang addressing a post-peace signing press conference: http://www.rayam.net/syasa.htm– 04/07/2005.

'Lou Awiz Taeesh biblash Ashtri Clash.' A Western Sudan war-time proverb literally meaning: 'If you want to live for free buy an AK-47 automatic rifle.'

Why do we need to study the processes that shaped the march to peace? The central argument of this chapter is that reconstruction is shaped greatly by the processes through which civil war ended and far less, if at all, by the initial conditions that triggered it. Licklider's study of the consequences of negotiated settlement in civil war presents some very complex scenarios and concludes with a list of questions aimed at answering the question of 'why some negotiated settlements in identity wars "stick" and others do not and why some victories are followed by mass murder and others aren't?' (Licklider, 1995, p. 687). Cramer (2004) provides a broader approach that transcends such narrow specifications: 'post-conflict and peace-building are not technical projects but are sharply political and largely determined by the coalition of interest groups that dominates the political process'. Interestingly, its overwhelmingly static approach, the new blueprint à la Collier, repeatedly emphasizes that each post-conflict situation is distinctive and 'that the general principles are merely broad lines' (Collier *et al.*, 2003, p. 152).

Consequently, this Chapter is an essential prelude for understanding the political terrain emerging out of negotiated settlement in the Sudan: new collisions, partnerships and various actors representing national, regional and international interests are all actively playing a role in the reconstruction process. The chapter traces the formation of such a terrain and goes beyond the technical construct of de-mobilization, disarmament and reintegration (DDR) to examine how the DDR mechanisms are essentially politically driven, providing a means for forging new alliances and partnerships in the context of a negotiated settlement. Thus, the options made viable for reconstructing war-produced economies and societies are shaped by the political terrain of the post-negotiation period.

The political terrain as emphasized in this chapter is far more complex than the terrain governed by the armed conflict. In the previous war-shaped terrain the armed contending forces had the upper hand in shaping the political governing sphere, forging alliances and silencing 'opponents' and flows of people and ideas within their held territories and beyond.[1] Once armed struggle was over, a plethora of political and social agents, previously dormant or less articulate, emerged. The seemingly chaotic and crowded political terrain of post-Nivasha in both the North and South is a testimony to this. Furthermore, the terrain is compounded by the multiplicity of regional and international actors who contributed to the negotiated settlement or in response to its outcome.

The long march to negotiations

The peace negotiations followed a long and complex process extending from 1997 until 2005 when the Comprehensive Peace Agreement (CPA) was finally signed. The second civil war in Southern Sudan, which broke out in 1983, engendered dramatic changes at national, regional as well as international levels. At the national level the civil war broke out during Nimeiri's regime, oversaw its demise in April 1986, and was shaped by the political turmoil in the North. The transitional Military Council that succeeded Nimeiri's regime stopped short of making a peaceful solution viable by rejecting the SPLA/M demand for freezing Shari'a Laws of 1983, the National Salvation Alliance (the Umbrella organization of the parties that overthrew the Nimeiri regime). Serious attempts at making a breakthrough based on the March 1986 Koka Dam meeting and the zigzagging policies that followed the parliamentary government preceded the NIF's engineered takeover in June 1989.

At the regional level, the 22 years of civil war was shaped partially by changing alliances with regimes of neighbouring countries (from Mengistu in Ethiopia, to Zenawi in Ethiopia and Musivini in Uganda). These changes took place within a fluid international context (the end of the Cold War political readjustments). With each shift in the neighbouring countries, Sudan's political groups were affected to varying degrees. The influence largely fell in the internal forces contending for external support, overall internal unity between Sudanese groups based on their alliance with outside regimes and, by implication, ideological and political orientation.

The peace agreement was heavily shaped by six important factors:

- Oil exports, which began in 1999.[2]
- War-Fatigue, better understood in Engel's definition as mutual exhaustion of the contending forces.
- As a consequence of War-Fatigue a heavily mediated peace process was inaugurated and concluded.
- As opposed to the pre-Addis Peace Agreement, the Nivasha Peace Agreement of 2005 took place against the backdrop of a sharply divided North and South.

- The gradual build-up of a national consensus on peace and the right to self-determination.
- As opposed to the pre-Addis situation, when only 1.7 million or 27.4 per cent of the estimated total population were displaced, by 2003 Southern Sudan was almost completely depopulated with 4 million in the North and 0.5 million refugees in the neighbouring countries out of 6.2 million (2003 estimation), and a significant number of its educated elites in diaspora.

These factors influenced the peace process, set certain limitations to the capacity of warring parties to manoeuvre and fixed a rigid ceiling to what might have been developed in terms of national consensus. At the same time, these factors shaped the transition to peace and the nature of the reconstruction process.

Deeply divided North and South

Naturally, the lengthy process of negotiation reflected, among other things, changing dynamics on the ground. During the second half of the 1980s, the Sudanese army was poorly equipped and seemed to be losing its grip on the South. Consequently, the SPLM's position was hardening. With the collapse of Mengistu's regime and the withering away of the Soviet Union and its allies' support for the SPLM at the end of the Cold War, the NIF hardened its position and hoped for outright victory. In fact, the Khartoum regime was able to retake most of the territories taken by the SPLM during the late 1980s.

The serious split of the SPLM in 1991 was devastating. However, by the mid-1990s the SPLM largely recovered lost territories but, despite the return of the 1991 splitters Drs Reik Machar and Lam Akol, their military backer did not succeed until two years after the signing of the CPA. Sudan's military was a conglomerate of informal military forces and militias loosely united, and the Southern Sudan Defence Force (SSDF) was a military front attached to the Southern Coordinating Council (SCC), which serves as a focal point of the Khartoum-based Southern Politician Signatures of the Sudan Peace Agreement (Khartoum, 21 April 1997). The SSDF may not represent a serious political rival to the SPLM, but it does represent a formidable spoiler for the peace process.

A recent Institute for Security Studies (ISS, April 2004) publication made a realistic estimation of the relative weight of the SSDF. While it is not easy to estimate accurately the size of the SSDF, its own claims of 'more formidable but less equipped than the SPLA' are certainly untrue. It has some several thousand members and can mobilize thousands more from village militias and the local citizenry. SPLA/M's claim that it holds 80 per cent of Southern Sudan and surrounds all GoS towns is false. The SSDF control much of the Upper Nile, part of Northern Bahr El-Gazal and of Bahr El-Jebel, and much of Eastern Equatoria. 'And it is not SPLA, but SSDF that surrounds and thus provides security for most GOS held towns in the South, for example, Bantiu, Rubkona, Wau, Juba, Torit, Nasir, Adar and Malaka.' The SSDF forces provide a curtail component of the oil fields of Western and Eastern Upper Nile. However, the SSDF, despite a heavy Nuer presence in its ranks, represents a wider ethnic coalition. Despite the seeming lack of political cohesion and institutional fragmentation, we need to recall that this is the same group that was opposed to Dinka domination in the post-Addis agreement. The group is overwhelmingly Nuer, whose history of expansionism (1818–1890) renders images of the displaced Anuak Dinka. Kelly (1985) describes that the 'Nuer displacement of the Dinka (The Anuak) represents one of the most prominent instances of tribal imperialism' (ibid., p. 1). Such a long historical incidence seems to be regenerated by the recent encroachment of the Nuer into Dinka areas.

The conflict cannot be portrayed in simple terms describing the deeply divided North and South. Rather, the erosion of all contending forces and the many factions within each must be considered seriously. Despite the return of Riek Machar and Lam Akol to the ranks of the SPLM/A, the 1991 split was symptomatic of broader breakdowns in the organization.

The December 2004 meeting of the SPLM/A[3]

While the minutes of the meeting were not officially released, opening remarks by the chairman on the second day of the meeting 'noted that the present meeting has come out on the Internet; and a warning was given to those who might have done so' (Rumbek Meeting, p. 11).

Despite the warning, the minutes of the three-day long meeting became available on the Internet no sooner than the meeting was over. Most of the debate focused on the latest institutionalized leadership and on dysfunctional committees locked in strife with one another. The second man in SPLA/M stated: 'There are also other major problems; the chain of command should be observed from today onward. Peter Gadet left the Movement because of a break down in the chain of command. Corruption has led to the collapse of services in our liberated areas. I urge the Chairman to immediately start a mechanism to fight corruption. Money, which was taken in order to bring New Sudan currency, can be brought back and directed to other programmes. The issue of "Radio SPLA" is not clear. Why is it not brought up publicly? Powers should be given whenever you are given something to do' (Rumbek Meeting, pp. 17–18).

The chairman responded to all the grievances and promised:

> We will begin to form formal structures of the Movement as soon as the agreement is signed. The political organs will be separated from the government structures. SPLM county secretaries will be political cadres of the Movement and commissioners will be appointed as career administrators. We must transform SPLM into a political party and the CNAs into a civil authority. There will be no ISCOORT since it creates parallel structure with the CNAs. Concerning the leadership council, was formed just for convenience but as soon as peace is signed we will adopt the structures which are the agreement so I ask you to be patient until such a time when peace is signed. So the life of the leadership council will come to an end on the date the agreement

is signed. The SPLA will be a national army upon signature of the agreement. (ibid., p. 19)

Nevertheless, he urged gradualism in the transformation processes. The argument as to whether or not the leakage of these minutes was intentional is beside the point. What is important however is that the difficulties and challenges of transforming an essentially guerrilla movement into a viable political and administrative institution became the organization's clear agenda. These challenges are indeed going to be central to the success or failure of the interim period.

War-Fatigue

The mutual exhaustion of the contending forces and the imminent danger of the country falling into an irreversible process of fragmentation was eloquently expressed by Garang addressing the post-signing of the CPA in Nairobi on 5 June 2005. Garang told his audience, 'Indeed, what makes this peace welcome is that it came as a result of a hurting stalemate which made both sides realize that a win-win peace is attainable and that the cost of the alternative of peace is far less than that of continuation of the war. Peace became possible because both parties realize that the country was dissipating, that the state seemed to be withering away without undergoing the famous Marxian transformation and that the "Old Sudan" we have known was heading blindly into an abyss of irreversible fragmentation.'

Yet another important manifestation of the path leading to War-Fatigue was the declining capacity of the state to finance war out of the shrinking revenue. As was noted in the JAM report (2005) the GoS's revenue mobilization lagged behind both inflation and GDP growth from the early 1980s to 1999 as total federal revenues deteriorated from 11.4 per cent of GDP during 1981/1982–1984/1985 to 8.0 per cent of GDP during 1996–2000.

Equally important is the fact that external support for the contending parties was drying up. The 'war-donors' fatigue', a common post-cold-war phenomenon, was further driven by the NIF regime increasing international and regional isolation. SPLA exports which included gold, livestock, coffee and timber (Douglas, 2003, p. 165) was accompanied by a great deal of lack of accountability and a disproportioned division of receipts between leaders, local people and the SPLA/M (ibid., p. 166).

As shown in Chapter 5, the de-population of war-affected areas was unprecedented. By the time of the signing of the CPA, Southern Sudan's population remaining in their home communities represented less than one-third of the total population. Despite the recent escalation of civil war in Darfur, by 2006 approximately 40 per cent of Darfur's people were living away from their homes.

National consensus on peace and self-determination

The NIF capitalized on a national consensus that it ferociously opposed for the previous two decades. In fact, opposition to any peaceful deal has been the cornerstone of its bid for power since 1993. For example, the early alliance with Nimeiri following the enactment of Islamic Shari'a laws (better known as the September laws) of 1983. The long process of building political consensus was spearheaded by secular forces, which led to the uprising against the Nimeiri regime in April 1986. A brief overview of the build up of a national consensus on peace settlement of the war in the South and the recognition of the right for self-determination was introduced in the Koka Dam meeting that took place in March 1986. The Asmara Declaration (officially named Declaration of Principles) in 1995, signed by major actors in the NDA, was the culmination of such a newly generated national consensus (see Box 6.1).

Box 6.1   The quest for peace: major initiatives, 1986–1989

1. The Koka Dam Declaration held on 24 March 1986. Participants: SPLM/SPLA (Kerubino Kuanyin, Arok Thon Arok) and National Alliance for National Salvation, NANS (Awad El Karim Mohamed), representing 14 political parties and 22 trades unions, including Umma, CPS but not the DUP or NIF.

    Agreements: National Constitutional Conference to be held in June, preceded by recognition by all that the problem is of Sudan not Southern Sudan, lifting of State of Emergency, repeal of 'September 1983 Laws' (a version of Shari'a), adoption of constitution based on 1956 Constitution, abrogation of Sudan's military pacts, cease-fire, and further discussion on dissolution of government in favour of a new interim government including SPLM/A.

2. Prime Minister's Working Paper for Peace (late 1988). Content: historical account of the background to conflict and peace initiatives; proposal for immediate meeting to discuss cease-fire, humanitarian relief and arrangements for the National Constitutional Conference (but ignoring most of the preconditions agreed at Koka Dam); draft agenda for NCC (leaving out some of the points agreed at Koka Dam, such as 'basic human rights' and 'natural resources'); outline of transitional arrangements including amnesty and reconstruction.

3. Sudanese Peace Initiative (August 1988 to 14 November 1988). Negotiators: SPLM/A (John Garang, Lam Akol and others), DUP (Mohamed Osman El-Mirghani, Sid Ahmed El-Hussein and others) with wider support from secular movements.

    Agreements: National Constitutional Conference to be held by 31/12/88, preceded by freezing of 'Hodoud' [Shari'a punishment] provisions in September 1983 laws, abrogation of Sudan's military pacts, lifting of state of emergency, cease-fire, and formation of national preparatory committee.

4. Ambo Workshop on Sudan: Problem and Prospects (or Koka Dam 2) (4/2/89–7/2/89). Participants: a few members of SPLM/A and intellectuals from inside Sudan not representing parties but 'the National Democratic Forces'.

Agreements (unsigned shared diagnosis of Sudan's problems): the principle of citizenship can be the only basis of national identity, Arabic is the shared language, equality for women, an anti-imperialist and anti-Zionist foreign policy, and a radical abandonment of the capitalist system, by revolutionary means.

Sources: Compiled from Tvedt (2004), Economist Intelligence Unit (EIU, 2007) and ISS (2004).

Naturally, the story was less positive than it was presented to be. The Prime Minister elect, Sadiq El-Mahdi, never endorsed wholeheartedly the Koka Dam principles. While in office and after the overthrow of his government he continued to pursue an alternative consensus that did not fully endorse secularism. Both his rivalry with the DUP and shared ideological grounds with the NIF made him hostile to the Koka Dam agreement and hesitant to accept any breakthrough between the DUP and the SPLA/M of 1988. This is not surprising, as the agreements included the freezing of Shari'a laws, the lifting of the state of emergency status and a ceasefire before the national conference on peaceful solutions was to take place.[4]

The Army memorandum, which virtually amounts to the threat of a take-over, was instrumental in bringing an end to the NIF–Umma party coalition of 1989 and facilitating the emergence of a new coalition with sizeable representation in the April 1986 uprising. Building on its breakthrough Sudan Peace Initiative of August 1986, the other major Northern political party, the DUP, proceeded successfully to buildup its alliances with the SPLA/M.

A national consensus on peace and the right to self-determination of the Southern population was achieved largely through the NDA's efforts. The principles adopted by the Asmara Declaration of 1995, later confirmed by even wider forces, were confirmed by the Massawa Declaration of 1998, where the nexus of a new national consensus forced even the hesitant Islamists to produce their own version of self-determination.

The Massawa Declaration reiterated the commitment to voluntary unity based on diversity, prohibition of abuse of religion for political ends, good governance and respect of human rights, equity of citizens regardless of religion, race or gender, democratic transformation and a balanced sustainable development.[5] Despite its relative ineffectiveness, in terms of representing a serious threat to the NIF regime, the NDA political influence is much wider, not even related to its immediate constituency. The 1995 declaration is thus a landmark in post-colonial Sudan's political development as it represents a point of no return in terms of the right to self-determination. The vibrant agency of secular Sudan and that SPLA/M and other regional movement was the driving force behind such a conclusion for a national discourse that covered the 1964–1995 period of post-independence. The 1995 declaration was an effective declaration by the overwhelming majority of the Sudanese political forces, that the 'old' Sudan-formula of centralized state is no longer viable. The consensus was achieved despite pressures from regional powers, most prominently Egypt, whose opposition to the notion of self-determination was the most pronounced.

As Egypt's closest political ally in Sudan, the DUP did not hesitate to recognize self-determination policies despite the Egyptian Government's outspoken opposition to the principles. Adar (2000) was right in observing that Egypt does not condone the growing Islamic fundamentalism in Sudan. The Egyptian leadership also takes into account the country's dependence on the Nile River water, which flows through Sudan. The Government of Egypt's emphasis is that a disintegrated Sudan – either through secession or self-determination – may have long-term negative implications for their country. In order to maintain official contacts with Sudan, Egypt re-opened its embassy in Khartoum in early 2000 (ibid., p. 8).

While Adar's observation is true, Egypt also maintained a very cautious policy towards the SPLA/M because of its delicate resource, the Jungeli Canal. As noticed by Hamad (1996), the impact of the drought during the early 1980s on the Nile water was very serious: 'high stored water declined from 84 billion average 69 billion in 1979/80, to 79 billion in 1980/81, rising again to 82 billions in 1981/82' (p. 545). The stored water maintained its downward trend, reaching the lowest level of storage since the construction of the High Dam (59 billion) in 1985/86. Hence, Haj Hamad concluded that the 1988 agreement was actually an Egyptian initiative acted upon through the DUP.

Despite its exclusive nature, the CPA was greatly facilitated by this build up of national consensus on a peaceful solution and on the right to self-determination. Ironically, Northern opposition to the NIF regime led the way for a wide acceptance of the peace agreement that gave new life to the exhausted regime they opposed.

The heavy mediated Comprehensive Peace Agreement

As mentioned earlier, the Comprehensive Peace Agreement (CPA) was an outcome of the heavily mediated peace process that took place in the radically altered political and socio-economic terrains both in the deeply divided North and the depopulated South and thus offered a milieu of immense challenges to the emerging coalition and peace-building process.

Despite the lengthy process and the voluminous package of detailed agreements, the CPA left unanswered many questions, gaps and loopholes. Some are central to the immediate phase of peace building. It is possible that the gaps and loopholes will usher in new processes and conflicts that might undermine the peace process. The following will examine these issues and the various responses by indirectly involved actors as well as the new partners (the NIF and SPLA/M).

In his report to the President, Danforth (2002) emphasized that all proposals for peace in Sudan were based on three basic premises: first and foremost, on protecting ordinary Sudanese civilians who often find themselves caught between the two opposing parties; second, they obliged the parties to change past patterns of behaviour and to make tough political choices; and third, the proposals provided for international involvement and monitoring so as to maximize the chances of being respected as previous agreements did not provide for international involvement and often collapsed because of the intense distrust of the parties who could neither monitor compliance nor verify implementation.

'The four proposals addressed specific areas of human suffering in Sudan. I presented the outlines of these proposals to the parties during my November visit to the region. Three weeks later a joint State/USAID/DOD team returned to Sudan to follow-up. The negotiations were intense because we were asking both sides to put the well-being and protection of the people and the prospects of peace above considerations of short-term military advantage. After eighteen years of war, this was not easy. Nevertheless, by dint of persuasion, pressure and perseverance, we were eventually able to secure agreement to all four of the proposals, as discussed below (Box 6.2)'

**Box 6.2   Highlights of the Comprehensive Peace Agreement,
9 January 2005**

The signing of the CPA by the GoS and the SPLM/A on 9 January 2005 successfully concluded the final phase of negotiations to address the issue of inclusiveness, identity and access to resources that were among the most significant structural causes of the conflict. The CPA builds on years of discussion and prior agreements, including the Machakos Protocol (July 2002), which established the right of the people of Southern Sudan to control and govern affairs in their region and participate equitably in the national government.

The CPA represents a complex and detailed set of arrangements and actions, all of which cannot be summarized here, but key features include the following elements:

The Power Sharing Agreement provides for a largely autonomous government for Southern Sudan, as well as a share for Southern Sudan in the NG, with a view of making unity attractive to the Southern Sudanese population before it votes in six years on whether to remain unified with the North or to become independent. The Agreement provides a basis for broader participation in government and the civil service, the restructuring of critical national institutions (e.g. the judiciary), and a new national constitution. It also recognizes the right of the Sudanese to elect their representatives in free and fair mid-term elections at all levels of government, and emphasizes internationally acknowledged human rights and freedoms, including a commitment to a bill of rights and basic freedoms of expression, religion and association.

The Wealth Sharing Agreement provides a framework for resource allocation and sustainable decentralization, establishing comparative underdevelopment and war-affected status as the key criteria for the prioritization of public revenue allocations. The Agreement assigns a share of oil and non-oil revenue to the South, as well as the right to collect additional domestic revenue and external assistance, and the right to have its own banking system within the framework of the Central Bank of Sudan.

The Security Protocol outlines a collaborative approach to security issues by providing for two armed forces and joint integrated units that will become the nucleus of a future national army, enabling the parties to gradually downsize their forces and allowing the GoSS to mobilize resources for the SPLA.

The particular factors that precipitated conflict in Abyei, Southern Kordofan and the Blue Nile (also referred to as the Three Areas) are recognized and special power and wealth-sharing arrangements have been agreed upon. These include the establishment of State Land Commissions, special provisions on education and security, the right to solicit external resources, popular consultation rights for the local population, and a unique administrative status for Abyei.

Sources: JAM, vol. 1, 18–19 March 2005.

CPA and wealth sharing

On the one hand, oil greatly facilitated the negotiation of the peace deal and in particular the economic aspects of it. On the other, oil overshadowed other central issues related to wealth and the root causes of conflict in the South and North. The 'Political Dutch Disease' effect of oil in the negotiated settlement was all too clear.[6] Emphasis on the sharing of the newly realized non-renewable wealth overshadowed the central issue of wealth creation. The marginalization of the South, West and East was not an outcome of the 'intended' distribution of oil revenue which started in 1999. Addressing the issue of the historically rooted lopsided development necessitates a common vision of reconstruction at least for the immediate transitional period. Two vague references to what could amount to a broad reference to some vision about reconstruction were included in the Machakos Protocol and the framework for negotiation between the GoS and NDA. These vague references, however, did not represent any kind of framework or terms of reference with regard to reconstruction.

The question of accountability and transparency with regard to oil should have been broadened to involve the use of funds. This has an immediate as well as long-term implication for the peace-building process and reconstruction. Despite the detailed protocol on wealth sharing including the provision of an 'oil stabilization account' and a fund for future generations, there was not a single word mentioned about the allocation of these funds. This presents serious challenges to achieving successful reconstruction at two levels.

First, the trade-off between reconstruction – addressing the larger task of rebuilding a sound economic base as well as the more immediate needs of the suffering people – and, second, the requirement of building a representative and effective civil administration in the war-torn areas. In the latter, this amounts to the construction of a nascent state out of scratch. The large task of building this administration in Southern Sudan is illustrated in Garang's description of the top-brass of such an administration. Addressing the South–South dialogue conference (Nairobi, 19 April 2005), Garang stressed:

> I say to all Southern Sudanese that there will be many rooms in the GOSS and GONU, and all are welcome. In the legislature for example we shall have 135 members in the Central Parliament, 170 in the Southern Parliament, and about 400 legislators. In the Executive Southern will have 10 full Ministers and at least 10 State Ministers in the GONU and about 20 Ministers in the GOSS and some 40 Ministers in the State Governments; these are more than 70 Ministers. Then you have the judiciary and civil service. And with the massive development we shall launch the private sector which will be very lucrative and full of jobs. As you can see there will be enough rolls for every one; our problem will actually be lack of manpower.

In the North there were already mammoth top-brass structures, whose ranks continued to be inflated by Islamic patronage policies aimed at enlarging its narrow-support basis through public offices within the divided Islamist movement. This is part of its policies directed at dividing opposition parties and the regional elites. By 2004 the state structure comprised the following high-ranking offices:[7]

36	Federal Ministers
6	Presidential Advisers
34	State Ministers
26	Governors
156	Regional Ministers
18	Regional Advisers
136	Country Governors
414	**total of High-Ranking Officials**

In addition to these top-ranking officials, there were 450 National Parliament members and another 900 at the state level. The collapsed pay structure was augmented at the official level by a whole parallel structure of invisible payments including: sitting allowances for senior officials on state-owned company boards; special contracts for key staff (covering political patronage appointments and key technocrats); the designation of certain cadres, especially lawyers and accountants, to receive pay above and outside the main pay structure; and ad hoc pay for performance incentives for staff called upon to put in extra efforts for special purposes such as getting the budget ready in time (World Bank, 2004, p. 79).

Given the almost non-existence of a private sector, the reproduction of a similar mammoth administrative structure in Southern Sudan is an even more attractive option for a shortcut to a state-sponsored elite formation. According to the Nivasha Agreement there is a four-tier structure of government relevant to the South:

1   A National Government/Government of National Unity (GoNU) in Khartoum. It is estimated that employment in June of 2004 in the federal government

was 28,305. Southern Sudan is entitled to up to 30 per cent of such employment, with no less than 20 per cent of the idle and upper positions filled by qualified people from the South. Depending on the actual number of already-employed Southern Sudanese, this amounts to roughly 10,000 slots (JAM background paper on Public Administration, p. 3).

2   Government of Southern Sudan (GoSS) composed of ten state governments in Southern Sudan. In addition, there are to be county councils (currently 90 with the possibility of being reduced to 60, amounting to 6 counties per state) (JAM, 2004, p. 3).

3   For Southern Sudan local government consisting of three levels was recommended:

   i   County administrative units, called Payams. It was suggested that each county will have between 3 and 6 Payams.
   ii   Village-level administration structure, called Boma. A Boma may comprise one or more villages.
   iii   Larger urban administrations will comprise: (a) municipalities for urban settlements with populations of more than 100,000; and (b) town councils for urban settlement.

4   Overall, it was recommended that a starting size of 35,000–40,000 would work for public services with a majority of the staff at the sub-state level and a ceiling of 100,000 persons (based on a norm of 1per cent of an estimated population of 10 million).

While there was virtually no administrative structure in SPLM-held territories, only a few hundred according to JAM (2005), there was an estimated 40,000–50,000 employed in the ten Southern states by the Government of Sudan. The Nairobi workshop recommended that staff working in garrison towns and other Southern Sudanese working for the Government of Sudan should be selectively included in the new public service.

Despite the sophisticated structure of the alternative administrative system envisioned by SPLM – that is, the Civil Authority for the New Sudan (CANS) – it implicitly assumed a tabula rasa. On paper, the 1998 SPLM programme, which amounted to a blueprint for state building, avoided any mention of the native administration. CANS was assumed to be the highest political and administrative authority in the New Sudan. It consisted of the National Liberation Council (NLC), the National Political and Executive Committee (NAPEC) and other organs of the movement from the regional level down to the Boma.

The CANS therefore represents the emerging administration of the New Sudan, which shall be developed and consolidated over time until it becomes the Government of the New Sudan as the NIF administration withers away, and as the New Sudan expands and develops.

On the ground, however, this revolutionary vision was diluted to accommodate the limited capacity as well as to meet the needs of well-established and thriving institutions. Johnson (1998) saw this as a major departure from the usual revolutionary paths: 'Whereas other revolutionary movements in the region have attacked institutions of the ancient regime, the SPLA has approached the "grassroots" through the institutions of native administration and chiefs' courts' (Johnson, 1998, p. 71).

The viability of this involuntary infusion of the traditional institutions into the SPLA military structure is questionable. Such partnership was not an easy one. Tensions between communal authorities and SPLA regional commanders were common. However, as an attempt to shortcut state development, it is neither unique in the narratives of state building during colonial and post-colonial times in Africa nor in terms of Sudan's own history. The crucial issues at hand are the implications of this process of political and economic post-war reconstruction, particularly in relation to two major issues. First, the reproduction of what Hughes and Sasse (2001) termed 'territorialized ethnicities', with the latent danger of destabilization, as in the case of the USSR. And, secondly, the implications with regard to land tenure reform, central to both the transformation of subsistent low-productivity agricultural methods and state building. Ethnic division within the Southern Sudan is deeply rooted and played a major role in the frictions and conflicts following the Addis Ababa Agreement. Such 'territorialized ethnicity' has been further accentuated by the marked polarization with Dinka dominance and Dinka–Nuer and Dinka–Equatorians rivalries.

The challenges facing this massive build-up of administration in Southern Sudan are obvious. They include organizational capacity, the transformation of military institutions into administrative ones and finding the qualified staff for recruitment. Both the North and South suffered from a serious brain drain through emigration but Southern Sudan's loss was immensely greater because of the relatively smaller initial population. Addressing the latter issue, the Nairobi Workshop proposed a weighted average wage for Southern Sudan of about $143 higher than the

Table 6.1 Comparison of average monthly wages in US dollars: current and proposed wages

Grade	Average monthly wages (US$)		
	SOFEP (current)	*GoSS (proposed)*	*GoS (current)*
1. Senior Level–Super Grades	33	50–100	210–301
1. Administrative Professional	20	170–340	148–188
2. Technical/Sub-professional	14	90–180	96–133
3. Clerical	12	50–100	70–92
4. Unclassified	9	30–60	51–57

Sources: Workshop proceedings and paper on the GoS, Nairobi Workshop, Nairobi, 2004; and JAM (2005: 'Sudan Peace Dividend Launched: The Development Plan for New Era').
Note
* GOS pay structure consists of 17 grades and 3 super grades. This correspondence is based on equating Grade 1+ of the GoSS to the Grades 1+ to 3 of the GoS; Grade 1 of the GoSS to Grades 4–6 of the GoS; Grade 2 of the GoSS to Grades 7–9 of the GoS; Grade 3 of the GoSS to Grades 10–14 of the GoSS; and Grade 4 of the GoSS to Grades 15–17 of the GoS.

previous pay in Northern Sudan (about $100) (see Table 6.1). The workshop recommendation was based on the need to attract and retain well-qualified staff in more senior positions.

To these immense needs of building a nascent administrative structure in Southern Sudan, one must add the enormous cost of both police and army forces, including the potential integration of the SSDF or part of it into either the SPLM army or the Central Government's army. On the one hand, JAM (2004) was right in observing that Sudan's civil service system has been steadily weakened since independence in 1956 through attrition, mismanagement and a series of purges based on changes in the political leadership. Further, the prolonged civil war has added to this by reducing the funds available for development and civil administration and by severely reducing the importance of the permanent bureaucracy relative to that of the political leadership and the military. As a result, moral is low, with adverse effects on efficiency and productivity (JAM, 2004).

On the other hand, the temptation to use the easy oil money to lubricate political patronage in the seriously divided South and North is a serious threat that might crowd out both reconstruction and development expenditures. By focusing on wealth sharing and ignoring how these funds are allocated, the CPA has laid down the foundation for serious trade-offs between the political interests of the two major partners and the needs to foster sustainable peace. Oil money may have accelerated the pace of negotiation but may well endanger the hard-won peace.

Power-sharing: exclusion and inclusion

The power arrangement which naturally gave the lion's share to the two new partners induced fierce political turmoil and changed radically the alliances and partnerships in both the North and South. All political parties welcomed peace, but not its passage. The fear that the power-sharing arrangement may amount to the establishment of a 'dual authoritarian regime' was common in both the North and South.

The power-sharing arrangement set a rigid limit that did not allow an effective process to build a more inclusive peace. The new partnership was based primarily on population share. Despite the lack of accurate figures available, estimates place the Southern Sudanese population at less than 25 per cent of the total population. Proportionate population representation in the power sharing was not a guiding principle as it is hard to apply to the major partner holding the reins of power. Thus, the arguments based on proportionate representation of the South and North are irrelevant. What matters most is the rigidity of the formula for power sharing that sets limits to the potential of building up inclusiveness in the peace process. The Nivasha peace process set a rigid limit to power sharing, virtually ignoring the sharply divided North and South and triggered, expectedly, a wave of 'proportionate representation demands' in Darfur, Kordofan and Eastern Sudan.

The other imbalance created by the Nivasha peace agreement is the asymmetrical structure whereby the South has its regional government and naturally shares power in the national government while the North does not enjoy a similar situation.

This is certainly a defect that served the narrow interest of the NIF regime, but it will prove to be a stumbling block for making peace more inclusive, especially when trying to accommodate regional demands for autonomy or some sort of loose confederation of regional powers. Mansour Khalid, the SPLM/A political adviser, argued that such an asymmetric structure is not unique, citing the example of the UK since unification in 1707 (Khalid, 2005, p. 7). While admittedly the Sudan is not a unique case, the asymmetric structure of Nivasha is neither conducive to lasting peace in the increasingly fragmented North nor for the ongoing intra-South factional hostilities. This became clear before a year elapsed after the signing of the CPA. At both Cairo talks between the government and NDA and Abuja Peace negotiation, the rigid ceiling and the asymmetric structure of the CPA became a stumbling block for a breakthrough.

This statement is equally relevant to Northern and Southern Sudan. The NDA's criticism of the presidential system in the country is justifiable, given the past experiences in the Sudan of authoritarian presidential councils that reflect the political and regional diversity of the country (Babikir, 2004, p. 226). Any accommodative peaceful solution to the conflicts in Darfur, Kordofan and Eastern Sudan escalated in part by the rising expectation triggered by Nivasha will require a major modification to the power-sharing protocol.

Peace inclusiveness: was it viable?

Much of the critique of the Nivasha Peace Agreement, by the 'left-out' political players, concentrated on its bilateral nature (as a deal between the SPLM/A and the NIF regime). These criticisms are legitimate and the concerns raised about various limitations, gaps and shortcomings of the peace agreement are all important. They are important, however, in pointing out the challenges that will be faced during the peace-building process. Considering that each of the contending forces were far away from outright victory, was there any other route to a more Comprehensive Peace Agreement available? The answer is an outright 'NO'. Ideally, a Comprehensive Peace Agreement in the case of Sudan should involve all actors in the Northern Sudan political opposition groups and non-SPLM/A Southern political and government-supported militias, assuming that both Darfur and Eastern Sudan movements are represented within the NDA. Such a scenario was neither attainable nor viable for a breakthrough in the peace statement for a number of reasons:

- This scenario implicitly assumes that the NIF government and SPLM/A were ready to relinquish their respective authorities to other forces not at parity with them.
- Despite its remarkable achievements in setting the tone of a national discourse, the NDA failed to create equality between the various militaries and its terms of political mobilization.
- A peace deal that met the needs of all parties from the beginning was the only possibility short of an anarchy similar to the case of Somali. To avert

this scenario, international mediation was necessitated in the peace-building process as Mansour Khalid rightly observed (Khalid, 2003, p. 19).

CPA: the lagging behind of the implementation process

One serious threat to the peace process is reflected in the extremely slow pace of the implementation process of the CPA. Madam Rebecca De Mabior, the widow of the founder of the SPLA/M and the minister of social affairs in the GoSS, in her briefing to the Sudanese diaspora in Nashville, Tennessee (13 February 2006), aptly summarized the balance sheet of what has and has not been completed. On the few steps been taken, she mentioned the following:

• At all levels, governments have been established.
• National and Southern Sudan State Assemblies have been operating.
• Interim constitutions have been enacted.
• Most Commissions, as stipulated in the CPA, have been formed.
• The Bank of Southern Sudan (BOSS) has been established.

Despite this modest progress, she suggested that the most critical steps included:

• Redeployment of the Sudanese the Armed Forces (SAF) north of the border has not occurred.
• The Abyei report has been shelved.
• Oil revenue shares are not being transferred as expected.
• The Commissions formed are not functioning.
• The Boundary Commission has not been formed.

This is certainly a very comprehensive account of the serious obstacles facing the implementation of the CPA. These obstacles are, however, an outcome of both the lack of political will of the ruling party (NIF) as well as a deficiency in the capacity of both partners in the peace agreement. For example, 'The lack of a reliable and well-trained police force in most of South Sudan, the abundance of small arms and light weapons and insufficient disarmament initiatives add to the problem. The presence of well armed militia groups in South Sudan also is a problem', as was noted by observers.[8]

Re-establishing a monopoly over violence: DDR strategies

By the time the CPA and DPA were signed, the Sudanese territory was awash with armed groups, hindering control over of vast territories and at best representing a serious threat to peace and security in seemingly low-intense conflict areas. The spill-over from conflicts in neighbouring countries, particularly Uganda, added to the mosaic of armed groups prominently represented by both the Lord's Resistance Army (LRA, led by J. Kory) and the West Nile Bank Front (WNBF), both fighting against the Ugandan Government. The response to the Ugandan support for the SPLA/M was typically reciprocated by support from Khartoum to both armed Ugandan groups. Despite the agreement reached by the signers of the CPA concerning the need to curb the security threat constituted by these two Ugandan armed groups, one year after the signing of the CPA the LRA still proved to be an additional threat to peace building in Southern Sudan.

Darfur exhibited similar characteristics of the breeding of armed groups. Multiple divisions within the contending armed groups further aggravated the deep divide within Darfur, which was based on the struggle for resources. The Central Government's policies of arming and siding with some of the contending forces was exacerbated by the spill-over from neighbouring countries. The multi-dimensional causes of Darfur's crisis were deeply rooted in the crisis of primary production and the competition for natural resources under the population programme and drought (Chapter 2). With the politicization of ethnicity during the Islamic ascendancy (Chapter 4), the spill-over of civil war and unrestrained factional policies in Chad coupled with Libyan involvement (1981–1987) and other powers (France, USA), Darfur became deeply enmeshed in the sub-regional conflict. Given similar ethnic networks, it is not difficult to see how the rise of some elites (e.g. Zaghawa) can be accounted for with the strength of cross-national networks of trade, smuggling and the ascendancy of new actors not tied especially to any boundaries of the existing 'nation state'.

The split within the SPLA/M in 1998 led to the creation of the UDSF and SPLA/M as two opposing armed groups, each representing a large ethnic group in the South (the Dinka and Nuer). This divide reflected the deep historical mistrust and rivalry between the two ethnic groups as was stressed earlier. The proliferation of armed groups based on ethnic links that started during El-Mahdi's rule in 1986 (the Murahelin of the Buggara Arab tribe of southern Kordofan) was aggravated by the NIF's oil exploration policies as well as the struggle over the future of the Abyei region.

Both the CPA and DPA addressed issues related to the demobilization, disarrangement and reintegration of armed groups. The security arrangements, however, reflected the essential differences between the two peace agreements. Thus, the Nivasha Agreement proposed to maintain two separated armies – the Sudanese Armed Forces (SAF) and Sudanese People Liberation Army (SPLA) – with a symbolic small joint unit, should the result of the referendum on self-determination confirm unity. Abuja, on other hand, was more concerned with equal access to the national army, as shown in Box 6.3.

Box 6.3   Armed forces, law enforcement agencies and national security

79. The Sudanese Armed Forces (SAF) shall be regular, professional and non-partisan. Darfurians shall be fairly represented at all levels therein, including in senior command positions, in accordance with Chapter 3 of this Agreement.

80. Qualified former combatants from the movements shall be integrated into the Sudanese armed forces, law enforcement agencies and security services, in accordance with Chapter 3 of the Agreement.

81. The GoS shall take appropriate measures to rectify any imbalances that may exist in the representation of Darfurians at senior levels of the Sudan Armed Forces in general and the intake into Military Academies in particular.

82. The Police, Customs, Immigration and Border Guards, the Prisons and Wildlife Services shall be open to all Sudanese including in particular Darfurians and nominees of the Movements, to reflect the diversity of the Sudanese society.

83. The National Security Service shall be representative of all people of the Sudan. Darfurians shall be fairly represented at all levels therein.

Furthermore, the CPA agreement emphasized the principles of the proportional downsizing of forces on both sides. With regard to what the agreement referred to as 'Other Armed Groups' the two parties to the CPA agreement agreed that:

No Armed group allied to either party shall be allowed to operate outside the two forces. The parties agree that those mentioned in (79a) who have the desire and qualify shall be incorporated into the organized forces of either Party (Army, Police, Prisons and Wildlife forces), while the rest shall be reintegrated into the civil service and civil society institutions. The parties agree to address the status of other Armed Groups in the country and to realize full inclusiveness in the transition process.

The first year after Nivasha was greatly shaped by the struggle to implement the interim security agreement. On the one hand, the principle of integrating the armed groups within the two armies proved to be a formidable task. On the other hand, the restriction of two officially recognized armies (SAF and PPLA) made possible a breakthrough in the deadlock in the first South–South Conference, held in Nairobi. It was Silva Kiir who brought a breakthrough in the talks with SSDF. During the Juba meeting of 8 January 2006 between the SPLA and SSDF, the parties agreed to a complete and unconditional unity and to immediately integrate their forces into a non-partisan army under the name of SPLA, as stipulated in the Comprehensive Peace Agreement.

Additionally, it was agreed that each party would:

- completely cease all forms of hostilities and ensure that all their forces and persons under their control observe and comply with this declaration;
- guarantee freedom of movement of people, goods and services in all areas in Southern Sudan;
- offer a declaration of general amnesty covering any criminal acts committed during the past period of hostilities between the two forces;

- appeal to any armed persons or groups outside the two forces to join the process of unity and reconciliation in order to promote peace, stability and development throughout Southern Sudan;
- mobilize the people of Southern Sudan behind this agreement to support its implementation.

Peace spoilers: too many contenders

Downs and Stedman (2002), in their study of the determinants of success in peace-implementation strategies, identified two sets of variables: one related to the conflict environment and one to the degree of international commitment. The authors noted that 'the three most important environmental sources of failure are the presence of spoilers, the presence of neighbouring states opposed to the peace agreement, and the presence of valuable commodities or spoils'. Post-peace agreement Sudan is no doubt a host of all three sources of failure.

By the time the CPA was signed, the Sudan seemed to be hosting every possible peace spoiler. Over two decades of war, conflicts, drought and the destabilizing overflow of conflicts in all major regions surrounding the Sudan made it a convoluted terrain of armed groups: within the South, in the transitional areas particularly in the oil-producing regions, in the West, where the Darfur crisis is looming, and, to a lesser extent, in the East.

This war-produced terrain of too many contending forces reflected the complexity of factors that shaped the process of war and conflict in the Sudan. Such complexity is well documented in a number of recent scholarly contributions (Lesch, 1998; Abdel Salam *et al.*, 2001; de Waal and Ajawin, 2002; and Johnson, 2003). As Johnson (2003) emphasizes, war is being fought over complicated and changing issues that encompass identity, culture, the rival claims of extremely diverse peoples and control over natural resources inducing grazing land, water and oil. Savage (2003) notes: 'the shifting alliances and counter alliances struck between various political and military factions over the last 20 years have left the country profoundly divided' (p. 3). What is crucial here is not the narration and documentation of how these sources of fragility were produced but rather their implications for the post-war situation and outcome.

Once the highly exclusive and extremely violent forms of power negotiations are over, the monopoly over violence secedes and new actors appear. Though not entirely new, they were less visible and less able to voice their opinions in full. It must be added that, unlike colonial wars, armed movements' claim to exclusive representation is extremely difficult to assert. This is particularly true in the case of prolonged conflicts. Sudan's conflicts provide a wealth of evidence on the non-viability of exclusive representation attempts by the contending parties. This non-viability, apart from its obvious limitations on the capacity to mobilize populations during the war, greatly curtailed the claim of the contending forces to the monopoly of representation. Post-war situations, with their proliferation of actors, sometimes magnify such limitations. This is demonstrated by two representative examples from the prolonged conflicts in the Sudan. The NIF's mobilization capacity which started by voluntary Jihad mobilization was soon dropped in favour of an involuntary and repressive recruitment programme based on new laws linked to national security services. Defection, fierce resistance and all forms of non-compliance with national security obligations became the norm. Similarly, the SPLA/M, following the short-lived voluntary mobilization in the early 1980s, resulted in all forms of non-voluntary recruitment of combatants including the notorious and well-publicized child soldier.

The post-Garang era: implications for the reconstruction process

The tragic death of John Garang on 30 July 2005 marked a radical shift in the power structure within the SPLM/A and Southern Sudan and ushered new changes in the direction of partnerships and coalitions within the SPLM/A and between it and other contending forces in the South and the country at large. The implications of these changes for the process of reconstruction and North–South relations are far reaching.

On the immediate task of addressing the challenge of the deeply divided South the succession of Kiir proved to be instrumental in making a breakthrough in the negotiation with contending anti-SPLM/A forces, particularly the conglomerate of Khartoum-supported armed groups loosely aligned under the umbrella of the Southern Sudan Defence Forces. Following the signing of the CPA, Garang started a process of internal reconciliation. In April 2004 Garang organized a South–South reconciliation conference in Kenya but the SSDF was excluded. It was only in July of the same year when Garang agreed to meet with the SSDF delegation led by Matiep in April 2005, but the meeting ended with a deadlock. Kiir's approach to South–South reconciliation was far more inclusive and accommodating. He started a series of meetings with the SSDF immediately following his inauguration as a first vice president in August 2005. As a gesture of goodwill he appointed 20 members from the SSDF as commissioners. On 8 January 2006 the Juba declaration was signed by Kiir and Matiep signalling a dramatic departure from SPLM/A monopoly over the South. The other important dimension of such a shift took place within the SPLM/A itself. The re-incorporation of the group that led to the 1991 split within the SPLM/A and the signing of the Khartoum Peace Agreement of 1997 was of equally important shift in the political matrix of the South. With the appointment of Dr Riek Machar as GoSS Vice President and Lam Akol as Minister of Foreign Affairs for the GoS, the power restructuring has been effectively done. The Juba declaration paved the way for further changes in SSDF–SPLM/A relations. By June 2007, over 50,000 former soldiers of the SSDF were officially integrated into the SPLA and the GoSS's civil service. 'The list of something going to 3,700 officers has been radioed through radio communication to all units of SPLA. This is how we do our things in the SPLA, then we make him known to all units of SPLA so he enjoys the respect with the rest of SPLA officers,' explained an SPLA spokesperson.[9]

On the one hand, the post-Garang major shifts have certainly facilitated greater inclusiveness and speeded up the process of DDR in war-torn Southern Sudan. On the other hand, these major changes in the political terrain of Southern Sudan underline major changes in the direction of the reconstruction processes as well as the future of North–South relations.

The loss of Garang as a visionary leader meant also a major transformation of reconstruction imaginaries. Within the South a more realistic, far less radical process of state building that takes into account sub-regional and ethnic division and balances is likely to prevail. A broader coalition that gives adequate weight to traditional communal structures in terms of both polity and economy is likely to emerge. The new coalition is also likely to depart a great deal from the 'New Sudan' advocacy with clear implications for North–South relations. The rapprochement between Kiir and other contending forces reflects a deeper and well-established suspicion of the 'New Sudan' thesis that is well entrenched within both sides. Kiir is perceived as a secessionist by many despite his ardent efforts to change such an image. In August 2005 he was emphasizing the need to give unity of the country a chance: 'We have to give unity of our country a chance and then to see how attractive it will be to Southerners so that they join into it. I am also committed to that unity until the other side proves otherwise' (ICG, 2005, p. 2). However, after two years in power and the emergence of the new coalition in the South, Kiir came out clearly in favour of an independent state. Addressing a congregation on 24 June 2007, Kiir noted in despair that the Government of Southern Sudan had been established in 2005 but nothing big had been achieved in a period of almost two years. Stressing the need for full participation in the coming election (2009) and referendum he declared, 'This time round, we South Sudanese should not allow somebody to dictate on us, rather let us bear in mind that we have two choices either to remain in united Sudan where we are subjected to being second class citizens or we remain an independent state of our own.' Despite his reference to the right to vote in any direction he was clear in emphasizing secession as the most popular choice: 'If unionists become the majority, then they would forge the unity of the country but should they become the minority, they will have to follow the separatists and I believe separatists in Southern Sudan are more than those seeking to unite Sudan' (*Sudan Tribune*, 25 June 2007). A similar strong position was expressed by the acting Archbishop of the Episcopal Church of Sudan who told the congregation that Southern Sudanese should all vote for independence in the referendum (ibid., 27 June 2007).

Challenges of governance and sustainable peace: towards a conclusion

In both the North and South, problems of governance are deep seated and the struggle for participation, transparency and accountability represent a formidable task for lasting peace. In the North, decades of old traditions of public participation were almost completely eroded by the NIF's ruthless policies of purging the military, judiciary, public administration, political parties, trade unions and all forms of civil association. The process of state privatization coupled with legal and constitutional frameworks to maintain control over all aspects of political, social and economic activity profoundly affected and undermined all the structural foundations of what was once a vibrant civil society. The enormity of the challenges of governance in the North is well represented by this summary from Savage's (2003) report entitled 'The Crisis of Governance and Challenges to Peace in the Sudan'. In the North, Savage identified the following:

- Unclear roles and responsibilities between the government and security services;
- Use of legal and constitutional frameworks to maintain control of all aspects of political and economic and social activity;
- Slow and non-transparent administrative procedures serve as a political tool to obstruct freedom of movement and organization;
- Legal and administrative restrictions on independent civil society;
- Lack of reform in all government departments;
- The military forces of Northern Sudan include semi-autonomous security forces, tribal militia and popular defence forces, armed bands and a large conscripted army;
- The renewal of the state of emergency and amendments to the National Security Forces Act give the security forces legal impunity for their abuses;
- An elite monopoly on the use of natural resources such as land and oil and links between economic strategies and military objectives;
- Lack of accountability in the management of state finances, including a pervasive lack of transparency and corruption;
- Neglect, marginalization and underdevelopment in many regions of the North (and government garrisons in the South) which lack basic social services and are unstable and impoverished;
- Formal economic activity, employment opportunities and credit are restricted to those who are politically affiliated with the current regime;
- Social and cultural marginalization through policies denying equal opportunity to many social groups (including women) and seizing land and assets from already marginalized people;
- The dismantling of what was a vibrant and active civil society and the creation of new organizations with limited ideological and religious visions under programmes of 'Islamic social planning'.

In the South, his detailed description can be summarized as follows:

- A militaristic mentality dominates the SPLM/A and the South generally despite efforts to form civil administration and despite the Southern leadership's wish to be seen as a Southern government-in-waiting;
- Political and military expediency often overrides the attempts to establish an effective and functioning civil administration and institutions;

- Factionalism and opportunistic warlordism and government-supported militias are still prevalent in the South – often to destabilize the SPLM and maintain instability and insecurity.

Taken in a broader sense DDR involves more than sheer demilitarization and reintegration. It involves the serious challenges of transforming a predominantly military group in to a viable institutionalized political party and civil administration. As an eyewitness and participant in the movement Nyaba (1997) describes the typical behaviour of the armed soldiers of the SPLA who were previously cattle herders, peasants and the 'lumpen' from town: 'The pride of carrying a gun and being part of a victorious army made many of these forget the purpose for which they were fighting and turn their guns on the unarmed civilian population... 'The arrogance of power of carrying an AKM rifle made them wasteful and brutal to civilian population' (ibid., p. 36). 'The neglect of political education in the course of military training is another important factor that contributed to this unfortunate behaviour' (p. 37).

Nyaba's description of the rank and file of the SPLA is important in understanding some of the potential challenges of post-conflict Sudar. In other words, disparity between those who were fighting and those who were studying internally or in diasporas. The post-conflict shift to priorities linked to institutional building and administration of the reconstruction processes may highlight such disparity as it translates into access to employment and administrative hierarchies. In the immediate transitional process this may signal one of the most important challenges of reintegration of the military as well as returnees. In Sorbo's words, 'employment is critical to reintegrate particularly volatile groups (ex-militias/soldiers, refugees/IDPs) and to create a sense of confidence in the future that will help to demilitarize politics' (Sorbo, 2004, p. 7). The transitory nature of such a challenge is not evident. Studies in post-reconstruction/revolution lends much support to the possible prolongation of such a transition (see Allen and Turton, 1996; Hammond, 2004).

Two years after the CPA and the GoSS, accusations of rampant corruption created a sense of despair among Southern Sudanese. Current investigations include the 60 million USD missing from the GoSS. This money was given out by the GoNU to the GoSS as their share of oil revenues, but this money was not invested for reconstruction or development in the South, but was redirected for private use. Another allegation made in the name of GoSS was the purchase of 300 land cruiser vehicles.[10] 'GoSS is reported to have paid $95,000 per vehicle for Toyota Land Cruisers valued at $50,000 each. The difference is alleged to have made its way into the pockets of procurement officials.'[11]

If the NIF regime continues to exert its firm exclusive control over oil revenues, the route to this new form of 'indirect monopoly over violence' may succeed in the short run. However, the formula for creating a conglomerate of militia leaders and warlords all incorporated in the administrative and security apparatuses may prove to be unsustainable even in the short run. The unstable peace in Darfur demonstrates such inherent limitations, unless of course the new 'royal family of armed contenders' can be enlarged indefinitely to accommodate the unrestrained reproduction of contenders for power.

The formula for the DDR, embedded in both the CPA and DPA, is a shortcut to re-establishing a monopoly over violence through the formalization and amalgamation of contending armed groups. This 'quick-fix' formula, lubricated by rising oil income, will inevitably lead to the creation of a mammoth administrative and military conglomerate and, eventually, crowd out reconstruction as an alternative to the failed development model. Despite the temptation of this easy route to ending the proliferation of violence, it carries far-reaching threats to sustainable peace. The CPA itself sets limits to power and wealth sharing, as was explained earlier in this chapter. Transcending such limits may amount to undermining the Nivasha agreement. The asymmetrical confederate system adopted by the CPA is already posing serious limitations to power-bargaining processes and the potential for accommodating new contending forces.

The pre-war situation is only important in understanding the emerging structures, institutions and actors in the economy and society. The cessation of hostilities and the fully fledged peace agreement is not the new social contract. It could however be the end of extremely violent re-negotiations of the pre-existing social contract. Even the actors who initiated the process are no closer to homogeneity! Signing of an effective peace agreement does not end or conclude the negotiation of social contracts. It does, however, shift the course of such negotiation into a more complex direction that denies the possibility of an easy categorization or prediction. Hence, understanding the changes that were produced by war is essential in identifying new actors, new institutions and new sites of polarization within the economies and societies of war-torn communities.

7 Post-Nivasha

Challenges of (re)-building a war-produced economy

'...take towns to people in countryside rather than people to towns.'
(John Garang addressing the South–South meeting, 2005)

This chapter is based on the theoretical debates that inform current attempts at theorizing both war and post-war situations (outlined in Chapter 2) and is set to examine challenges and viable routes to the reconstruction of a war-produced economy. As noted earlier, the limitations and in most cases the irrelevance of the conventional approach to reconstruction, based on a narrowly defined engineering-economic notion of rebuilding devastated areas, is evident. Furthermore, as stressed in the theoretical sections, prolonged civil war produces a number of irreversibilities in socio-economic structures and triggers new processes and dynamics for societal change. These irreversibilities are a direct result of abrupt and massive flows affecting not only populations but also their institutions, assets, skills, levels of entrepreneurship and means of reproduction. The production of these irreversibilities seriously undermines the validity of the main assumptions underlying the conventional approach to post-conflict reconstruction: 'retrievability' of the pre-war situation, that war is a temporary instance of disequilibria, the localized nature of war effects, and finally its emphasis on macro variables or alternatively negligence of the vital and profound impact of micro variables. War produces new forms of multilayered and overlapping urbanities, ruralities and extensive and interactive local, translocal and transnational networks that are constantly reshaping institutions and unleashing new transformative potential. Understanding such transformative potential and its dynamics is an essential step towards building a sound framework for addressing post-war reconstruction.

In this respect there are many lessons to be learned from the experiences of countries well ahead in the reconstruction process. Perhaps Bosnia and Herzegovina in Southeast Europe is the best example. First, it represents a reconstruction process at an advanced level and, second, it represents an advanced initial condition for reconstruction (medium human development) as opposed to the majority of a war-torn country (mostly residing within the low human development category of the UNDP human development categories). Using the words of Pugh and Cooper (2004) the Bosnian experience 'demonstrates that the legacies of wartime economies are far from eclipsed, despite more than eight years of external aid and guidance' (ibid., p. 12). The implications are far more interesting for countries just emerging out of a prolonged conflict. Lack of recognition of the persistence of a war-produced economy was determined to be the success of a post-war reconstruction. With little or no recognition of this fact, the neo-liberal model reconstruction focused on macroeconomic reforms as a principal strategy. 'Not only have these reforms made little difference to the lives of the bulk of the population in terms of their ability to take care of basic needs, if anything their situation has worsened, but also they have done very little to revive production or attract the level of foreign direct investment that external agencies have investment that external agencies have spuriously insisted is essential for long term development' (ibid., p. 12). The implications of the Bosnian experience is indicative of the nature of the challenges of the process of reconstruction currently under way in the Sudan and in particular Southern Sudan.

The previous chapter on the sources of fragility and challenges of governance showed how the political and socio-economic terrains were shaped and reshaped by the processes leading to and resulting from negotiated peace. This chapter places heavy emphasis on the issues related to rural transformation, addressing the root causes of the crisis in primary production, as well as land tenure reform, as key to sustainable peace and successful reconstruction. The chapter also addresses the often neglected war-driven multi-layered urbanities, which is the site for both potential threats to peace as well as progressive and development-enhancing potential. The specificities of negotiated settlement have also been highlighted. The most important conclusion with a direct bearing on the reconstruction phase is the erosion of various alliances, partnerships and coalitions following the cessation of hostilities and in the transitional phase following negotiated settlement. By definition, following negotiated settlements means that visions for reconstruction advocated by various contending forces are not the only guidelines.

A war-produced economy

Central to the new thinking about reconstruction is the emergence of a new structural foundation for the economy, society and political order, implying an irretrievability of pre-war situations and thus the complete departure from a 'conventional' approach to reconstruction thinking. The emerging post-war situation is based on new demographics, new rural and urban economies and skill endowments that bear no resemblance to the previous pre-war situation. This is due to the population transformation. The new post-war economy was essentially shaped by demographic changes that brought large, involuntary population flows that resulted in depopulation in rural areas, a changing composition of households, massive influx to urban sites and various forms of disruption and discontinuities in institutions and structures. However, massive population flows are most often defined in narrow terms. As demonstrated in Chapter 5 in the case of both Southern Sudan and Darfur, such flows are invariably accompanied by assets and entrepreneurial flows[1] that strips these marginalized areas of their already 'meagre' physical and human resources. The flow-back or reversal of such flows constitutes a serious challenge to successful reconstruction. Where such flows of capital and entrepreneurship is by and large of non-indigenous origin, in both Southern Sudan and Darfur, the deepening ethnic hostilities represent the single most important barrier. There are four major sites for changes and new dynamics following prolonged civil strife. These are:

- The economics of a new rural setting (depopulation and depletion of assets and resources).
- The economics of new urbanities (accelerated informalization, new dynamics of urban poverty, child labour and youth unemployment, as well as skills gain).
- Human capital formation (multiple forms of skills and brain-drain within and outside the country).
- Eroded/failed state (the challenges of post-war: capacity to manage/administer reconstruction, re-establishing the state, partnership conflicts between emerging new factors).

This plethora of changes and emerging dynamics are closely interrelated and interactive and criss-crossed by a number of issues: networks of illicit activities and warlords; changing gender composition of the labour process; new consumption habits and needs; erosion of the structural foundation of old values, norms and institutions; changing family dynamics and loss of intra-generational channels of transmission of knowledge and values because of war; and internal as well as external displacement.

Central challenges in war-produced economies

The emerging structures of the war-produced economy suggest four central priorities:

- Rehabilitation (buildings in most cases) of physical infrastructure as a precondition even for the initial phase of both reconstruction and nascent state building.
- Rehabilitation and transformation of primitive low-productivity agriculture, which brings to the forefront the urgency of land tenure reform.
- Rehabilitation of human capital in its broadest sense involving the capacity to work, voluntary repatriation of the displaced population and upgrading of all skills in a sustainable basis, as well as measures aimed at addressing the serious brain-drain.
- Rehabilitation and building of a viable urban economy that can accommodate the current and expected influx of new 'no-more' rural residents.

The potential for voluntary repatriation, whether urban–rural or rural–rural, is completely lost. Reallocation/repopulation of rural areas becomes dependent upon a comprehensive package that compensates for lost assets and creates an attractive environment comparable to that of the urban setting including its deprived shanty towns. Paradoxically that is not only unattainable given the limited resources but not foreseeable in the short and medium terms. Hence, the post-war situation may pave the way for some deep transformations in the urban and the rural economy that were not attainable in the pre-war situation. For example, the loss of asserts may lead to totally new comparative advantages based on a new distribution of the population, completely changed consumption habits and lower population intensities in rural areas. In some African cases, a shift away from communal ownerships of land based on previous and discontinued mixed farming/pastoral activities may prove to be structurally inevitable. Equally, the massive population movement may render communal boundaries of land ownership obsolete. In other words, what had not been achieved by the failed modernization project seems to be attainable by the radical changes brought about by war.

Pre-negotiated peace visions: the SPLM vision and programme – a pre-Nivasha document

As was discussed earlier the SPLA/M programme underwent several radical phases corresponding to international, regional and national shifts in political alliances and backing. From the Marxian populist version of radical transformation to 'cohabitation' with the neo-liberal ideology, the SPLA/M vision underwent several shifts. In the newest version of SPLA/M before the peace negotiation the new programme adopted a 'mixed economy' outlook. Thus the economy of the New Sudan shall be a liberal and mixed free market in which both public and private sectors shall complement each other and be encouraged with the public sector based on social welfare, competitiveness, efficiency and provision of social overhead services. The principal basis for economic development of the New Sudan shall be the individual human being.

Foreign investment in the New Sudan, including joint ventures, shall be allowed and encouraged and the repatriation of profits shall be guaranteed and facilitated. Small and large-scale industrial projects shall be established in the New Sudan by the movement and/or their autonomous investment interests, by individual entrepreneurs, or through joint ventures with foreign investors.

Agricultural production shall be aimed primarily at self-sufficiency in food as well as cash crops for export to earn foreign exchange for farm families and for the movement. The SPLM will strive to promote the mechanization of agriculture, beginning with the ox-plough and tractors as this becomes feasible. The SPLM shall stimulate agricultural, industrial, technological and scientific development by adopting the necessary policies and laws that foster initiative and encourage local and foreign investment. However, in furtherance of social justice, the SPLM may regulate the acquisition, ownership, use and disposition of land and other non-renewable natural resources, in order to protect the environment and in advocacy of the interests of posterity.

The SPLM shall work to modernize and transform the economy of the New Sudan from its present agrarian and backward state to an agro-industrial and industrial economy through the promotion of mechanized agriculture, integrated industrialization, entrepreneurship and science and technology, all aimed at and leading to the modernization of the economy.

Selected items from: The Fifteen-Point Programme of the SPLM, SPLM Political Secretariat, Yei, New Cush, New Sudan, March 1998.

The SPLM comprehensive development plan, found in a document known as *The SPLM Strategic Framework for War-to-Peace Transition*, did not fail to identify these areas, albeit with obvious neglect of the fourth issue related to the urbanities. The downplaying of urban centres stems from two reasons. First, a wrong assumption based on the pre-war situation is made about 95 per cent of the Southern Sudan population in the previously mentioned document it was stated: 'The SPLM plan is focused on development of rural areas, which are home to 95%.' Such a statement ignores both the depopulation of rural areas as well as the fact that half of the four million southern IDPs (roughly two-thirds of the population) became fully integrated in urban life in the North. Their voluntary return to a deprived urban centre in the North is doubtful let alone their return to rural life. Second, the wrong assumption is very much based on ideological convention rather than empirical evidence. Such an ideological convention was echoed several times in Garang's speeches when he reiterates slogans like 'taking the town to the rural areas', 'industrializing the rural areas', etc. In a live broadcast on Sudanese TV (28 May 2005) Garang introduced Sudan's priorities by saying that Over 90 percent of our people are in rural areas. We have a vision to take towns. There are not enough towns in the South. We will start new towns for our people in rural areas. We will provide them with everything: Whatever can be found in towns will also be found in rural areas, such as electricity. This is possible in the South. There are many rivers. One can build micro-dams to generate electricity. One can use wind and solar energy in order to generate electricity' (*Sudan Tribune*, 28 May 2005). The statement is consistent with Garang's deep mistrust about urban potential expressed earlier in 1987 (Garang, 1992): 'Our city is not a productive city but a consumptive, exploitive, cancerous growth living on rural areas and like cancer, our cities are killing the rural areas making both the cities and rural areas unproductive and inducing famine in magnitudes which has never been experienced before in Africa' (ibid., p. 255).

Relevance

The question of the direct bearing on the process of shaping and implementation of the reconstruction phase is: 'How are these initial visions for reconstruction going to influence the process?' the multiplicity of approaches and visions could be seen, given the appropriate enabling conditions, as a continuation of the negotiation of a social contract between various contending forces by 'less violent' or ideally peaceful means. This may ideally lead to a build-up of a broad-based consensus on national priorities and/or a regional mess. Such a smooth path to the peaceful negotiation of a social contract is hard to predict. The previous chapter identified the main sources', fragility in the peace process and challenges to governance as the two determinant factors of the process of the successful, broadly based reconstruction phase. The interlocking nature between the 'political' and the 'economical', and between a 'quick-fix' solution in the initial phase of the peace-building process and long-term objectives, is the source of the constant production of trade-offs and deviations.

Post-Nivasha visions: from radical to accommodative programmes

As discussed in the previous chapter, Garang's sudden departure led to tremendous changes in the political terrain of Southern Sudan with far-reaching implications or the process of rebuilding the war-torn economy. On the one hand, it is true that the CPA left unresolved a number of key issues. These issues can be summed up together in one binding phrase: the CPA's emphasis was on wealth sharing and not on wealth making. On the other hand, the departure from Garang's grand revolutionary strategy was made effective through a much wider new coalition of political forces. Within the SPLM itself the grand strategy of social transformation advocated by Garang hardly commanded a majority and was to a great extent the revolutionary minority advocacy within the movement. Kiir, not known to be among this minority, headed towards a wider coalition of political forces that could hardly agree on a common vision for transformation. SPLM terms of reference for reconstruction and development continue to be the post-Nivasha programme. Yet the direction and content of such a transformation will be the net outcome of the bargaining processes within the new coalition. For example, the opportunity for a radical land tenure and agrarian reform which was traditionally used to speed up the state-building process (Eritrea, Ethiopia and Zimbabwe are among the recent and relevant examples) is no longer available.

The agrarian crisis: the centrality of land issue

Chapters 3 and 4 discussed the root causes of the crisis in primary production in both modern and subsistent agriculture. In the conflict-torn subsistent agriculture, the struggle over access to land and natural resources was accelerated by population pressure, devastating droughts and squeezing of land available for both subsistent farming and grazing. During the 1980s and 1990s, the combination of the three aforementioned factors coupled with the active politicization and ethnicization of the struggle over resources brought the crisis in the largely, yet not exclusively, subsistent economy to its ultimate conclusion, rendering both its sustainability and institutional structures dysfunctional. As early as 1993, the magnitude of the depletion of assets (mostly cattle) was revealed by the IDPs who moved to Greater Khartoum, as reflected in Table 7.1.

Table 7.1 IDP asset losses

How many animals lost?	Frequency	Per cent
All	28	3.3
Most	518	61.8
Some	11	1.3
Don't know	33	3.9
Who took them?		
Marheel (Raids)	357	41.9
Rebels	100	12.0
People we don't know	11	1.3
Combination	146	17.5
Not applicable	219	25.3

Source: DPSG files, 1993.

The findings of the early 1990s were recently confirmed by Deng's (2004) study on the magnitude of depletion of assets at the other end of the migratory flow:

> It is clear that while the level of household cattle ownership in 1998 declined by almost 60 per cent of the level in 1988 in Abyei area, households in Gogrial experienced about a 90 per cent decline in the level of their cattle ownership. The decline in the level of cattle ownership was significantly higher during 1993–1998 than between 1988–1993, particularly in Gogrial area when endogenous counter-insurgency warfare intensified. (p. 13)

Within Southern Sudan, JAM (2005) identified the following factors as being the factors facilitating the low-productivity trap for each sub-sector.

- Crop production: based on slash and burn rotations, primitive technology, no purchased inputs and a substitute orientation, isolation from domestic and international markets implies weak incentives for surplus production. Because most households have access to some land on which they produce their own food, the domestic market for food is thin, except in drought years (but then additional food supplies have been provided by the WFP).
- Livestock producer: isolation from markets, inefficient marketing infrastructure, low productivity exacerbated by periodic droughts and heavy disease burden. However, markets for livestock appear to be less distorted than those for food crops.
- Fisher folks: very primitive equipment for fishing, rudimentary fish processing equipment to make fish available for use over time, is rationed from market, and low productivity of cropping/livestock activities for those who also have lent.
- Forest-based enterprises: maintenance, replanting and management of government-owned forests for long-term production is weak; likely that lack of roads means little is logged, yet evidence of considerable falling of trees for housing, firewood and sale.

Table 7.2 Level of household cattle ownership in the 1990s

Research communities	Years	Average number of cattle owned by households			
		Initial level of household/Wealth status			
		Poor	Middle	Non-poor	Total
Abyei	1988	15.1	25.9	112.0	52.6
	1993	11.2	26.1	97.3	47.3
	1998	5.3	13.4	37.5	20.2
Gogrial	1988	5.9	54.4	97.0	59.3
	1993	16.8	47.0	40.7	39.3
	1998	1.6	7.8	6.7	6.3

Source: Deng (2003), http://www.ids.ac.uk/ids/bookshop/dp/dp381.pdf.

The issue of land tenure was largely thought to be a firmly concluded thesis, within the linear perception of development. The centrality of the agrarian question and land tenure systems, in conflict making and in the post-conflict situation, as well as in the paradigm shift in development thinking, has been subjected to serious scholarly investigations in the last two decades. Furthermore, for countries striving to rebuild state legitimacy or where the state hardly existed before, the land tenure and agrarian issue is deeply untargeted in the process of nation state building (Eritrea, Ethiopia, Zimbabwe, Southern Sudan and in Northern Sudan). In the Eritrean case, the new legislation repeals all other tenure agreement, and provides for ownership of all land by the Eritrean state. 'The individual peasant farmer is allowed a lifetime lease of the land currently held, and new usufruct rights in the land be distributed to all Eritrean citizens above the age of 18, without any discrimination of sex, religion, tribalism, and side, for the right of life long use of a specific plot of land. The land cannot be sold or re-leased' (Tronvoll, 1998, p. 1).

The World Bank seems to be departing from the 1960s and 1970s tenure reform debate that tended to focus narrowly on the merits of converting an informal traditional system of communal rights into a modern formal system, by a process of adjudication and individual titling.

Land tenure reform is central to any attempt at transforming traditional agriculture in both the North and South. Pollani (2005), who acted as a Senior Policy Adviser for JAM, acknowledged the centrality of land use to conflict making and peace building in both parts of Sudan. In 'Conflict over land' he wrote that, the conflict analysis guidelines:

> are still mushrooming all over the Sudan as a consequence of competition over scarce resources between nomads and settlers, worsened by a particular regime of native administration that denied some nomadic groups the right to their own tribal home-land, therefore to secure land tenure. This competition is a key factor in the ongoing Darfur crisis. In other cases, the conflict over land revolved around the expansion of privately owned mechanized farming at the

expense of the communal subsistence of agriculture and pastoralism. Again, the conflict has been exacerbated by the flaws of current land legislation: where tribal communities failed to register land as their own, out of ignorance of the law, land was attributed to the state and could thereafter be sold to Sudanese foreign absentee landlords; especially the transitional areas of central Sudan but also Eastern Sudan and parts of the upper Nile (Renk) features. (ibid., p. 12)

The matrix of current land-based conflict roaming in Darfur (Annex) is quite representative of the other parts in Southern Sudan, Nuba Mountains, Abyei and all over the transitional zone between Northern and Southern Sudan. Thus with the exception of Northern Sudan, in all of these areas multiple forms of indigenous land tenure systems prevail with some correspondence to particular ethnic groups. However, such systems are neither static nor egalitarian and over time these forms of communal organization have been defined by the interplay of various factors.

Sudan: land policy and land tenure

Let us recall some of the basic characteristics of the land policy and land tenure rights in the Sudan. Under the 1929 Land Ordinance, private land was confined to agricultural land along the Nile and a few areas along other courses. This accounts for about 1 per cent of all land in Sudan. The Unregistered Land Act of 1970 acknowledged this freehold but declared all other land formally owned by the Government of Sudan. Apart from freehold land, all other agricultural land can be classified into one of three types:

Type I: Registered leases on government land that has been surveyed usually referring to land under cultivation of large-scale semi-mechanized schemes, or in traditional irrigated farming. Since land cannot be leased or sold, the lease cannot be used as collateral for credit.

Type II: Registered land with usufruct rights on government land that has been surveyed and is usually cultivated. Cultivation rights are held in perpetuity, but leases are held for specific periods of time.

Type III: Unregistered land with traditional usufruct rights deemed to be government land. The use of these lands (often referred to as 'un-demarcated' lands has usually been established through unlawful settlement and unlawful clearing and cultivation by individuals or groups. Eventual registration of this land merely formalizes an unauthorized occupation.[2] Within these three types, there are many variants depending on location and type of land. They include:

   i   Communal land owned by the government, under the community or village leader, and usually allocated to households from the village or a local ethnic group for exclusive use. Although it can be inherited it cannot be used as collateral;

ii   Leaseholds are allocated by the government to private farmers with water licences to draw from the Nile for 25 years. Leases on land for foreign investors in rain-fed areas have been granted for 25–99 years and can be used as collateral;

iii   Some land is rented by the government by decree, or owned within the command area of an irrigated scheme, such as parts of the Gezira irrigation scheme, and leased to tenants. Owners receive a negligible rent, cannot sell and land cannot be used as collateral.[3]

In both colonial and post-colonial versions of 'indirect rule', the partnership between the central administration and native administration altered and reshaped the communal tenure system. The trend, however, was always towards the shrinking of the communal tenure system in favour of commercial large-scale agriculture: first, during the colonial period to accommodate growing cotton schemes and, second, during the post-colonial regime, expanding systematically mechanized agriculture as was previously elaborated in Chapters 2 and 3. Nimeiri's socialist orientation brought this trend of encroaching into communal land to its conclusion by the 1970 legislation which set aside customary laws and all land was made into government land which allowed people access to it through lease arrangements. In practice, customary rights, albeit over constantly shrinking areas, were operating. Thus, both colonial and post-colonial authorities used land tenure as a mechanism for elite formation all over the country and constantly lubricating their 'uneasy alliance' with the traditional administration by unequal access to whatever remained of the communal land. Neither the notion of homogeneity nor the notion of 'paradise of equalitarianism' with regard to the communal land system holds. Intervention in the land tenure system was, and continues to be, a powerful mechanism for state building and for enhancing various forms of partnership in this excessively large terrain of land. The Southern Sudan, albeit not in its transitional areas within the North, may have survived relatively better but it is hard to imagine that it could survive the urgent tasks of nascent state building.

'Whose land?' committee, The Nuba Mountains committee, 1996

Perhaps it is indicative to look at fairly recent attempts (1996) to address the land tenure system as a major factor underlying conflict in the Nuba Mountains. El Imam and Egemi's (2005) paper addressing the land question in the Nuba Mountains summarized the experience as follows.

In 1996 a presidential decree established a committee responsible for the redistribution of land in the Nuba Mountains composed of representatives of all ethnic groups in the region (Nuba, Baggara and Jellaba – Northern Sudanese traders) and by type of activity (pastoralists, farmers and owners of mechanized farms) as well as various relevant officials. The committee developed and applied the following criteria:

- The applicant should be an inhabitant of the area irrespective of whether he is Nuba, Beggara, Jellaba or Fullani origin.
- Commitment not to sell the land.
- 'The relative ability to cultivate the land. This was defended by the committee on grounds that those with the relative ability are usually part of the power structure and have the ability of manipulating others and therefore cheating or contributing to conflicts.' (ibid., p. 2)

Despite some success in distributing and redistributing schemes whose licenses expired, the land was obviously distributed to the relatively able as the average size of farms distributed fell within three categories:

I   300–500 feddans (roughly an acre)
II 150–250 feddans
III 75–100 feddans

The authors rightly noted that such distribution did not address the needs of the very poor. The term 'very poor' used by the authors can hardly describe farmers who can afford to utilize 75 feddans. To comprehend the failure the committee was *ad hoc* and did not have the powers to pass the title of land to the new owners. The Nuba Mountains' experience with setting a committee to review the land issue highlights both the highly political nature of the process and the dangers involved when there is an overall vision for such reform.

The 'perhaps later' approach

Despite the centrality of land tenure to the root causes of conflict in both Southern and Northern Sudan, the CPA, and later DPA, adopted an attitude of 'perhaps later'. 'The Parties agree to establish a process to resolve this issue' (Article 2.1), and Article 2.3 of the wealth sharing protocol states: 'The Parties record that the regulation of land tenure, usage and exercise of rights in land is to be a concurrent competency exercised at the appropriate levels of government.'

A national land commission is entrusted with the following functions:

- Arbitrate between willing contending parties on claims over land and sort out such claims.
- The party or group making claims in respect of land may make a claim against the relevant government and/or other parties interested in the land.
- The National Land Commission may at its discretion entertain such claims. (Articles 2.6.0 to 2.6.3 of the CPA)

It will be naïve, however, to assume that both parties were not aware of the centrality of the land issue to both peace building and reconstruction. Both parties had their own agenda immediately following the signing of the ACP. In the short period between the signing of the ACP (January 2005) and swearing in of Garang as first vice president (June 2005), the NIF government hurriedly passed a new law on land tenure in Gezira (19 June 2005), distributed residential lands in Khartoum that were pending since 1990, confiscated the riverain holding of the Blue Nile east of Khartoum (Al Ayaam, 6/7/2005) and allotted its top-ranking officials agricultural plots north of Khartoum. During the same period, hurriedly signed contracts for new projects in Northern Sudan with a total of several billions of US dollars were arranged in a relatively short time. For the SPLA, land tenure is obviously a rational choice. While land tenure is central to ongoing conflicts in both Northern and Southern Sudan, it is also central to the state-building process as the experience elsewhere in Africa has shown.

Despite the centrality of the agrarian question to conflict making and resolution in both Northern and Southern Sudan, the reconstruction framework adopted by the GoS, SPLA and IFIs and donors seem to evade any direct guidelines or more precisely left for 'Up-coming Land Commission'. Land policy in Southern Sudan is currently based on Customary Law, and there are considerable inconsistencies in how the Customary Law applies in different regions. One common principle is that 'land belongs to the people', which is different from the North where all land (apart from relatively small numbers of free-hold titles along the Nile and in cities and towns) has been declared government land. It is generally agreed that land laws in Southern Sudan are not sound because of the lack of tenure security. Moreover, land use conditions are not clear. Lack of security of land rights and clarity on land use conditions weaken incentives to invest, hence the need for review of the land policy. The interim constitution for Southern Sudan is expected to contain some core policies on future land policy. The Up-coming Land Commission for Southern Sudan will consider future land policy in detail and it is anticipated that land policy in future constitutions will be based on the conclusions and recommendations of the 'Land Commission' (JAM, Economic Policy, p. 133).

Possible options

One possible avenue, albeit not inherently egalitarian, is to allow land titling in Southern Sudan within the confines of the traditional tenure system. I would argue that that is an available path given the war-induced depopulation of the rural areas and the subsequent de facto urbanization of over half of the southern IDPs whose voluntary or involuntary repatriation to rural areas is certainly doubtful. One virtue of such an approach to land reform is that it will avert a Zimbabwean model of land reform à la Ndebele and the Shona Violence in Matabeleland 1983–1987 (see Alexander *et al.*, 2000) that could trigger inter-ethnic and inter-communal conflicts in the deeply divided South.

An alliance with the traditional system, driven by the immediate political challenges facing the nascent new administration, may result in a tenure system that is neither conducive to equity consideration nor productivity enhancement. In fact, state control over access to land was functional to the forging of such an alliance. Control of the access to land is both a functional and effective means of establishing a nascent state legitimacy. Its distributional impact is an open question. If it follows the Northern Sudan model of land tenure, not in reverse, it could be a recipe for disaster not only ecologically but also in fermenting the foundation for conflict reproduction or, as Giordano *et al.* (2005) aptly noted, 'in particular, conflict is most likely to emerge in those areas where (1) recourses to sovereignty is ill-defined or non-existent, (2) existing institutional regimes are destroyed by political change and/or (3) rapid changes in resource environment out pace the capacity of institutions to deal with the change' (ibid., p. 47).

Furthermore, such an option is not available in the three transitional areas and certainly in Darfur (Nuba Mountains, Abyei and Southern Blue Nile) where there are already conflicting claims on traditional ownership and tribal/ethnic boundaries. In all these conflict-ridden areas both the de facto emerging land tenure as well as claims to some traditional notion of a 'traditional/communal land tenure' is being contested by deeply divided communities. As such, the happy return to 'customary rights' seems to be a recipe for deepening conflict. Harragain (2003) suggested another important limitation in the notion of a return to the customary laws in the case of the Nuba Mountains: 'One locally comprehensive solution' to the land tenure system is 'to support the tribal territorial boundaries as people currently understand them. This would cause dispute between Nuba and non-Nuba groups as Nuba effectively claim the whole of the Nuba Mountains' (ibid., p. 16).

The egalitarian nature of the communal land tenure system is extremely doubtful, at least, at two levels:

- Gender-wise as most of these systems are paternalistic, with extremely few exceptions.[4]
- Community leader 'patron–client' relationship making the notion of communal ownership a powerful mechanism in the power structure of traditional communities.

The looming ecological crisis in Darfur since the 1980s suggests that the communal land tenure system is neither retrievable nor functional. There are a plethora of in-depth studies (Ibrahim, 1978, 1982, 1984 and 1998; Abdulrahman, 1988; Amin, 1986). Given population pressures, overstocking and the destructive impact of mechanized agriculture in the fragile eco-system of Darfur, the old communal system is no longer functional, but, as these studies suggest, existing patterns of traditional agriculture and shifting grazing strategies are no longer viable in Darfur and similar areas (Nuba Mountains, Abyei and Southern Blue Nile); re-establishing the pre-conflict land tenure system is a recipe for the continuous breeding of conflicts, not reconstruction.

Despite the less dramatic population and livestock pressures in Southern Sudan, immense population flows changed dramatically the boundaries of communities, tribes and ethnic groupings, rendering old communal-land boundaries irrelevant.

Furthermore, for countries striving to rebuild state legitimacy or where the state hardly existed before, the land tenure and agrarian system is deeply entangled in the process of nation-state building (Eritrea, Ethiopia, Zimbabwe, Southern Sudan and rural Northern Sudan). Studies from these areas do not provide a road-map or a straightforward conclusion as each land tenure system, communal or non-communal, has been and continues to be shaped and reshaped by a complex matrix of processes (chained authority, post-colonial state and conflicts).

While maintaining the present structure of communal ownership is obviously not viable, 'the present land tenure system in the communal areas cannot cater for land pressure and a fair land distribution in general and the development needs of the individual holding in particular. Instead, the present land tenure system is hampering a large extent rural development' (ibid., p. 2).

The tenure issue may suit both the CPA's principal parties but the absence of a clear framework for land reform is proving to be a serious challenge for the peace-building process. The multiplicity of actors crowding the post-war scene within JAM itself has produced multiple visions of how to reconstruct the war-produced economy. This is a major challenge to which the next chapter speaks.

The temptations of following Northern Sudan's easy route to a surplus extraction of agriculture and in particular a traditional one are relatively strong. Since independence, successive governments have not embarked on serious plans to transform traditional agriculture but instead they have restricted intervention to a limited injection of modern techniques. Within traditional animal production, the state intervention was limited to basic veterinary services and water provision along the migratory route of nomadic groups. Save a few attempts at improving traditional agriculture research services, the major emphasis has been on controlling the marketing of the products of traditional agriculture heading to external markets; as was previously stated, state policies of the unlimited and uncontrolled expansion of modern mechanized agriculture meant, by the end of the day, killing the goose that lays the golden egg. The lack, so far, of a coherent and well-integrated approach to agricultural transformation in Southern Sudan suggests that the dangers of following the easy route to surplus extraction maximization in the short term are strong. So far JAM, which represents a sort of negotiation platform for all stakeholders in the process of policy making (SPLM, NIF, IFIs and other donors), has presented a framework that might constitute some broad framework. JAM (2004) suggested a more equitable/pro-poor approach whereby market reforms and technological change should be complemented by a programme of land reform leading to structural change in the semi-mechanized and traditional rain-fed areas and leading to reductions in very large holdings that are at present not using land efficiently. Furthermore the plan emphasized that policies should allow small holdings not capable of providing a typical family with an adequate income to be increased in size. The JAM document was, however, very clear on the need to rely on market forces:

> Land tenure arrangements such as the right to buy and sell lease rights, and the termination of long term leases on very large parcels of land as the leases fall due would make such structural changes possible – mainly through market forces. A restructuring of the rural sector should improve the economics of farming in rainfed agriculture (in Northern and Southern Sudan) and go hand in hand with a process of rural development that provides better social services in rural areas. (ibid., p. 17)

Multiple visions

Three different versions of agrarian policy seem to have emerged in the reconstruction process in Southern Sudan: a modified but essentially pre-Nivasha SPLM programme, an alternative vision from within the SPLM technical apparatus represented by Deng (2005) and a USAID-sponsored programme. The three approaches to agricultural transformation are not the same in terms of the approach to agrarian questions including land tenure.

The SPLM pre-Nivasha position is well reflected in Garang's (May 2005) address. In his address to the Southern-Sudan Dialogue Conference, Nairobi, Garang outlined briefly a very broad framework for economic development in Southern Sudan. In addition to conforming with the millennium development goals he emphasized:

> The SPLA/M shall adopt an economic development vision and programme that emphasized economic growth through rural development and transformation of traditional agriculture that is integrated with agro-industries 'we aim' he added to transform the present subsistence traditional agriculture in South Sudan and other areas through technological innovations, and make agriculture the engine of growth.

Along lines of SPLA/M slogans 'use the Oil revenue to fuel agriculture' and 'take towns to people in countryside rather than people to towns' 'where they end up in slums without skills and without employment and consequently their quality of life deteriorates. Rural small towns and rural electrification will therefore be priorities, so that small rural towns become the focal points of rural development and thus eradicating poverty and rapidly lifting the living conditions for rural people who constitute more than 90 per cent of the population of Southern Sudan. The USAID-sponsored agrarian programme is a gradualist transformative injection of modernity within traditional agriculture through mobile technology providers, training, microfinance and the gradual build-up of marketing networks. Deng presented a similar version supporting the maintenance and revitalizing of communal traditional structures, the Five Year Southern Sudan Agricultural Revitalization Programme (SSARP).

A comprehensive package for the revitalization of Southern Sudan's agriculture was developed in direct support of USAID. The SSARP addresses three main areas in agricultural building:

- Increasing access to agricultural skills and technology.
- Increasing access to capital for agricultural enterprises.
- Increasing capacity and commodity networks to facilitate expanded trade.

The SSARP targets all groups in the opposition-held areas of Southern Sudan, Southern Blue Nile and Nuba Mountains. The programme directs particular attention to:

1   the support of agriculture and business skills in six sub-sectors (crops, agricultural technology, forestry, livestock, wildlife, and fisheries);
2   the establishment of a Central Information and Data Analysis Unit: The New Sudan Centre for Statistics and Evaluation (NSCSE);
3   providing capital to agricultural enterprises through a sustainable micro finance institution; and
4   strengthening the agricultural-commodity network. (SSARP Info link, 2003)

The programme features some interesting aspects. Namely, it marks a departure from previously assisted projects, which are no longer able to provide both on-site and outreach business and technical skills training. This is certainly a positive orientation for the vastly spread primary activities in Southern Sudan. A good example is the project to reach fishing communities through mobile training and through the training of community resource persons to increase the number of people having access to improved business and fisheries skills. The programme also includes the establishment of micro finance institutions (AFEP) as a component of the SSARP.

Both USAID and Deng's version of transformation ascribe to the newly founded enthusiasm of the World Bank concerning the preservation of tradition in the bank's envisioned route of rural poverty eradication. The SPLM agribusiness programme does not explicitly specify any version of land tenure but its emphasis on mechanization, export orientation and encouragement of local and foreign investment betray a clear option for state capacity to reshape land tenure. This is not surprising as the land tenure policy is intrinsically functional to the state-building process. The experiences of reconstruction in several countries emerging out of protracted conflict support such a priority, for example Ethiopia, Zimbabwe and Eritrea.

The post-Garang era witnessed a further retreat to a radical, albeit not well defined, approach to land tenure. 'Land belongs to the Community and the Government, says Lt General Kiir.' 'There is a big problem in Juba in regard to the issue of land.' He went on to say: 'GOSS is a guest and is not responsible for land distribution ... Central Equatoria State has even requested GOSS to rent houses in Juba.' He stated that there is no investment coming in because there is no land. He said that he has talked to the Governor but they have not reached a solution on the land issue.[5]

Competing priorities: rehabilitation of human resources and others

The three principal priorities of reconstruction (transformation of agriculture, rehabilitation of human resources and physical infrastructure and the building of the nascent state) are so meshed together, complementary as well as embedding that there is, always the danger of a trade off. In the previous chapter discussing the challenges of governance and peace-building, it was shown how short-run tasks may crowd out long-term tasks or render them unattainable. In this chapter, we have seen how the war-produced new urbanities were largely ignored by various actors with an implicit assumption of temporality or because of ideological leanings. Both new urbanities and new urban structures are central sites for any serious efforts at rehabilitation of human resources. The primary task in such rehabilitation is increasing the work force. In both war-devastated areas as well as in the urban slums where war refugees landed, this capacity has been eroded considerably.

The new forms of urbanity are largely associated with the simultaneous growth of informalization and, in the case of war-stricken economies, with high levels of destitution shaped by the new dynamics of urban poverty. The recent concept of 'Decent Work Deficit' introduced by the ILO well captures the determinants of such new dynamics. As Thomas (2002) explained, the point of departure brought by this new definition is that the previous emphasis on informality was targeting small enterprises or job-creating units. The new concept of decent work and the decent work deficits shifts the focus from enterprises to people, particularly onto the poor with the largest deficits.

> The goal of decent work is best expressed through the eyes of people. It is about your job and future prospects; about your working conditions; about balancing work and family life, putting you kids through school or getting them out of child labour. It is about gender equality, equal recognition, and enabling women to make choices and take control of their lives. It is about your personal abilities to compete in the market place, keep up with new technological skills, about receiving a fair share of the wealth that you have helped to create and not being discriminated against; it is about having a voice in your workplace and your community. In the most extreme situations, it is about moving from subsistence to existence. For many it is the primary route out of poverty. For many more, it is about realizing personal aspirations in their daily existence and about solidarity with others. And everywhere, and for everybody, decent work is about securing human dignity. (ILO, 2001a, pp. 7–8)

In the context of the previous definition of work, the initial condition of a war-produced rural–urban setting, the population deserves further attention especially with regard to access to work as assumed in the modern resource allocation theory. In its general form, the modern resource allocation theory assumes that people have sufficient resources at their command as an initial endowment. Furthermore, even if a person owns no physical assets he owns one inalienable asset, namely labour. Recent studies on nutrition have proved that such a presumption is false. However, Dasgupta's (1993) seminal contribution points out that

> what an assetless person owns is potential labour power, nothing more. Conversion of potential into actual labour can be realized if the person finds the mean of making the conversion, not otherwise. Nutrition and health care are a necessary means to this. The economics of destitution inquires into the circumstances in which this conversion is realizable, and when it isn't. (Dasgupta, 1993, p. 4)

Dasgupta's reconstruction of the distribution theory has serious implications for poverty alleviation policies:

- If the economy is vastly poor in assets, it is technologically not feasible to enjoy an adequate diet and health care. There has to be a sufficient accumulation of productive capability before this is possible. Therefore, the initial distribution of assets would play a crucial role in determining whether or not all citizens have their basic needs met. In other words, if the distribution of assets were equal, the labour market would be capable of absorbing all and no one will suffer from malnutrition.
- Involuntary unemployment, as distinct from surplus labour, will not be due to demand deficiency. Poor economy markets on their own are incapable of empowering all people with the opportunity to convert their potential labour power into actual labour. In other words, assetless people become involuntarily unemployed and hence rationed out of the labour market and forced to live on common property resources. The market equilibrates by rationing the labour market, which means that there are no policies open to the government for alleviating the extent of undernourishment other than those that amount to consumption or asset transfers. A policy of transfer from the well-off to the undernourished can enhance output via increased productivity of the assetless.

Dasgupta's Economics of Destitution model is important to the understanding of both the new dimension of urban poverty, particularly in war-torn communities, and offers a rare insight into the relevance of some of the critiques of current humanitarian aid polices. Furthermore, extreme deprivation may negatively impact the potential for collective action despite the fact that the rural population movement into urban space makes them far more visible and may improve their plight. However, the abrupt and massive nature of war and natural-disaster-related rural–urban migration has serious implications for the trajectories predicted by Turner's model. As opposed to the gradual, often-invisible growth of shanty towns under normal urban–rural migration, disaster-related migration is massive and glaringly visible. Both bulldozing and relocation became a permanent feature of the official policy of the 1990s (Elnur *et al.*, 1993, 1994). Studies on extreme deprivation in the global North, suggests that such a potential may be inversely related to need (see Harrison, 1985, p. 403):

> Deprivation is frequently multiple, emulative, self reinforcing, and self perpetuating thought generations, there is indeed a cycle of deprivation, but the disadvantaged and many of their children are trapped in it less by their own personal shortcomings than by the structures of social and geographical inequality. (ibid., p. 424)

Ironically, however, despite the absolute priority given to both health and education, actual spending so far, is the favoured cost of building new partnerships. Following Darfur's recent peace agreement, the presidential institutions comprised two vice presidents and a staggering 12 advisers (Minister of Finance, Al Ayaam, 29 August 2006). El-Affendi (2006) was right in observing that the budget for the presidential institution (177 billion Dinars) is 50 per cent greater than the health budget for the whole country (ibid., p. 2).

Reconstruction with too many actors

The multiplicity of visions as we have seen in the Sudanese version of DDR has been further exacerbated by the drive to establish a shortcut to a monopoly of violence leading to a successive integration of previously opposed groups under one umbrella. A war of visions and approaches or, alternatively, balance of various interests will decide the outcome in terms of policies aiming at reconstruction within the new coalition in power. As typical in all negotiated settlements, external actors are part of this process of shaping post-war reconstruction. The heavily mediated negotiated peace settlement in the Sudan will inevitably be mediated equally by external actors. As Cramer (2004) emphasized, post-conflict reconstruction and peace-building projects are not technical projects but are sharply political and largely determined by the interests of coalition groups that dominate the peace process. The multiplicity of donors involved in the reconstruction process is well reflected in Table 7.3. Within each of the donor countries, a number of NGOs are typically the donor-country agents in the process of implementation of various donor-funded projects.

Abbink (2004) warns against the danger of the massive NGO and donor-country onslaught to 'providing large sums of money and plethora of development schemes', stating that 'local people are bypassed and urged to follow foreign agendas' (ibid., p. 6). This is certainly one aspect of the negative impact of externally driven and managed assistance but its most serious impact is for long-term

Table 7.3 Post-negotiation donors' pledges

Donor	Pledge in Oslo total	Pledge in Oslo of which development	MDTF	Total recorded funding in 2005	% of total pledge	North (of which MDTF)	South (of which MDTF)	Total (of which MDTF)
Norway	250	–	100	56.3	23	11.2	20.3	31.5
Sweden	110	40	28.6	38.4	35	3.3	6.3	9.7
Germany	165	8	26	29.9	18	–	–	–
Netherlands	227	33.5	195	115.7	51	23.4	23.4	46.8
Italy	78	2.6	5.2	14.8	19	–	–	–
EC	767	400	45.5	164.2	21	–	28.2	28.2
Denmark	91	–	15	14.3	16	–	6.2	6.2
UK	545	464.5	80.7	164.1	30	11.8	11.8	23.6
Japan	100	–	–	58.7	59	–	–	–
US	1,700	430	–	601.4	35	–	–	–
Canada	73	–	–	27.5	38	–	–	–
Finland	16	–	16	4.4	28	–	4.4	4.4
France	40	40	–	6.7	17	–	–	–
Arab League	200	200	50	–	–	–	–	–
Australia	10	–	–	10	100	–	–	–
Others	180	13.9	12.5	1001.6	58	0.1	0.1	0.2
Total	4,552	1,632.5	574.5	2,308	31	49.9	100.7	150.5

Source: ADB (2006, p. 15) Pledge in Oslo.

Table 7.4 Sudan: selected economic and financial indicators

Item	2001	2002	2003	2004	2005	2006 (Proj)
Nominal GDP in million of US dollars	13,369	15,109	17,680	21,610	26,698	49,298
Crude oil production (in thousands barrels per day)	209	232	262	288	575	492
GNP per capita (US dollars)	374	425	486	579	740	1,060
(in per cent of GDP)						
Gross investment	17.6	19.4	20.0	22.5	23.3	25.3
Gross savings	8.2	13.4	15.3	18.7	14.8	20.1
Central govt. revenue	10.7	11.8	16.1	19.8	21.8	23.0
Central govt. expenditure	11.6	8.7	15.4	18.3	23.6	22.0
(in millions of US dollars)						
Exports f.o.b	1,699	1,949	2,577	3,778	4,825	7.8
Of which oil	1,377	1,511	2,082	3,101	4,187	5.9
Imports	2,031	2,153	2,536	3,586	5,946	8.7
Foreign direct investment	650	633	1,092	1,481	2,355	2,232
Exchange rate D/$	258	263	261	258	244	201
External debt (billions of US dollars)	20.9	23.6	25.7	26.0	27.7	28.8

Source: Adapted from IMF (2006) and World Bank (2003).

sustainability, crowding out the nascent state by eroding its claim to legitimacy. Such a scenario was evident in the previous, albeit far less massive reconstruction programme following the first civil war (1955–1973). As Tvedt (1998, Chapter 4) eloquently demonstrated, even a relatively efficient international NGO may crowd out the state-building process because of its very efficiency. A similar conclusion was reached by Riehel (2001), who titled his paper:? 'Who is ruling South Sudan?', He concluded his assessment of the role of the INGOs in the areas controlled by the SPLA suggesting that 'The SPLA has won the war against GoS, but lost against armies of INGOs which occupied their territories in the name of humanitarianism' (ibid., p. 17).

The oil factor: beyond the Dutch Disease proper

By 2005, only six years after the start of the oil export, the third shift in the country's export orientation was fully realized (from cotton to livestock and labour export). Crude oil revenues constituted a staggering 61.5 per cent of total central government revenue and 91 per cent of the total value of the country export earnings, and annual inflow of FDI reached 2.6 billion (IMF, 2006, p. 21).

The impact of oil on war intensification, making a negotiated peace viable and on focusing negotiation on 'wealth sharing' rather than 'wealth making' was discussed earlier in Chapter 6, suggesting a 'Political Dutch Disease' effect. In addition, as was explained earlier, the lack of transparency and accountability in oil accounts continued to be a constant source of difference between the SPLM and NIF and constituted one source of fragility during the peace process.

The long-term possible negative impact of oil on the reconstruction process is even greater. The possible negative impact of a sudden surge in a country's income from minerals export is commonly known as the 'Dutch Disease'. In the strict economic sense, as developed by W. Max Corden and J. Peter Neary in 1982, the model predicts that a resource boom will affect the economy in two ways. First, via a resource movement effect as a result of an increased demand for labour which causes production to shift towards a booming sector, away from a lagging sector. This will lead to de-industrialization. However, this effect can be negligible since hydrocarbon and mineral sectors are generally not labour intensive. Second, through the appreciation of the exchange rate as foreign revenues start flowing. An appreciation of the exchange rate coupled with the increase in factor prices mentioned earlier undermines the competitiveness of the non-boom export product. While the model was mainly concerned with the impact on the industrial sector, its relevance to LDCs, usually with a low level of industrialization, is not less significant with regard to its exports of primary products. Within a broader political economy approach the Dutch Disease effect may result in a large inflow of foreign currency, including a sharp surge in natural resource prices, foreign assistance, and foreign direct investment (FDI) (IMF, 2003).

As shown in Table 7.3, post-war Sudan is already a host of all these factors (a surge of FDI, surge in foreign assistance-Oslo pledges, fast appreciation of the exchange rate, etc.) and escalating international prices of oil. The combined amount of foreign investment and exceptional finance increased from almost zero in 1996 to about 5 per cent of GDP in 2001, well above inflows in other African countries, as noted by the World Bank (World Bank, 2003, Vol. 1, p. 60). The oil saving account (OSA), established by the Bank of Sudan in 2002, will allow the government to save windfall revenues resulting from oil prices exceeding budgeted oil prices. As reported by ADBC (2006) the OSA has accumulated a sizeable balance (2 per cent of GDP by the end of 2005), driven by the increase in output and international prices (ibid., p. 5). 'The purpose of OSA is to enable the authorities smooth fiscal adjustment in case of lower oil prices with accumulated financing margin' (ADB, 2003, p. 5). At the same time, the government is maintaining its high taxation policy in an attempt to strengthen non-oil revenues, in order to reduce the vulnerability of the budget to volatile oil prices (IMF, 2006). However, the twin effect of foreign exchange appreciation and raising no oil taxes will certainly deepen the crisis of the non-oil commodity production reducing further its dwindling profitability and competitiveness. The overall impact of the oil revenue so far is mostly concentrated on meeting the escalating cost of DDR, the cost of building modern administrative structures in war-torn regions in the South, West and East, and the ever-growing presidential institution that keeps growing with each subsequent negotiated peace agreement which could justifiably be labelled as 'buying peace'. In Southern Sudan, the weak, almost non-existent administrative structure may prove to be a major obstacle to enhancing an absorptive capacity, crowding out both the initial phase as well as long-term reconstruction efforts. 'Donors' fatigue', particularly with the escalation of the humanitarian crisis in Darfur, is very much highlighted in the assessment of post-Nivasha minimal achievements. While this is partially true, the major problem in Southern Sudan remains its low absorptive capacity. In the North, the NIF's almost total control of oil revenue is engaged in a hectic programme for building political support through hurriedly and unplanned investment in the North. Immediately following the signing of the CPA and before the inauguration of the government of national unity, tens of new contracts were signed with foreign firms and construction companies. These included seven new bridges across the Nile in the capital and Northern state, a number of electricity generation stations, a water pipeline for Eastern Sudan and two new airports. Thus another impact of oil could be seen in terms of crowding out any coherent and integrated approach to reconstruction with the imminent threat that the transitional period may turn into a hectic and excessively costly struggle for political survival rather than creating a basis for sustainable development.

Reconstruction and the illusive return migration

In the previous chapters, in the context of both the transformative potential of migratory flows and challenges of nascent state-building, I maintained an assumption of no massive or immediate returns. Despite almost three years of concentrated efforts by local UN agencies international and local NGOs and, the projected massive population return migration seems to be a remote possibility. On the one hand, given Southern Sudan's stagnant infrastructure, limited capacity to police an orderly and safe return and the embryonic state in the rehabilitation and building of infrastructure for both health and education provision, the negligible return may have spared the new administration of Southern Sudan efforts to which it is hardly prepared. On the other hand, a slow or extremely limited return has a serious negative implication for reconstruction efforts in both the medium and long term. An estimated 80 per cent of the Southern Sudan population have been displaced at least once during the second civil war (Global IDP Database, 2005, p. 88). In this respect Phelan and Wood (2006) are right in suggesting that nearly everyone is a returnee (ibid., p. 14). By mid-2006 an estimated 82,871 returnees from 21,525 households were tracked at 28 tracking points in North Sudan (10 Newsletters, April–August 2006). The latest survey conducted by 107 revealed that 62.5 per cent of IDPs in Northern Sudan stated that they will return; 25 per cent stated that they had no intention of returning; and 11 per cent were undecided (ibid.).

The data on voluntary repatriation (assisted or not) reveal the following patterns:

- The majority of the returnees were rural–rural refugees (from neighbouring East African countries) or rural–rural IDPs.[6]
- So far the trend is the voluntary return of the less educated or altogether illiterate, less skilled and more recent displaced.[7]

Divergent paths of integration

The SPLA/M seems to lay heavy emphasis on its links to the Southeast. Great emphasis has been laid on links with both Kenya and Uganda according to Al-Qadai: 'The movement has also secured a loan from the German government to finance a railway linking Southern Sudan to Kenya, Uganda and elsewhere in East Africa with Southern Oil revenues as collateral 'Addressing the Nairobi South-South Conference (19 April 2005) Garang both railways link either Uganda or Kenya and also access to the Atlantic through revil link to the D.R Congo. In addition to the South-South linking roads a priority was given to links with Blue Nile (Melut-Adar- Ulu- Kurmuk – Damazine road), Darfur through Wau – Rga – Nyala road and Nuba Mountains, Abyei, through Wau-warp – Abyei – Kadogli (ibid., p. 9). 'This transportation network will link Southern Sudan with Northern Sudan and with the Greater Horn of Africa and the Great lakes Are, and create a major market of some 300 million people. It is a win-win strategy for all stock holders in the Sudan, in the region and the rest of the world' (ibid., p. 9).

Conclusion

This chapter outlined the main challenges facing the reconstruction of the war-produced economy. It was shown how the economic and political issues are so meshed together, defying any attempt at untangling them into separate and well-defined spheres of activity. The pre-negotiated settlement and visions of various contending forces are relevant as far as the post-war non-violent negotiation of an alternative social contract is concerned. But, as shown, these visions and approaches are constantly being defined and redefined with the break-ups and formation and reformation of political alliances and partnerships. Within the three major and competing priorities in the reconstruction process (i.e. rehabilitation of human resources, infrastructure and agrarian transformation), a central emphasis has been placed on the issues related to land tenure. As was shown, the centrality of the land tenure reform stems, first, from both conflict creation and in the creation of the foundation for lasting peace. Second, its centrality to the state-building process out of the consolidation of the existing state structures. And, third, because of the centrality of the tenure reforms to the agrarian transformation in all war-torn communities in the Sudan. All negotiation partners, whether in the CPA, DPA or EPA, are well aware of the centrality of the land issue but they all opted for a 'perhaps later' option. The rationale of all contending parties is the simple recognition that the land issue is also central to the political processes implied in state-building, elite creation and reproduction and to the creation and reproduction of strategic alliances and partnerships.

War also produced new multi-layered urbanities. Both the initial conditions as well as the ideological perceptions seem to ignore that, after prolonged civil strife, new ruralities and new multi-layered urbanities are sites for challenges, sources of peace fragility as well as the potential for transformation. A programme addressing the new urbanities, with object poverty, unemployment among the relatively better educated young people as well as the transformative potential shaped over more than two decades of war, is almost absent from the current reconstruction programme. Such an absence betrays the lingering 'retrievability' of the pre-war situation thesis as well as an underestimation of the magnitude of transformations that have already taken place. In plans of both contending parties as well as donors, the voluntary repatriation of IDPs, supported by a survey of intentions to return, prevails in JAM documents, reflecting the collective reflection of all contending parties and donors, and largely ignores the war-produced multi-layered urbanities. Ironically, following prolonged conflict, sources of peace fragility may have greatly shifted, from the depopulated rural areas to overpopulated, actual and potential, new urbanities.

As Hobson and Phillipson (2006) noted, recent works have linked an analysis of violence to poorly managed rapid urbanization. Typically urban violence emerges in the context of high inequality where a sense of citizenship is weak. 'Large-scale unemployment of young men in cities, associated with a "youth bulge" as well as with economic restructuring, creates frustration and has been associated with increased gender-based violence and with armed conflict' (ibid., p. 49).

One possible focus that might transcend the rural–urban dichotomy is to emphasize the rural–urban linkages in the reconstruction programmes. Programmes focusing on the loose-bounded ruralities and urbanities may help to transcend such a dichotomy. In this sense, land tenure reform is equally important as urban settings, if such linkages are to be cultivated. This chapter mapped out various sources of challenges including the syndrome of excessive activity in the post-war situation and by implication of the crisis of coordination. As the chapter suggests, the immediate post-war phase is a phase of continuing negotiation through non-violent processes, and that the post-war situation seems as chaotic as war itself. The process of negotiation of the reconstruction direction is, however, far more inclusive than the initial process that ended the war. New actors, dormant or seemingly dormant during war, take an active part in the negotiation reconstruction. In other words, reconstruction is seen as a dynamic process unleashed by the cessation of violence.

Part 4

Potential scenarios

8 Conclusion

A two-tier conclusion is very much in harmony with the readings provided by this book: first, the major wars have ended but the process of peace is still ongoing and, second, 'old' Sudan is dead but a 'new' Sudan has not yet been born. Both echo the 'Gramscian' sense of crisis where the old is dead and the new has yet to emerge.

Conceptually, this book departs completely from the conventional approach to reconstruction. It stresses both the 'irretrievability' of the pre-war situation and the 'irreversibilities' characterizing changes brought about by war. The theoretical framework also departs from the prevailing and influential 'blueprints' for reconstruction, most prominently represented by the influential World Bank report 'Breaking the Conflict Trap: Civil and Development Policy' of 2003 and previous and other works by Collier (1999, 2003) who was the major author of such 'blueprints' adopted by the World Bank. The report assesses causes and consequences of civil wars and suggests policies to reduce the likelihood that war will break out again. Different policy packages are suggested to match different causes of war. What is dominant however in these packages is the emphasis on retrieving pre-war institutions, particularly in the state. The Sudan 'blueprints' ignore almost completely that the dynamics unleashed by civil war undermines such a possibility of a 'happy' retrieval.

Wars produce new demographic dynamics that transcend the limited notion of counting heads across spatial divides. These new dynamics, I argue, are central to understanding and recognizing that war itself is the ultimate expression of failed modernity projects. In addition, the processes at work in the economy and society leading to war are shaped and reshaped by war itself. These become new forms of social and economic practices that shape the post-war environment. In other words, war produces essentially new political, social and economic spaces. Such alternative readings of the new dynamics unleashed by war itself, as has been explained in Chapters 6 and 7, further shaped and reshaped by the processes leading to the end of war and peace building, brings about significant implications to 'post-development' thinking. Such significant implications may include: low priority assigned to urban questions in conventional developmental thinking, the need to understand the informal economy beyond the notion of re-organization/formalization and how to top the potential of such informality, the primacy of human capital and how to address problems of its war-led deficit including new mechanisms for enhancing the reproduction of human resources and cultivating the potential of the existing translocal and transnational networks.

The primacy of a state is undoubtedly an important issue, but the question is, 'What state?' The emergence of a non-Weberian state is most prominently reflected in the diversity of centres of monopoly over violence and the multiplicity of actors in the provision of public goods (international NGOs, national NGOs including faith-based ones, community initiatives and the private sector).

The study of the crisis in the Sudan that led to the erosion of the feeble basis of the nation state is of direct relevance to current discourses on state failure and collapse. State collapse plays a central role in studies dealing with conflict marginalization and reconstruction in Africa (Chabal and Daloz, 1999; Migdal, 1988; Milliken and Krause, 2002). The 'weak state' thesis may provide a useful insight and an enabling tool into understanding the working of the emerging complex economic structures and networks into which the centralized immediate post-colonial state has degenerated. However, the thesis needs a further breaking down to capture the complex diversities involved in the sub-Saharan African scenery pertaining to the structural foundations of various economies and different historical paths as well as modes of configuration of political socio-economic formations. The temptation to generalize is strong. Many students of African politics cannot resist such a temptation, yet some others keep reminding the reader of an increasingly shrinking African category. For example, Chabal and Daloz (ibid., p. xxi) exclude North Africa and the Horn of and Southern Africa because they have 'dissimilar social structures and have had a different political experience'.

Most importantly, the 'weak state' thesis does not situate such weakness in the broader structural foundations of the African state. Before proceeding any further let us recall that the structural foundation of the immediate post-colonial state in most sub-Saharan countries was characterized by:

- relatively stable subsistence with stable institutions, limited and manageable flows and almost clear boundaries between the small niche of urban space and the vast ocean of rural space, mostly dominated by small-scale agriculture;
- extraction and siphoning of the surplus that was equally manageable with the high-level visibility of trade and other flows and stable, relatively efficient forms of taxing largely pre-capitalist formations;
- a gradual, manageable and controllable pace of urbanization with a relatively low level of informality that was fictional to and supportive for the emerging formal sector.

There were institutionalized low levels of linkages between rural–urban and local–international spheres with clear boundaries and the state being able to manage and control flows of people, commodities, ideas, patterns of consumption and organized/localized patterns of intervention by external actors even when such intervention assumed an extreme form (orchestrated coups or assassination of leaders and rarely direct military intervention). Thus the boundaries between the local and the external were visible and functioning.

On top of such well-bounded spheres, the state played a central role in resource allocation and capital accumulation management, albeit with varying degrees of relative autonomy.

With the collapse of the modernization drive, the maintenance of such bounded linkages, exchanges and flows became increasingly unattainable. Hence, the destruction of the basis of subsistence, failure to transform the rural communities and rural–urban exodus became inevitable. The ultimate collapse of the modernity project marked by prolonged civil strife brought the process of state collapse to its conclusion, producing many ungovernable flows and blurring the boundaries between the local, the national and the international. The collapsing state was neither able to maintain boundaries nor manage flows of people and transactions and oversee the once visible internal–external linkages. In the extreme cases such as Maputo's Congo, the state was hardly controlling anything beyond the capital. In the case of Somalia, the state degenerated into a multiple autonomous domain of warlord control and translocal and transnational networks that were made viable because of the minimal role of central government in a largely pastoral economy. It is the unsustainably nascent immediate post-colonial state particularly in Africa that led many analysts to question the existence of such a state and terming it a quasi or pseudo-statehood. As Milliken and Krause (2002, p. 763) noted, this 'pseudo-statehood' was in some cases converted into 'real' statehood, especially in Asia. But in many instances, especially in Africa, post-colonial state building resulted in the formation of what Robert Jackson (1990) has called the 'quasi-state'. The relevance of the state collapse thesis needs to be situated in this broader context of failing structural support of the nascent statehood. Despite the obvious commonalities represented in the process of erosion of the weak structural foundation of the immediate post-colonial state, there are multiple forms of state break-up corresponding to different initial conditions and the multiplicity of forms of wealth production and surplus extraction. Such multiplicity is well reflected in the alleged homogeneous residual of Africa à la Chabal and Daloz (ibid.).

This book has provided an interpretation of the processes that led to crisis in post-colonial Sudan. It has traced the history of crisis making in Sudan with the main focus on two important periods. The 1969–1983 period witnessed the intensification of the struggle over the future direction of development and simultaneously laid the structural foundation of the crisis. The NIF coup of post-1989 brought such a crisis to its ultimate conclusion of complete erosion of the foundation of the post-colonial state. A lasting peace and transition to a truly democratic system will depend very much on a more comprehensive inclusive process at the national level but also in the South, Northeast and in particular in Darfur.

There are, however, serious threats to the attainment of such inclusiveness. First, if in the present power sharing between the various contending forces, the armed groups and the NIF, both with narrow bases of representation, claim by virtue of their control over violence a political monopoly. Once armed contestation is over, far more representative actors who were hitherto dormant or less visible will naturally become more active actors (political parties and civil society). Repressing them in the old manner is not an available option. Second, both the CPA and DPA have emphasized a transition to democracy and set dates for parliamentary elections – whether such elections will translate into democracy is an open question. One of the challenges facing the process of democratization, and hence the task of making peace an inclusive process, is the erosion of the structural foundation built of a once vibrant political and civil society movement, particularly in Northern Sudan. The loss of such vibrancy was instrumental in the ascendancy of the NIF, as was thoroughly discussed in Chapters 4 and 5. The less vibrant political and social movement in South Sudan was equally weakened. As Akec (2007) rightly observed:

> Southern Sudanese-based parties that were founded in the 1960s such as Southern Front (SF) and Sudan African Nationalist Union (SANU) have either shrunk to insignificant size or have completely disappeared from the political scene. The only legacy left behind is old comradeship or labels passed down family lines which can be used by some to favour or discriminate against one politician or another: 'this is a Front diehard, you know', is not an uncommon whisper … Least mentioned in many analyses, however, are the political risks posed by increasingly fragmented party system and culture in South Sudan, in addition to the all too apparent political immaturity. By fragmented political system and culture I mean the dearth of political parties with clear vision, programme of action, sound ideological underpinning, and healthy political mind set.
>
> (*Sudan Tribune*, 19 February 2007)

The NIF, however, through its extreme repression, re-tribalization and polarization of ethnicity, succeeded in the fragmentation and erosion of the nuclei of the political and social movement that transcends narrow loyalties based on clan and ethnic identities in the traditional communities. In urban communities, a phenomenal degree of migration among the educated and middle class has taken place. Such massive migration led to the reshaping of such social classes. Elites' reproduction trajectories were radically altered and reshaped with significant loss of inter- and intra-generational transmission of knowledge and traditions, and the continuity and potential for dynamism has also been lost. Beyond the limited notion of the brain-drain argument, this massive involuntary migration of educated elites and social actors deprived the political and social arena of what Gramsci called the 'organic intellectual'. Years of savage political suppression and purges of state apparatus and trade union movements led to the emigration of significant numbers of active social organizers (trade unionists, activists and 'social entrepreneurs' with an unrepairable loss of inter- and intra-generational transmission of knowledge and experience).

With regard to the changing political terrain resulting from the massive emigration and limited but selective return migration, there are some central questions that need to be answered in order to read future trends beyond speculations. Thus, it is important to see these interactions as networks reshaping the political terrain; how political elites are reproduced; how inter- and intra-generational transmissions of knowledge and traditions are maintained or lost; and how the closely and interactive diasporic/local communities are compensating for the loss of what Gramsci termed the 'organic intellectual'. Additionally, one must address the issue of how the diaspora is contributing to the reproduction of an educated elite and how the over-diversified educational experience is marking the process of social reproduction of educated elites in particular.

Experience in post-conflict communities does not lend much support to such optimism examining post-conflict elections in Mozambique and Angola, as Karbo and Mutisi (2006) noted: 'Both Angola and Mozambique reflected electoral processes which have been undermined by the monopoly and domination of ruling parties regarding access to and the utilization of state resources. The consequences have been that the party in power ends up winning elections outrights' (ibid., p. 22). The likelihood of such a scenario is much reinforced by the findings in Chapters 6 and 7 on the NIF policies that transformed the state resources into a party domain. Weak accountability and transparency may carry a similar threat in Southern Sudan. An independent state in Southern Sudan following the referendum cannot be ruled out. Given, however, the serious challenges to state building, the possible repetition of the post-Addis experience of too many actors crowding out the state-building process cannot be ruled out. The actual integration of Southern Sudan labour into the Northern economy and challenges of transforming the Southern Sudan into a viable economy may reduce such an independent state to a labour-export enclave. Closer integration into the Eastern African regional economy, as envisioned by the SPLM and reflected in actual priorities revealed in infrastructure plans (see the previous chapter), is not likely to produce an effective alternative.

As was discussed in Chapters 6 and 7, Garang's tragic departure triggered important changes within the SPLM/A and paved the way for a much wider Southern coalition. On the one hand this new coalition is an outcome of a relatively successful DDR incorporating the most significant sections of the conglomerate of armed groups opposed to the movement. On the other hand, the loss of the visionary leadership of Garang meant a serious setback to the ideals of 'New Sudan', advocating some, albeit less precise, notions of radical transformation within a united Sudan. A post-Garang political coalition drive for a separate state is openly expressed but far less so in terms of creating the enabling conditions for such an option. In the post-first civil war period (1955–1973) such an option was almost readily available. The second civil war (1983–2005) resulted in a number of significant transformations in people, their characteristics, institutions and aspirations, as outlined in Chapter 5, that cannot be reversed nor ignored. Neither the North nor the South of post-Addis 1972 exist. A different North and South, politically, socially and economically, emerged out of over two decades of war. None of them resembles the earlier one and boundaries between the two are blurred by years of mobility erosion of the structural foundations of these boundaries. The currently popular term 'making unity an attractive option' applies equally to the case of the separate state option. At the end of the day making 'separation an attractive option' is an equally challenging option involving the capacity to build a viable state: a viable urban and rural economy that can facilitate the voluntary return of roughly two-thirds of the Southern Sudan population; and a stable political system that can prevent chaos.

In both Darfur and Eastern Sudan, the option of a separate state has neither been negotiated nor appears to be feasible. Within those two regions, greater so in the case of Darfur, a more inclusive peace formula that can accommodate their diversities is an urgent prerequisite for sustainable peace and a stable regional autonomy. The unresolved issues of the three regions (Abyei, South Blue Nile and Nuba Mountains), as was discussed in Chapter 6, is another site of an extremely complex situation where neither separation nor integration seems to be attainable. Over two decades of mobilization and counter-mobilization and polarization of ethnic boundaries and proliferation of small arms has rendered traditional mechanisms of conflict resolution dysfunctional. The oil discoveries in and around the Abyei region intensified the struggle for the centrality of the region, rendering the recommendations made by the International Committee of Exports, based on some interpretation of the history of the region, an 'irrelevant' academic exercise. Nothing short of an inclusive peace negotiation that will bring together all contending parties, armed or not armed, seems to be the only viable path to stable peace in the three regions.

One possible scenario, albeit inherently wrought with dangers of instability, lies with a possible symmetricalization of the peace accord (i.e. giving regional autonomy to the North similar to that of Southern Sudan). According to such a scenario a loose confederation of states, as Crawford (1951) described the 'Fung Kingdom of Sennar', may arise. Alternatively we might think of a local version of the North American state formation where local state structure has been quite powerful in providing the primary source of legitimacy (see de Tocqueville and others). The excessive polarization resulting from politicization and ethnicity and the erosion of the structural foundation of the tranquil coexistence between different modes of production surviving on an ample supply of resources may pose the single most important impediment to such a model for state formation.

If not representing a broad-based consensus at regional level, a very remote possibility in places like Darfur, such a scenario may not lead to stable peace. Worse, it may lead to a process of fragmentation closer to the predictions of some international relations (IR) theorists about the emerging 'new medievalism' (Friedrichs, 2001; Korbin, 1998; Trainor, 1998) or in its dramatic version of the collapse of the Roman Empire in Kaplan (1996), where collapse gave way to the dark ages. In such a scenario of fragmented power, citizens loyalties are shared by a plethora of new agencies extending from international NGOs, drug gangs, transnational networks and corporations and regionalist and ethnic movements, heralding 'the beginning of a new age that will more closely resemble the medieval Western Europe than the state system to which we have grown accustomed' (Rapley, 2006, p. 170). This may give credence to Hamad's notion that, given the dialectic of Sudan's composition, only a centralized state based on equal rights citizenship and an equitable balanced development of various regions can survive. The alternative according to Hamad is either cessation or a much looser confederation within a regional block (e.g. the Horn of Africa; Hamad, 1996, p. 708).

If the peace-building process transcends the enormous challenges of the constant breeding of the sources of peace fragility and the tendency for the fragmentation of power outlined previously, a possible far more optimistic scenario may arise. In post-war Sudan, a real sense of realism or 'pragmatism' is prevailing, transcending ideological, political and social debates. This was especially felt in the public debates on the forms of provision of both health and education (that is, fee payment and cost recovery schemes). The misery and social upheaval resulting from the erosion of post-independence gains in health and education left no room for differences. The focus of the debates were, however, on higher levels of provision of such services (curative medicine and higher education). Moreover, the question of provision of educational services goes beyond the sheer size of resources allocated to education or health per se but also to the allocation of resources within the education and/or health pyramids.

In the difficult terrain of policy such as agriculture and macro policy, the overwhelming nature of the crisis is also forcing its 'moderating' impact. In agriculture, for example, there is an increasing awareness that the old model of agricultural development based on horizontal expansion and dichotomies between its three main components (traditional rain-fed, mechanized and livestock) can no longer be maintained.

The debate is, hence, on the alternative paths to growth that are sustainable and more equitable. Resolving the debate in this and other areas and building a consensus on alternative policy has important consequences for the direction of resource allocation and the development strategy debate.

In most cases, the debate on macro policy and economic reforms tended to assess the present NIF's 'ruthless' structural adjustment policies that have been carried out since 1992. Some viewing these measures have saved the policy debate from the embarrassing and socially, if not economically, difficult question of 'How far should reforms aiming at restoring balances in the economy go?' Or even the more difficult question: 'At what pace?' However, the 1992 NIF surgery was too drastic – to the extent of perhaps killing the patient (pushing millions below the poverty line, escalating inequalities within and between peoples and regions and wiping out post-independence social gains in terms of education and health) – and because of its failure, creating internal and external imbalances far greater than the initial ones of 1989.

While the NIF's structural adjustment policies may have saved economists, planners and decision makers the 'embarrassment' of taking unpopular decisions (removing subsidies, introducing fees for social services and repressing wages below the bare minimum for survival), it left them with an even more difficult task of addressing the social upheavals that resulted from ruthless 'textbook' reforms. This leaves little or no room for manoeuvre in terms of resource allocation in particular at the micro level that involves allocation between sectors and groups.

With peace, whatever its form, strong pressure for a more equitable resource allocation between regions will be high on the agenda and that will also leave very little room for manoeuvre for policy makers, in terms of efficient resource allocation. In other words, a trade-off between efficient growth-maximizing resource allocation and sub-optimal, perhaps excessively inefficient, resource allocation is likely to prop-up as a result of strong regional pressures. Except for oil revenue, the CPA provided very broad principles for the equitable share of wealth: 'the sharing and allocation of wealth emanating from the resources of the Sudan shall ensure the quality of life, dignity, and living conditions of all citizens are promoted without discrimination on grounds of gender, race, religion, political affiliation, ethnicity, or region. The sharing and allocation of this wealth shall be based on the premise that all parts of Sudan are entitled to development.' At best these broad formulations serve as a platform for negotiating the future vision, direction and content of development programmes. However, even with regard to oil with its quantifiable and traceable value, an equitable share that does not trickle down from the mammoth power-sharing structures both at the national and regional levels may end up creating isolated elites that at best breeds new rounds of competition over representation. Therefore much of the policy formulation effort should try to address these possible trade-offs by designing realistic policies that will not 'ignore' the drive for a more equitable resource allocation between regions and at the same time attempt to minimize inefficiencies and link short/medium-term policies to the overall development strategy. Furthermore, with rising oil revenues, the Sudan may at last be able to transcend the paucity of infrastructure which (The Economist 1986) described as the 'the primary reason for the country's inability to form a single cohesive national unit' (ibid., p. 11). Again, war is over, but the struggle for peace is yet to be concluded, seems to be the answer.

Appendices

Appendix I: Selected Documents on British Policies
on Southern Sudan

Volume 2, 1945–1946

ENCLOSURE TO KHARTOUM DISPATCH No. 89 of 4 August 1945

**Civil Secretary Office,
Khartoum,
3 April 1944**

CS/SCR/1 . c . 14
Secretary to council.

1. A meeting of all Governors of Provinces, the three Secretaries and the Directors of Agriculture; Medical, and Education was held at the Palace on 7.2.44 under His Excellency's Chairmanship and it was generally agreed that a policy of more intensive and rapid economic and educational development of the Southern Sudan. was desirable and should now be planned and executed.

2. At an ad hoc meeting on 9.2.44, attended by Financial and Civil Secretaries, Director of agriculture Governors Equatorial and Upper Nile and the General manager Sudan Railways (who had not been able to attend the meeting on 7.2.44 a preliminary discussion tool: place on possible lines of economic development and on communications and it was agreed that in order to secure continuity and execution of development Council should be asked formally to endorse : policy of development and to ask the Directors of agriculture and Educations to formulate concrete programmes.

3. There is no need to stress to the Council the backwardness of the Southern Sudan We have a moral obligation to redeem its inhabitants from ignorance superstition, poverty, malnutrition, etc. and although devoted efforts have been made for many years by the Administration aid the missions with some remarkable individual results, progress has been on the whole, only spasmodic and sporadic compared with the Northern Sudan.

4. A number of factors contributed to this in the past – the great distances and Pool' communications: climatic factors; tribal apathy and conservatism; certain disabilities inherent in mission education, chief of which is that the Government is using as educational agents people to whom education is only a secondary objective; a recurring scepticism in Khartoum about the economic possibilities of the South; a natural preoccupation in Khartoum with Northern problems of greater urgency or, proximity; a tendency in the South to interpret the Southern policy, as laid down in 1930, on Arcadian lines and an ignoring of the political time factor: aryl for the lust 4 years, of course, the World War.

5. Some of these limiting factors are natural and historic some are man-made Recrimination about the latter would be futile', because even if every one had been agreed before this are the urgent need for development and its method, the funds were not available. Not only are funds now available but official opinion both in the South and Khartoum seems to be more favourable to a firm development policy.

6. Lastly, I must stress that, apart from moral or economic reasons, there are strong political reasons to adopt u more positive policy in the South. The eyes of Egypt and of the Northern Sudanese are on the South, and our Southern Policy (or lack of policy) has been heavily criticised both in Cairo and Omdurman. Part a of the policy will never command themselves to the Northern Sudanese and some of the criticisms have been hard to answer. If we are to carry Northern enlightened opinion with us at all, over our Southern policy, it is imperative that we go faster in both education and material development de may also have to consider external e.g. American opinion after the war, and the impression which the present state of the Southern Sudan would give to a mandates Commission or a Regional African Council. Ar. Cox in his recent report on his visit wrote: 'One of my strongest impressions on- this visit is of the urgency of speeding up developments in the South, if it is to stand any chance of -being able to hold its own ...... The south is being left further and further behind'. Sir. Cox is a friendly and shrewd critic who is in close touch with recent trends of Colonial policy.

7. I ask Council, therefore, to approve a policy of more intensive economic end educational development in the Southern Sudan, and I suggest the best way of initiating this is (1) to instruct the Director of Education to submit to Council a programme for expansion of' Southern education, both sideways and upwards, using both Government and mission institutions, and bearing in mind Uganda facilities. (11) to instruct the Board of Economics and Trade, now to be revived, to review the existing and proposed scheme of Director of Agriculture, the need for improved communications whether by air, river, road and rail, and any industrial possibilities.

8. It Council approves this policy, 1t is likely that sore change in the Southern provincial machinery will be necessary. Two possibilities stand out, firstly the re-division of Equatoria Province into two provinces secondly the appointment

of a Lieut. Governor for the South The former, I believe, is essential. Over the latter I have an open mini, as I have not time during the war to study its manifold implications, but there is a strong school of thought in its favour. In neither case, however, would the manpower situation permit the change for some time and I am not asking Council approve major administrative changes at such short notice and without some idea of stuff and financial implications But I want to place on record that 1 consider the present administrative layout in Equatoria at least, is not fully suited to a development policy.

(Signed) D. NEWBOLD.

CIVIL SECRETARY,

KHARTOUM:

ENCLOSURE TO KHARTOUM DESPATCH No. 89 of 4 August 1945

10TH STATISTICAL REPORT ON PROGRESS OF *EDUCATIONAL* AID ADMINISTRATIVE POLICY IN THE SOUTHERN SUDAN IN 1942, 1943 AND 1944

Government Staff Proportion of Southern Sudanese	1941	1944
(a) Administrative		
(i) Foreigners (British, Egyptian etc.)	39	37
(ii) Northern Sudanese .	8	8
(iii) Southern Sudanese	1	2
Total	48	47
Percentage of Southern Sudanese		4%
(b) Clerical		
(i) Foreigners	12	20
(ii) Northern Sudanese	105	111
(iii) Southern Sudanese	81	136
Total	198	267
Percentage of Southern Sudanese	$W\%$	51%
(c) Technical		

It has always been the endeavour in furtherance of the policy of advancing local culture rather than that of the Northern policy to select Northern Sudanese officials, when their employment in the South is unavoidable, from among those thought to be sympathetic rather than antagonistic. Southern culture, In 1943 and **1944** selection was not always successful: many Northern Sudanese officials proved to have little sympathy with and no regard for the Southerner and some discontent arose among southern employees at the higher rates of pay earned (generally with less labour) by Northern Sudanese staff, especially as their influence on the young southern employee fresh from the intermediate school was not always good. The policy of substituting Northern Sudanese for British (and other foreign) officials in the Northern Sudan involves to some extent the replacement by Northern Sudanese of British officials (especially doctors) in the South, and this adds to the importance of this problem. No opportunity occurred for special training of Southerners as administrative assistants to district commissioners the two appointments to such posts were made from among police non-commissioned officers who are literate in English. The majority of the Southern services is yet young and suitable candidates may be expected from the clerical cadre as they approach n more responsible age in the early thirties.

The output and standard of the government post-intermediate training contras at Juba wore greatly improved Clerical and accounting, training remained a two-year course, elementary medical training a three-year course and now two-year courses for agriculture and telegraphic work to begin in 1945 was arranged and for forestry were initiated and similar course for postal and telegraphic work to begin in 1945 visa arranged for.

The output of the training centres was as follows:#

Equatoria Headquarters:	1942	1943	1944
Clerical and Accounting	9	9	9

Sudan Medical Services:			
Medical Assistants	12	—	7
Sanitary Overseers	2	1	—
Laboratory Assistants	—	1	—

Agriculture and Forest:			
Agriculture	2	—	5
Forests	—	—	—

The experiment referred to in the last report of appointing Southern under-officers to the Equatorial Corps has had lose than a normal chance of success in the exacting conditions which war in remote areas imposes. It could not be given enough supervision, and the individuals chosen were perforce mostly of the clerical typo (there being no other Southerners of sufficient education) and in consequence tended by their own inclination (and by that of their British officers) towards sedentary quartermaster work.

The figures give no information regarding the employment of Northern Sudanese personnel in the Equatorial Corps of the Sudan Defense Force, which with the necessary adoption of part-mechanisation and of increasingly complicated ancillary services such as signals and motor transport maintenance units, had considerably to be increased. Recruitment of Southern Sudanese into Northern units of the Sudan Defence Force, and in some cases their subsequent transfer to service with the Equatorial Corps, led to unfortunate contrasts between Southern and Northern rates of pay; but by the full cooperation of the Major-General Commanding measures were take n to reduce the occurrence of such anomalies by confining recruitment of Southerners to the Equatorial Corps. Instructions in the rune sense regarding permanent recruitment of Southerners into Government service in the Northern Sudan were issued to Governors of Northern Provinces and to all Heads of Departments.

2. Staff of the Egyptian Irrigation Department in the Upper Nile Province

(a) Clerical	1944
(i) Foreigners	33
(ii) Northern Sudanese	4
(iii) Southern Sudanese	0
	37

(b) Technical	1944
(i) Foreigner a	38
(ii) Northern Sudanese	168
(iii) Southern Sudanese	77

Total	283
Percentage of Southern Sudanese	27%

3. Non-Official Immigrants

The number of Northern Sudanese trading in the South was as follows

1927	1930	1932	1934	1936	1938	1940	1942	1944
795	632	466	435	411	416	426	455	421

During the abnormal wartime conditions of demand for cattle to provide meat for forces in the Middle East a number of Northern Sudanese traders were specially licensed to tap the herds of the Nilotic southern tribes, though the total decreased ¢o shown partly owing to the difficult trading conditions end partly to* increased employment of Southerners ¢s shop assistants. Permits to trade in the Southern Sudan granted to Northern traders do not cover their sons when those become of sufficient age to support themselves.

Year/Item	1927	1930	1932	1934	1936	1938	1940	1942	1944
Outschools Village Schools	-	-	189	310	392	519	404	464	317

Elementary (Boys)	27	32	29	31	34	34	34	34	37
Elementary Girls	-	-	5	16	17	18	19	13	19
Central School Boys	-	-	-	-	-	-	-	3	8
Central School Girls	-	-	-	-	-	-	-	1	3
Intermediate Schools	3	3	3	3	3	3	3	3	3
Trade Schools	2	3	3	3	3	3	3	3	3
Normal Schools	-	1	1	2	3	2	2	2	-

The total of village schools for 1944 excludes a number of catechist centres and village schools without buildings previously included under the classification of village schools. Two new elementary schools are included, one established by the American Mission in the Upper Nile Province and one by the Church Missionary Society in Equatoria of the eight Central Schools four are under the Church Missionary Society and four under the Verona Fathers Mission. Normal schools, as such, have been replaced by these central schools. There are also fifth year classes for teacher training tit certain elementary schools and a beginning has been made in sending boys for post-intermediate education to Uganda: It was happily possible by the end of 1944 in agreement with the Military authorities to remove the restraints made necessary by war upon the movements and activities of the Italian staff of the Verona Fathers' Mission and action to secure the return both from Italy and from England of their staff detained there since the outbreak of war is in training.

(b) <u>Attendances at Mission Schools</u>
Attendances at schools in 1943 and 1944 were (so far as accurate figures in local circumstances are obtainable) the following:

Year	1943	1944
village schools	4,298	5,993
Elementary Schools (Boys)	2,713	2,466
Momentary Schools (Girls)	456	667
Central Schools (boys)	234	225
Intermediate Schools	242	562
Trades School	74	89
Total	8,217	9,702

	1943	1944
Dinka Village school, Tonj, Equatoria	-	19
Central School, Abwong, Upper Nile Province	-	32

Both these schools are new undertakings, the main object of which is to supplement the educational work of the missions among the Nilotic tribes; they are described more fully in Appendix' 'D'.

(d) Expenditure on Education in £E.

1927	1930	1932	1934	1936	1938	1940	1942	1944

(i) Subventions to Mission Schools

3800	7925	7805	9085	10035	9255	15305	15890	18017

(ii) Cost of Government Schools

1326	1952	-	-	-	-	-	88	1633

(iii) Cost of Government Supervisory Staff and Services

852	2239	1315	1659	2511	2669	3913	4216	5039

The population of the two provinces concerned is estimated at about 1,710,000 souls: of those therefore but 9702 attended school in 1944 at an expenditure by Government of £E. 24,789.

In January 1943 all educational council was formed in the zande district of Equatoria and five further councils wore subsequently formed for other districts in that province

These will it is hoped in time emerge into larger councils each concerned with a major vernacular language area. The councils arc constituted of tribal authorities and representatives of missions and of departments of' Government working in the areas. They are to advise on curricula and on school sites and terms, to encourage association between parents and schools and to help in fitting hygiene nutrition, agriculture crafts and animal husbandry in the educational framework and in looking after boys who have left school to ensure the boat use of their training.

5: Language
(1) English

While the Governor considers that the use of English in the Upper Nile Province has made little pro rose, the Governor of Equatoria reports that the knowledge of English is spreading rapidly in his province and that it will gain impetus from the teaching of English now being undertaken at the primary level in the schools. He adds however that the 'Wongalla Arabic' patois will remain for some time the vehicle of expression amongst those who speak differing vernaculars and especially amongst the rank and file of the police and Equatorial Corps and among prisoners.

Council at their 510th Heating on 12.6.43 approved the payment at two standards of a small allowance for literacy in English to N.G.O's and men of the Southern provinces Police and of the Equatorial Corps of the Sudan Defence Force. The criteria upon which payment is based are

(a) ability to speak English for ordinary duty matters
(b) ability to read, write and speak English

The same criteria were adopted in assessing the pay of subordinate Government and local Government staff; the results were satisfactory. A Syrian junior Inspector of English was appointed to help the teaching of English by local staff and to hold tests in the higher standard. 77 employees satisfied the examiner in the higher standard and 257 in the lower.

(11) Local Languages
The number of British officials qualified in local languages was as follows;

1927	1930	1932	1934	1936	1938	1940	1942	1944
5	11	24	35	31	25	16	20	16

Of the 16 British officials qualified in local languages 12 are serving in Equatoria Micro there is a total of 53 British officials and 4 are serving in the Upper Nile Province where there is a total of 21 British officials. The number of those qualified at present is therefore low. It can to some extent be explained by the use of English in technical departments, by recent transfers (many due to ill-health) to the Northern Sudan and by wartime preoccupations but there is great room for improvement especially among technical officials. Two Northern Sudanese officials serving in the Upper Nile province were qualified in local languages.

(iii) Publications.
The paper shortage has reduced publication of textbooks to a minimum. There are a large number translated and ready for publication as soon as the paper is available.
    The following translations into the vernacular have been published during the period:-

In Bari	First Arithmetic
In Dinka	The Acts of the Apostles- St. John.
In Acholi	Pilgrim's Progress - Composition Book II.
In Latuko	Sudan History - Native Study - Catechism
In Maaban	Folk Tales
In Zande	Children fight the enemies of health.
	Readers I and II

Frimer III

Fruits Of the Ground.

No new grammars have been published, but Part II of
Dr. Trudinger's Northern Dinka Dictionary has been duplicated.

6. Administration.

Administration has continued with depleted wartime staffs on normal lines and
chiefs' courts representing both larger and smaller territorial or tribal groups are
slowly assuming under careful tuition further functions of Local Government.
Their principal difficulty is not in arriving at sane and practical resolutions
on the normal problems of their areas – e.g. increased food production, soil
conservation, or rationalisation of social sanctions such as bride wealth or adultery
compensation – but in ensuring by executive, action – for which few competent
agents exist that their resolutions are carried out. General meetings of District
Commissioners and chiefs in administering the great nilotic blocks of the Nuer
and Dinka tribes have been told to discuss problems affecting each tribe as a whole;
at those major issues were defined and valuable agreements reached upon tribal
administration proper and upon future economic and educational development.

7. Economics.

The outstanding obstacle to development *or* exports from the Southern Sudan is
the cost of transport, whether Southwards or Northwards, owing to the length,
paucity and difficulty of communications with the whole area inland from the
White Nile. But a sound export trade (perhaps in timber oil-seeds, beeswax etc.,
in addition to products of the scheme described in Appendix 'C') is essential to
produce the import of useful and valuable consumers' goods without which the
general standard of living particular that of health cannot be raised. It has hitherto
been strongly held that exports from the South can only be developed to compete
without subsidy in the Northern Sudan, in West Africa, or abroad, on equal terms
with those of more fortunately situated areas, by keeping the level of wages in
the south low enough to discount the very high cost of transport to the external
market. In consequence however of the increased cost of living, of increasing
sophistication, and of greater demands for labour as government works (including
work on improving communications) increase, the level of wages necessary to
secure voluntary labour, and to retain the services of locally recruited staff, has
risen, and will continue to rise. The Southerner with very few exceptions need
not work for wages in order to live, but can maintain an Arcadian but stagnant
existence in his traditional pastoral or agricultural pursuits; the few who have
become so accustomed to wage-earning as to be unwilling to return to so primitive
an existence, can always find casual employment in the Northern Sudan at rates
which the South can never afford to pay. The conditions however in the North
deprive them of a future planned on indigenous lines in which they can play a
full citizen's part, and they are condemned to a role of inferior and almost servile

drudgery as degrading for them as for their Northern employers an unregulated raising of Southern wages, whether in cash or in kind, at the present time it might at first therefore perhaps attract labourers who are now obtained only with some difficulty, (e.g. for the government saw-mills) it would soon cease to be effective and the value of money fell with inflation.

To acquiesce in the continuation of traditional Arcadian existence of the South would be to abandon hope of the economic and educational progress necessary to fit the Southerner for survival in the closer contacts with the outside world which must inevitably sooner or later be forced upon him. Government cannot hold the ring for him forever or even perhaps for very long. The problem therefore is to balance the necessity of discounting the coat of transport for Southern produce against the inevitability (and desirability of a general uplift, not of wages by themselves, but of health, education, husbandry, social standards, labour conditions, revenue etc., together with wages. The problem is not an easy one and is now engaging the close attention of all concerned. The only firm conclusions so far reached are that self-sufficiency in a balance range of foodstuffs must be the first aim and that the production of exports or of local cash crops must take second place. It is necessary also, at any rate so far as the Southern ports of Equatoria are concerned, that improvement of communications with East Africa and possible markets there, and even perhaps possible exports by way of Mombasa should be explored when conditions permit, if necessary at Government expense.

The Zando development scheme described in Appendix 'C' will not therefore exclude but will rather complement a general campaign to increase and improve food crops and animal husbandry. It is recognised that the scheme involves assumptions which if they prove false may result in failure and loss but the scheme has in fact been approved as an act of faith in the innate capacity of the Southerner to make good, given the capital with which to start: as the Northern Sudan has made good having, by geographical and other accidents, been given capital first – in the form of railway, port, dam, and irrigation schemes.

8. Political Situation:
Should no extraneous considerations prevent the eventual decision on the political future of the Southern Sudan being taken solely with a view to the welfare and future prosperity of the Southern peoples themselves it seems clear that it must be founded largely on an attempt to ensure that their political allegiance will be given in such a direction or directions as will coincide with their natural economic ties. Those ties have not yet been firmly established, and the urgency of investigating them therefore has high political as well as economic and social significance. Their own future is at present not a subject of speculation among Southerners, so much Northerners (whether serving in the South or not) can stir up trouble in the Northern Sudan, in Egypt or in the South itself – not for the benefit of the Southerners but for their own extraneous political ends. Apart from evidence that such trouble-making has occurred in one or two instances, there is no 'political situation' inside the Southern Sudan – yet. There are however indications that many of the educated Southern Sudanese – though their total number is still small – are

puzzled and resentful about the backwardness of the Southern Sudan, apart from their own personal ambitions. One unfortunate result of those feelings has been the same of their number – whose services the South can ill-afford to lose – have succumbed whether of their own accord, or as a result of Northern persuasion, to the glamour of supposedly far higher real wages and wider opportunities in the North – a glamour which disappears after arrival in the North, whom the greater cost of living, and the limited social and professional prospects open to those not of Northern Sudanese origin and upbringing, are learnt. The Church Missionary Society in conjunction with the Anglican diocesan authorities have done good work by the recent provision of welfare clubs – one in Khartoum and one in Omdurman – where the exiled Southerner may enjoy some social contact as among equals, and where he may be helped over his affairs – in particular his matrimonial affairs were he has left a wife behind him at home – and through which he can also be assisted should he wish, to return to his own country.

Khartoum:
4 August 1945.

Appendix II: Sudan Long Peace Negotiation Marathon:

Appendix II: A. Key Texts on Peace Agreements and Declarations*

(From Addis 1972 to 2006)

Pre-1989

*   **Addis Ababa Agreement** between the Government of Sudan and the SSLM/ Anya Nya, Addis Ababa, 27 February 1972
*   **Koka Dam Declaration** by the SPLM/A and NANS, Koka Dam. 24 March 1986
*   **November Accords** between the SPLM/A and DUP, Addis Ababa, 16 November 1988

1989–2001

*   **Frankfurt Declaration** by the Government of Sudan and the SPLM/A-Nasir, Frankfurt, January 1992
*   **Agreement on Reconciliation of the divided SPLM/SPLA,** between the SPLM/A-Torit and SPLM/A-Nasir, Abuja, 19 June 1992
*   **The Nairobi Communiqué** of the National Democratic Alliance, Nairobi, 17 April 1993
*   **The Washington Declaration** by the SPLM/A and SPLM/A-United, Washington, DC, October 1993

- **Declaration of Principles** (IGADD), Nairobi, 20 July 1994 (signed by the Government of Sudan July 1997)
- **Chukudum Agreement** between the SPLM/A and Umma Party, Chukudum, Sudan, December 1994
- **Political Charter** between the Government of Sudan and the SPLA-United, 26 April 1995
- **Asmara Declaration** by the NDA (DUP, Umma, SCP, USAP (Surur), SPLM/A, Trades Union, Legitimate command, Beja Congress, SAF, Independents), Asmara, June 1995
- **Operation Lifeline Sudan Agreement on Groundrules** between the SPLM/A and UNICEF, July 1995; between the SSIM/S and UNICEF, August 1995; between the SPLM/A-United and UNICEF, May 1996
- **Political Charter** between the Government of Sudan, the SSIM/A and SPLM/A-Bahr el Ghazal Group, 10 April 1996
- **Declaration of Principles for the Resolution of the Nuba Mountains' Problem** between the Government of Sudan and the Nuba Mountains United SPLM/A, Nairobi, 31 July 1996
- **Sudan Peace Agreement (or Khartoum Peace Agreement)** between the Government of Sudan, the SSDF, the SPLM/A Bahr el-Ghazal; the SSIG; the EDF; the USAP and the Bor Group, Khartoum, 21 April 1997
- **Fashoda Peace Agreement** between the Government of Sudan and the SPLM/A-United, Fashoda, 20 September 1997
- **Wunlit Dinka-Nuer Covenant**, Wunlit, 10 March 1999
- **Waat Lou-Nuer Covenant**, Waat, 8 November 1999
- **Liliir Covenant** (Anyuak, Dinka, Jie, Kachipo, Murle Nuer) Liliir, May 2000
- **Memorandum of Understanding** between the SPLM and the Popular National Congress, Geneva, 19 February 2001
- **Kisumu Declaration**, Kisumu, June 2001

2002

- **Nairobi Declaration on Unity** by the SPLM/A and the SPDF, 6 January 2002
- **Nuba Mountains Ceasefire Agreement** between the Government of Sudan, the SPLM-Nuba, Burgenstock, 19 January 2002
- **Machakos Protocol** between the Government of Sudan and the SPLM/A, Machakos, 20 July 2002
- **Memorandum of Understanding on the Cessation of Hostilities** between the Government of Sudan and the SPLM/A, Machakos, 15 October 2002
- **Agreement on the extension of the Memorandum of Understanding on the Cessation of Hostilities** between the Government of Sudan and the SPLM/A, Nairobi, 18 November 2002
- **Memorandum of Understanding on Aspects of Structures of Government** between the Government of Sudan and the SPLM/A, Nairobi, 18 November 2002

- **Kampala Declaration**, (civil society groups), Kampala, 24 November 2002
- **Towards a brighter future for the Nuba Mountains** (Resolutions of the All-Nuba Conference), Kauda, 5 December 2002

2003

- **Memorandum of Understanding regarding Points of Agreement on Power Sharing and Wealth Sharing** between the Government of the Sudan and the SPLM/A, Karen, 6 February 2003
- **Addendum to the Memorandum of Understanding on Cessation of Hostilities** between the Government of Sudan and the SPLM/A, Karen, 4 February 2003
- **Cairo Declaration** by the SPLM/A, the DUP and the Umma Party, Cairo, 24 May 2003
- **Ceasefire Agreement** between the Government of Sudan and the SLA, Abeche, 3 September 2003
- **Framework Agreement on Security Arrangements during the Interim Period** between the Government of the Sudan and the SPLM/A, Naivasha, 25 September 2003 (see CPA)
- **Project of a Final Agreement on Appendices** between the Government of Sudan and the Sudan Liberation Army, Abeche, November 2003
- **Joint statement** by the Government of Sudan and SLA delegations, Abeche, 4 November 2003
- **Jeddah Agreement** between the Government of Sudan and the NDA, Jeddah, December 2003

2004

- **Agreement on wealth sharing during the pre-interim and interim period** between the Government of Sudan and the SPLM/A, Naivasha, 7 January 2004 (see CPA)
- **A Charter for Peace agreed at the Nuer Fangak People's Peace Conference**, Fangak, 4 April 2004

2005

- The **CPA** was signed in **Nivasha** on January 9, 2005:

2006

- **Darfur Peace Agreement**, 5 May 2006, **Abuja (2006),** signed May 5, 2006, by the largest rebel group, the Sudan Liberation Movement, led by Mini Menawi, and the Sudanese Government.
- **Eastern Sudan Peace Agreement**, 19 October 2006.

Appendix II: B. A Summary of the Comprehensive Peace Agreement

Machakos Protocol (2002)

A six-year interim period [dated from 9 July 2005] is established during which the Southern Sudanese will have the right to govern affairs in their region and participate equitably in the national government.

Peace implementation is to be conducted in ways that make the unity of Sudan attractive.

After the interim period, Southern Sudan will have the right to vote in an internationally monitored referendum either to confirm Sudan's unity or vote for secession.

Shari'a law is to remain applicable in the North and parts of the constitution are to be re-written so that *shari'a* does not apply to any non-Muslims throughout Sudan. The status of *shari'a* in Khartoum is to be decided by an elected assembly.

Power Sharing (2004)

Sudan will have both a national government with representation from both sides of the North-South conflict, and a separate Government of Southern Sudan (GoSS). The Southern Sudan Constitution and state constitution must comply with the Interim National Constitution.

A Government of National Unity is to be formed. There shall be a decentralized system of government, granting more power to individual states.

Positions in the state governments are to be split 70:30 in favour of the NCP in Northern states (20% for other Northern parties and 10% for the SPLM) and 70:30 in favour of the SPLM in Southern states (15% for other southern parties and 15% for the NCP). In Abyei, the Blue Nile State and Nuba Mountains the division will be 55% for the NCP and 45% for the SPLM.

The executive will consist of the Presidency and the Council of Ministers. Two Vice-Presidents will be appointed by the President. The First Vice President is the Chair of the SPLM.

A bicameral national legislature will be established: the National Assembly will be comprised of specific percentages (NCP 52% SPLM 28% other Northern parties 14% other Southern parties 6%); two representatives from each state will be represented in the Council of States.

Elections will be held by the end of the third year of the interim period.

Wealth Sharing (2004)

A National Land Commission, Southern Sudan Land Commission and state land commissions are to be established. A National Petroleum Commission is to be established to manage petroleum resources.

2% of oil revenue will go to oil-producing states in Southern Sudan in proportion to their output. The remaining net revenue will be divided evenly with 50% allocated to the GoSS and 50% allocated to the national government. The GoSS has no power to negotiate any of the oil leases granted by the national government prior to the CPA.

The National Government is able to collect revenue from personal income, corporate and customs taxes; the GoSS can collect revenue from personal income taxes, luxury taxes and business taxes in Southern Sudan. Taxes that can be collected by states are also outlined. A commission to ensure the transparency of collection and use of revenues will be formed.

Two banking systems will be formed in the two areas, with the Bank of Southern Sudan as a branch of the Central Bank of Sudan. Essentially, the dual banking system means that banks will be commonly stationed with two different windows for service.

Two separate currencies in the North and South are to be recognized until the Central Bank has designed a new currency that reflects the cultural diversity of Sudan.

National and Southern funds for reconstruction and development will be established along with two multi-donor trust funds.

The Resolution of the Abyei Conflict (2004)

Abyei will be accorded special administrative status during the interim period, following the definition of the Abyei areas by the Abyei Border Commission.

Abyei will have representation in the legislature of Southern Kordofan and Warap states; at the end of the six-year interim period, Abyei residents will vote in a referendum either to maintain special administrative status in the North or to become part of Bahr al-Ghazal (Warap) state in the South.

Wealth-sharing of oil revenues from Abyei is to be split between the North and South (50:42) with small percentages of revenues allocated to other states and ethnic groups: 2% each to: the Ngok Dinka people, the Misseriyya people, Bahr al-Ghazal (Warap) state, and 1% each to Southern Kordofan state (SKS) and the Western Kordofan sub-state component of SKS.

The Resolution of Conflict in Southern Kordofan and Blue Nile States (2004)

The two states will be represented at the national level in proportion to their population size. At the state level, the NCP will comprise 55% and the SPLM 45% of the State Executive and State Legislature.

Southern Kordofan State (SKS): the southern portion of West Kordofan State (WKS) will be incorporated into the SKS. The state legislature will have 36 members from the SKS component and 18 from the former WKS component, subject to readjustment following a census. The state executive will have 7 from SKS and 4 from WKS. Al-Fula will have branches of all state ministries and institutions headed by a deputy. The legislature will convene sessions alternatively at Kadugli and Al-Fula.

Governorship of each state shall rotate between the NCP and SPLM during the interim period.

Wealth sharing: the 2% of SKS oil due to the state is to be shared between the two state components. The 2% share of Abyei's oil due to the state shall be equally divided between two state components. The 2% forming the Misseriyya share in Abyei oil shall benefit the previous Western Kordofan component.

The legislature of the two states will evaluate the implementation of the CPA.

State Land Commissions are to be established (in case decision clashes with National Land Commission and cannot be reconciled, the Constitutional Court will decide the matter).

Security Arrangements (2003 and 2004)

During the six-year interim period, Joint Integrated Units (JIUs) of 21,000 soldiers are to be formed with equal numbers from the Sudan Armed Forces (SAF) and the SPLA. They are to be deployed to sensitive areas such as the three disputed areas and will be commonly stationed but maintain separate command and control structures. If, after the interim period, the South decides to secede, the JIUs will unify into a 39,000 strong force.

The SAF and the SPLA will also continue to operate as separate armies with both considered part of Sudan's National Armed Forces. Each army is to be downsized and the parties are to implement demobilization, disarmament and reintegration (DDR) programmes. No other armed group will be tolerated outside the umbrella of the three services.

There is to be a redeployment of 91,000 SAF troops from the South to North within 2 years. The SPLA has 8 months to withdraw its force from the North.

A permanent cessation of hostilities is provided for, detailing disengagement and the creation of various committees for enforcement and oversight.

DDR and reconciliation are provided for through a number of commissions.

Monitoring is to be carried out by a UN mission to support implementation, as provided for under Chapter VI of the UN Charter.

Appendix III: A Summary of the Darfur Peace Agreement (DPA) and Estern Sudan Peace Agreement (ESPA):

Basic principles.
Both agreements state the superiority of modern constitutional law over traditional customary law, endorse affirmative action, and reiterate the importance of sovereignty, diversity, human rights, devolution, transparency, electoral process, the rule of law and equality before the law.

Darfur Peace Agreement

5 May 2006

Permanent status of Darfur

A referendum on whether to retain Darfur's three states or create a Darfur region is to be held within 12 months of the general elections (by July 2010). The Transitional Darfur Regional Authority (TDRA) is responsible for coordinating the implementation and follow-up of the DPA and facilitating better cooperation between the three state governments.

Participation in government

Pending elections, the SLM/A and JEM are to nominate people to the following posts, making a special effort to nominate women:

- 1 Special Assistant to the President (also chair of the TDRA), and 1 presidential advisor
- 1 cabinet minister and 2 state ministers (in addition to 3 cabinet minister and 3 state minister posts which will continue to be filled by Darfurians)
- 12 seats in the National Assembly and chairmanship of one of the National Assembly's parliamentary committees
- 1 ministerial position in the Khartoum State government
- The governor of one of Darfur's states and deputy governor of each of the other two, plus 2 ministers and 1 advisor in each of the states and a senior member of each state ministry

- 21 of the 73 seats in each state assembly, including the deputy speaker of each
- 6 local commissioners and 6 executive directors in Darfur

Membership of the Council of States is to be non-partisan and to follow consultation with Darfurians. 50 per cent of places in Darfurian universities and 15 per cent of places in Khartoum's universities are reserved for Darfurians. Historical land rights (*hawakeer*) are recognized, subject to rulings by state-level Land Commissions.

Development priorities

A Darfur Reconstruction and Development Fund (DRDF) is established, with seed funding of US$300m in 2006 and a further US$200m per annum in 2007 and 2008.

A Joint Assessment Mission (JAM) is to determine priorities.

Protection and compensation

A Darfur Rehabilitation and Resettlement Commission (DRRC) is established to coordinate humanitarian provision and access and the safe and voluntary return of IDPs and refugees. A Property Claims Committees will resolve disputes. A Compensation Commission is established with an initial budget of US$30m.

A comprehensive ceasefire comes into force within 72 hours of signing; free movement of people, goods and services; the *janjaweed* is to disarm within 150 days.

A Joint Humanitarian Facilitation and Monitoring Unit (including representatives of AMIS, the UN, the international community and the parties) is to monitor and report.

4000 former combatants from the movements are to be incorporated into the SAF; education and training are to be provided for a further 3000.

Dialogue and consultation

Darfur-Darfur Dialogue and Consultation (DDDC) is to serve as a mechanism for mobilizing support for, and implementing, the DPA. 60 per cent of delegates will be tribal and community representatives, the remaining 40 per cent from political parties, civil society, religious organizations and the diaspora; observers are to be sent by international community and others.

Eastern Sudan Peace Agreement

19 October 2006

Permanent status of Eastern Sudan

A Coordinating Council is established, comprising 3 state governors, 3 state assembly speakers and 3 Eastern Front (EF) nominees who together nominate the remaining 6 council members.

The ESPA is to be implemented by a Joint Implementation Committee (with 50:50 government/ EF representation) with disputes mediated by Eritrea.

Participation in government

Pending elections, the EF is to nominate people to the following posts, making a special effort to nominate women:

- 1 Assistant to the President (also vice-chair of the Joint Implementation Committee) and 1 presidential advisor
- 1 state minister (in addition to 2 cabinet minister and 1 state minister posts which continue to be filled by eastern Sudanese)
- 8 seats in the National Assembly
- 1 advisory position in the Khartoum State government
- The deputy governor in each of Kassala and al-Qadarif states, plus 1 minister and 1 advisor in each of the three eastern states
- 10 seats in each of the three state legislatures (in each of which at least one committee will be chaired by the EF)
- 3 administrators in each of the three states and an average of 5 members in each local government assembly
- 3 nominees to 11-member Eastern Sudan Reconstruction and Development Fund (ESRDF) board

The government is to consult citizens before developing land and to compensate them if they are adversely affected. Eastern Sudanese are to benefit from the development of Port Sudan and the nation's coastal area and fish and marine resources.

Development priorities

An Eastern Sudan Reconstruction and Development Plan is to determine service, infrastructural and other priorities.

The ESRDF is to be operational within 90 days of the ESPA (i.e. mid-January 2007), with US$100m in 2007 and US$125m per annum 2008-11.

Security arrangements

A comprehensive and permanent ceasefire comes into force within 72 hours of the signing the ESPA; all militias or other armed groups in Eastern Sudan to be absorbed into the Sudanese Armed Forces (SAF).

Monitoring is conducted by the High Joint Military Committee, chaired by Eritrean government. Willing and qualified EF combatants are to be incorporated into the SAF for a minimum of 2 years. A Joint Committee for Integration (5 government and 5 EF representatives, chaired by the SAF) are to identify those who are 'willing and qualified' and ensure adequate training for those who are integrated into SAF and proper support for those who return to civilian life. Prisoners associated with the conflict will be released within a week of the ESPA's signature.

Dialogue

A National Conference on Sudan's administration is to be convened by the end of 2007; the government is to implement recommendations.

An ESPA Consultative Conference is envisaged; a joint preparatory committee is to be established within a week of the signature.

Source: http://www.c-r.org/our-work/accord/sudan/dpa-espa-summary.php

A summary of the Comprehensive Peace Agreement

Machakos Protocol (2002)

A six-year interim period [dated from 9 July 2005] is established during which the Southern Sudanese will have the right to govern affairs in their region and participate equitably in the national government.

Peace implementation is to be conducted in ways that make the unity of Sudan attractive.

After the interim period, Southern Sudan will have the right to vote in an internationally monitored referendum either to confirm Sudan's unity or vote for secession.

Shari'a law is to remain applicable in the North and parts of the constitution are to be re-written so that *shari'a* does not apply to any non-Muslims throughout Sudan. The status of *shari'a* in Khartoum is to be decided by an elected assembly.

Power Sharing (2004)

Sudan will have both a national government with representation from both sides of the North-South conflict, and a separate Government of Southern Sudan (GoSS). The Southern Sudan Constitution and state constitution must comply with the Interim National Constitution.

A Government of National Unity is to be formed. There shall be a decentralized system of government, granting more power to individual states.

Positions in the state governments are to be split 70:30 in favour of the NCP in Northern states (20% for other Northern parties and 10% for the SPLM) and 70:30 in favour of the SPLM in Southern states (15% for other Southern parties and 15% for the NCP). In Abyei, the Blue Nile State and Nuba Mountains the division will be 55% for the NCP and 45% for the SPLM.

The executive will consist of the Presidency and the Council of Ministers. Two Vice-Presidents will be appointed by the President. The First Vice President is the Chair of the SPLM.

A bicameral national legislature will be established: the National Assembly will be comprised of specific percentages (NCP 52% SPLM 28% other Northern parties 14% other Southern parties 6%); two representatives from each state will be represented in the Council of States.

Elections will be held by the end of the third year of the interim period.

Wealth Sharing (2004)

A National Land Commission, Southern Sudan Land Commission and state land commissions are to be established. A National Petroleum Commission is to be established to manage petroleum resources.

2% of oil revenue will go to oil-producing states in Southern Sudan in proportion to their output. The remaining net revenue will be divided evenly with 50% allocated to the GoSS and 50% allocated to the national government. The GoSS has no power to negotiate any of the oil leases granted by the national government prior to the CPA.

The National Government is able to collect revenue from personal income, corporate and customs taxes; the GoSS can collect revenue from personal income taxes, luxury taxes and business taxes in southern Sudan. Taxes that can be collected by states are also outlined. A commission to ensure the transparency of collection and use of revenues will be formed.

Two banking systems will be formed in the two areas, with the Bank of Southern Sudan as a branch of the Central Bank of Sudan. Essentially, the dual banking system means that banks will be commonly stationed with two different windows for service.

Two separate currencies in the North and South are to be recognized until the Central Bank has designed a new currency that reflects the cultural diversity of Sudan.

National and Southern funds for reconstruction and development will be established along with two multi-donor trust funds.

The Resolution of the Abyei Conflict (2004)

Abyei will be accorded special administrative status during the interim period, following the definition of the Abyei areas by the Abyei Border Commission.

Abyei will have representation in the legislature of Southern Kordofan and Warap states; at the end of the six-year interim period, Abyei residents will vote in a referendum either to maintain special administrative status in the North or to become part of Bahr al-Ghazal (Warap) state in the South.

Wealth-sharing of oil revenues from Abyei is to be split between the North and South (50:42) with small percentages of revenues allocated to other states and ethnic groups: 2% each to: the Ngok Dinka people, the Misseriyya people, Bahr al-Ghazal (Warap) state, and 1% each to Southern Kordofan state (SKS) and the Western Kordofan sub-state component of SKS.

The Resolution of Conflict in Southern Kordofan and Blue Nile States (2004)

The two states will be represented at the national level in proportion to their population size. At the state level, the NCP will comprise 55% and the SPLM 45% of the State Executive and State Legislature.

Southern Kordofan State (SKS): the southern portion of West Kordofan State (WKS) will be incorporated into the SKS. The state legislature will have 36 members from the SKS component and 18 from the former WKS component, subject to readjustment following a census. The state executive will have 7 from SKS and 4 from WKS. Al-Fula will have branches of all state ministries and institutions headed by a deputy. The legislature will convene sessions alternatively at Kadugli and Al-Fula.

Governorship of each state shall rotate between the NCP and SPLM during the interim period.

Wealth sharing: the 2% of SKS oil due to the state is to be shared between the two state components. The 2% share of Abyei's oil due to the state shall be equally divided between two state components. The 2% forming the Misseriyya share in Abyei oil shall benefit the previous Western Kordofan component.

The legislature of the two states will evaluate the implementation of the CPA.

State Land Commissions are to be established (in case decision clashes with National Land Commission and cannot be reconciled, the Constitutional Court will decide the matter).

Security Arrangements (2003 and 2004)

During the six-year interim period, Joint Integrated Units (JIUs) of 21,000 soldiers are to be formed with equal numbers from the Sudan Armed Forces (SAF) and the SPLA. They are to be deployed to sensitive areas such as the three disputed areas and will be commonly stationed but maintain separate command and control structures. If, after the interim period, the south decides to secede, the JIUs will unify into a 39,000 strong force.

The SAF and the SPLA will also continue to operate as separate armies with both considered part of Sudan's National Armed Forces. Each army is to be downsized and the parties are to implement demobilization, disarmament and reintegration (DDR) programmes. No other armed group will be tolerated outside the umbrella of the three services.

There is to be a redeployment of 91,000 SAF troops from the South to North within 2 years. The SPLA has 8 months to withdraw its force from the North.

A permanent cessation of hostilities is provided for, detailing disengagement and the creation of various committees for enforcement and oversight.

DDR and reconciliation are provided for through a number of commissions.

Monitoring is to be carried out by a UN mission to support implementation, as provided for under Chapter VI of the UN Charter.

A summary of the DPA and ESPA

Basic principles
Both agreements state the superiority of modern constitutional law over traditional customary law, endorse affirmative action, and reiterate the importance of sovereignty, diversity, human rights, devolution, transparency, electoral process, the rule of law and equality before the law.

Darfur Peace Agreement

5 May 2006

Permanent status of Darfur

A referendum on whether to retain Darfur's three states or create a Darfur region is to be held within 12 months of the general elections (by July 2010). The Transitional Darfur Regional Authority (TDRA) is responsible for coordinating the implementation and follow-up of the DPA and facilitating better cooperation between the three state governments.

Participation in government

Pending elections, the SLM/A and JEM are to nominate people to the following posts, making a special effort to nominate women:

* 1 Special Assistant to the President (also chair of the TDRA), and 1 presidential advisor
* 1 cabinet minister and 2 state ministers (in addition to 3 cabinet minister and 3 state minister posts which will continue to be filled by Darfurians)
* 12 seats in the National Assembly and chairmanship of one of the National Assembly's parliamentary committees
* 1 ministerial position in the Khartoum State government
* The governor of one of Darfur's states and deputy governor of each of the other two, plus 2 ministers and 1 advisor in each of the states and a senior member of each state ministry
* 21 of the 73 seats in each state assembly, including the deputy speaker of each
* 6 local commissioners and 6 executive directors in Darfur

Membership of the Council of States is to be non-partisan and to follow consultation with Darfurians. 50 per cent of places in Darfurian universities and 15 per cent of places in Khartoum's universities are reserved for Darfurians. Historical land rights (*hawakeer*) are recognized, subject to rulings by state-level Land Commissions.

Development priorities

A Darfur Reconstruction and Development Fund (DRDF) is established, with seed funding of US$300m in 2006 and a further US$200m per annum in 2007 and 2008.

A Joint Assessment Mission (JAM) is to determine priorities.

Protection and compensation

A Darfur Rehabilitation and Resettlement Commission (DRRC) is established to coordinate humanitarian provision and access and the safe and voluntary return of IDPs and refugees. A Property Claims Committees will resolve disputes. A Compensation Commission is established with an initial budget of US$30m.

A comprehensive ceasefire comes into force within 72 hours of signing; free movement of people, goods and services; the *janjaweed* is to disarm within 150 days.

A Joint Humanitarian Facilitation and Monitoring Unit (including representatives of AMIS, the UN, the international community and the parties) is to monitor and report.

4000 former combatants from the movements are to be incorporated into the SAF; education and training are to be provided for a further 3000.

Dialogue and consultation

Darfur-Darfur Dialogue and Consultation (DDDC) is to serve as a mechanism for mobilizing support for, and implementing, the DPA. 60 per cent of delegates will be tribal and community representatives, the remaining 40 per cent from political parties, civil society, religious organizations and the diaspora; observers are to be sent by international community and others.

Eastern Sudan Peace Agreement

19 October 2006

Permanent status of Eastern Sudan

A Coordinating Council is established, comprising 3 state governors, 3 state assembly speakers and 3 Eastern Front (EF) nominees who together nominate the remaining 6 council members.

The ESPA is to be implemented by a Joint Implementation Committee (with 50:50 government/ EF representation) with disputes mediated by Eritrea.

Participation in government

Pending elections, the EF is to nominate people to the following posts, making a special effort to nominate women:

- 1 Assistant to the President (also vice-chair of the Joint Implementation Committee) and 1 presidential advisor
- 1 state minister (in addition to 2 cabinet minister and 1 state minister posts which continue to be filled by eastern Sudanese)
- 8 seats in the National Assembly
- 1 advisory position in the Khartoum State government
- The deputy governor in each of Kassala and al-Qadarif states, plus 1 minister and 1 advisor in each of the three eastern states
- 10 seats in each of the three state legislatures (in each of which at least one committee will be chaired by the EF)
- 3 administrators in each of the three states and an average of 5 members in each local government assembly
- 3 nominees to 11-member Eastern Sudan Reconstruction and Development Fund (ESRDF) board

The government is to consult citizens before developing land and to compensate them if they are adversely affected. Eastern Sudanese are to benefit from the development of Port Sudan and the nation's coastal area and fish and marine resources.

Development priorities

An Eastern Sudan Reconstruction and Development Plan is to determine service, infrastructural and other priorities.

The ESRDF is to be operational within 90 days of the ESPA (ie mid-January 2007), with US$100m in 2007 and US$125m per annum 2008–11.

Security arrangements

A comprehensive and permanent ceasefire comes into force within 72 hours of the signing the ESPA; all militias or other armed groups in Eastern Sudan to be absorbed into the Sudanese Armed Forces (SAF).

Monitoring is conducted by the High Joint Military Committee, chaired by Eritrean government. Willing and qualified EF combatants are to be incorporated into the SAF for a minimum of 2 years. A Joint Committee for Integration (5 government and 5 EF representatives, chaired by the SAF) are to identify those who are 'willing and qualified' and ensure adequate training for those who are integrated into SAF and proper support for those who return to civilian life. Prisoners associated with the conflict will be released within a week of the ESPA's signature.

Dialogue

A National Conference on Sudan's administration is to be convened by the end of 2007; the government is to implement recommendations.

An ESPA Consultative Conference is envisaged; a joint preparatory committee is to be established within a week of the signature.

Source: http://www.c-r.org/our-work/accord/sudan/dpa-espa-summary.php

Notes

1 Introduction

1 Earlier discourses on these issues were initiated within literary circles. The reference is here to the rich debates among Sudanese writers about Sudan being a product of a desert–forest encounter (particularly in the two acclaimed Sudanese poets Mohamed El Maki Ibrahim and Mohamed Abdel El Hai) and the rich extension of this debate in the Abadamak Sudanese writers group. Sayed Hamid Hurreiz's (1971) *Ja'aliyyin Folktales* provides an interesting reading of the interplay of African, Arabian and Islamic elements in riverain Sudan.

2 Studies on the process of conversion from Christianity to Islam are scarce indeed. Yet the dominance of Mahas *Sheikhs* of Nubian origin in the spread of Islam along the Nile and in Central Sudan is the most clear evidence of such continuity.

3 As a child, even though in Khartoum, I was taken to the Nile shores on the seventh day of my circumcision (evidently an ancient Nubian custom). My grandmother dipped her right fingers in the water and drew a cross on my forehead (in my case more than 400 years of my ancestors converting to Islam and migrating to Khartoum to preach it).

4 The term 'Jellaba' and 'Jellabi' meaning 'traders' and 'trader' is of Arabic origin but not widely used in modern Arabic perhaps except in Sudan and Iraq (see the poem of the famous Iraqi poet Badr El Sayab, '*Shansil Ibmat El Jalabi*', literally meaning 'The of the earings of daughter of the trader'). The jellaba institution as a term came to have a meaning defining this class of people that played an important role in Sudanese history (El Gadal, 1993, p. 118).

5 This view is not entirely different from the views expressed by Hamad (1996) on the three spheres of cultural influence in Sudan (Mediterranean in riverain Sudan, West African in Darfur and East African in South Sudan) nor different from the controversial statement by the ex-Minister of NIF finance, Hamdy, about the historical triangle of Sennar, Dongola and El Obeid (see www.sudaneseonline.com for Hamdy's statement).

6 Mohammed Ali Collection, Egyptian Museum, LB19MT, No.354, 7 February 1825, cited in Hill (1959, p. 73).

7 For a very interesting and well-documented survey of studies on the decline of the local cottage-based industry in the Gezira region during the 1600–1940 period see Pollard (1984, pp. 168–180).

8 This is often understated or altogether neglected. Notable exceptions are El Gadal (1993) and more recently Sikainga (1996) and Nugud (1995).

9 See the rich documentation of the British colonial policies of 1940–1956 in Saleh (2002) and on the 1940s effort to compensate for over four decades of colonial administration neglect of Southern Sudan (selected items are shown in Appendix I).

2 War and the transformative potential

1 'Chaos theory, in mathematics and physics, deals with the behavior of certain nonlinear dynamical systems that (under certain conditions) exhibit the phenomenon known as chaos, most famously characterized by sensitivity to initial conditions (see butterfly effect). Examples of such systems include the atmosphere, the solar system, plate tectonics, turbulent fluids, economies, and population growth' (from Wikipedia, the free encyclopedia). From interesting applications in social science see Richards (1990) Beyerchen (1992/93) and Grossmann and Mayer-Kress (1989).

2 The term modernities rather than modernity allows substantial conceptual flexibility that can accommodate the historical specificities of various experiences as was articulated by several contributors such as Taylor (2004), Martin (2005), Wagner (2000) and Eisenstadt (2000). See for example: Eisenstadt, S.E. (2000), 'Multiple Modernities', *Daedalus*, Winter, 129(1): 1–29. (Note: the entire issue of *Daedalus*, Winter, 129(1), is devoted to 'Multiple Modernities'.)

3 Cited in Yannis (2002, p. 817).

4 In Goldman's pioneering work he suggested three plausible scenarios of triggering the pressure cooker explosion. These were: reform from within the party; reform from outside the party; and a popular uprising. His prediction was that the first scenario is the most likely one.

5 See the rich discourse on characteristics of natural resources and the likelihood of conflict occurrence. A good overview of the literature on the synergies between natural resources and occurrence of civil wars is provided in Ross (2003). Ross suggests that the role played by any natural resources depend largely on its lootability, and to a lesser extent on its obstructionability and its legality (ibid., p. 54).

6 I am aware that the authors rightly alerted the reader that their analysis does not apply to the Horn of Africa countries, namely Ethiopia, Northern Sudan, Eritrea and Somalia. All these countries, as the authors argued, have dissimilar social structures and have had different political experiences (Chabal and Daloz, 1999, p. xxi). Yet, the argument is about the potential rather than the immediacy.

3 The failed modernity I

1 A three-year period of parliamentary democracy (1956–1958) was immediately followed by the first military rule (1958–1964); the short post-popular uprising of October 1964 was brought to an end by Nimeiri in May 1969, which lasted until the second popular uprising of 1985. In June 1989, the Islamist coup signalled the end of the popularly known third democracy.

2 The drying out of the early sources of capitalist accumulation in agriculture and industry led to fierce competition over the foreign-dominated spheres of accumulation, particularly foreign trade and finance (see Elnur, 1988).

3 In a stable but almost stagnant economy of the immediate post-independence's first two decades, the accumulation crisis was one of competition over the control of the commanding heights of the economy between the growing indigenous capital and the largely foreign and expatriate leading enterprises controlling exports, imports and finance activities. The Sudan communist party publication ('Marxism and the Questions of Sudanese Revolution') adopted by the party congress in 1965 provides a wealth of analysis on this struggle (SCP, 1965).

4 Despite the revolutionary rhetoric that accompanied the nationalization – confiscation policies, the communist members of the revolutionary council, led by Nimeiri, were strongly opposed to its timing, magnitude and indiscriminate nature (see Khalid 1984, pp. 37–38).

5 For a detailed account of the use of state allocations see Niblock, 1987, Chapter: Social forces under condominium, pp. 49–166.

6 Given the relatively small market and tight administrative control over imports, the emergence of a new single group of nouveau riche was associated with a sudden ban on imports of a certain commodity or a temporary monopoly over a certain imported commodity.

7 I would maintain that the Breadbasket-driven horizontal expansion and the extractive rather than transformative intervention in the traditional sector (particularly that focused on tapping the resources of the livestock sub-sector) laid the foundation for the structural crisis in primary production.

8 For detailed accounts of these generous terms see Elsheikh (1981) and ACR (1970/71, section B, p. 55).

9 SYP planners anticipated two different patterns investment for Sudanese and foreign private sectors. As for Arab oil-exporting countries, it is possible to argue that these countries were willing to pay a premium to delink from the US-dominated world food market. Hence, a different Arab investment pattern is still plausible.

10 Nimeiri's regime lasted until April 1985, but for all practical reasons the 1983–1985 period was practically a transitional one of sheer survival (see Glandar, 2005).

4 The failed modernity II

1 In the course of finalizing the manuscript of this book a number of publications by a number of ex and current members of the Islamist movement and others revealed interesting dimensions of the Islamist ascendancy strategies and discourses. While providing very interesting insights, these studies tend to confirm our main findings (see for example Mahy Eldin, Abdel Rahim (2006), Talha, Sabry (2006), Zein El Abdeen (2003) and a plethora of writings in the Khartoum dailies.

2 The second *Intifada* of April 1985 (first was in October 1964) that restored democracy in Sudan took place during the closing years of the cold war. Encouragement of the transition to democratic rule was not on the agenda of superpowers, least on the agenda of the close neighbours who were extremely suspicious of the forces that ended their close ally. In this sense Sadig El Mahadi is right in his notion of a conspiracy against the hard-won democracy but also one would agree with Khalid (1993, vol. 2, pp. 137–140) that there was a great degree of confusion and narrow party manoeuvres between Umma and NDP parties (see also Elsawi, 1993, pp. 227–228; and Elturabi, 1993, pp. 459–481).

3 For a very interesting historical record of the early years of the movement foundation in Egypt and Sudan see Radi, 1982, pp. 103–114.

4 Turabi acknowledged the tremendous gains to the Islamic movement from its alliance with the discredited regime of Nimeiri, particularly in its decay phase (Turabi, 1991, pp. 199–203). Ex-Nimeiri ministers and officials are still part of the NIF government.

5 Turabi was well aware of the implications of the changing urban terrain. He wrote: '… with the deterioration of the modern sector of the economy, the working class political influence deteriorated and so the communist'(Turabi, 1991, p. 146).

6 In the 1986 election 38.2 per cent of the votes went to the Umma party 29.48 per cent to DUP, 18.38 per cent to the Islamists, 1.72 per cent to the Communists and 0.905 per cent to the Baathists. In Khartoum alone 29.8 per cent voted for the Islamists, 30.48 per cent for the DUP 20.71 per cent for the Umma party, 5.6 per cent for the Communists and 2.1 per cent for the Baathists. (Elsawi, 1993, p. 227).

7 The extent of post-oil boom external support or the Islamist movements is well reflected in this quote based on a report by Alex Alexiev, 'Terrorism: Growing Wahhabi Influence in the United States', Testimony before the US Senate Committee on the Judiciary, Subcommittee on Terrorism, Technology and Homeland Security, 26 June 2003: 'While Saudi citizens remain the vanguard of Islamic theofascism around the world, the growth potential for this ideology lies outside the Kingdom. The Saudis have spent at least

$87 billion propagating Wahhabism abroad during the past two decades' (cited in Winsor, 2007).

8 This tension between the two strategies survived an open split within the Islamic movement in the 1995–1999 period. The 1999 anti-Turabi memorandum known as the memorandum of ten singled out the open rivalry between the two contending factions within the NIF (see Mohy Eldin, 2006, pp. 362–427).

9 See Abdel Gadir, Eltigani: 'The Islamic Capitalists', *Alsahafa*, no. 4849, 10 December 2006.

10 The counter popular response to this wishful thinking and the hardships imposed on the population was 'We shall eat what we wear'.

11 The serious limitations imposed by the Islamic formula for finance of non-trade activities was the single most important negative aspect of the Islamic Banking formula. As noted by Jamal (1991, p. 16), 'The investment pattern of these banks encouraged the growth of small and medium-sized-businesses (over 9 per cent of their investments are allocated to export/imports and only 4 per cent to agriculture).'

12 According to Winsor (2007) the Egyptian Brotherhood, fleeing Nasser's persecution and taking refuge in Saudi Arabia, paved the way for the cross-fertilization between Wahhabism and the Salafi jihadist teaching of Sayyid Qutb, breeding a militant variety of Wahhabist 'Al-Qaeda.' However, given the Sudanese experience one would suggest a more diverse output of such cross-fertilization.

5 Sudan's war-produced economy and society

1 DPSG is the Displaced Population Study Group, a collaborative research group co-led by the author, the late Dr Fatima El Rahseed and Dr Yasir Yacoub. The group undertook an extensive field among the internally displaced population in Greater Khartoum. The sample covered 1,060 households mostly from Southern Sudan but also included a representative of drought victims from Western Sudan.

2 An interesting and well-documented set of studies covers this aspect. See Christian Aid (2001 and 2002), and Duffield (1991), among others.

3 According to estimates in April 2005 2.6 million people were affected while there were 200,000 refugees in Darfur (see Guha-Sapir, 2006, p. 4).

4 The fieldwork that informs this section is based on DPSG files (1990–1993) as well as subsequent follow-up visits by the author in 2000 and 2004.

5 Cited in Hamimi, Nessreen (2007): 'Challenges to Return, Reintegration and Reconstruction of Refugees and Internally Displaced Persons: The Case of South Sudan', MA dissertation, The American University in Cairo, May 2007.

6 Among the refugee population those in Egypt (estimated at 300,000) and other Arab countries experienced a similar process of Arabization.

7 The emergence of gangster youth groups among both IDPs and refugee communities (Egypt) was widely reported, signalling an erosion of traditional authority based on age hierarchy (see IRC, 2004).

6 From Addis to Nivasha War-Fatigue-driven peace agreement

1 For example, both within internal diasporas of IDPs as well as external diasporas, the SPLM/A was able to silence or reduce the active presence of non-SPLM/A political groups. The Khartoum regime was less successful in external diasporas. (Notes from extended fieldwork, DPSG (1990–1993) files and Nyaba, 1997).

2 Oil was always on the agenda since the late 1970s when exploration started and the first successful drilling was undertaken then but oil, as long as no export plans were envisaged or successfully realized, remained a far less important factor. It was the shift from 'potential' to actual plans that triggered its serious development in the civil war.

For a detailed account see Christian Aid (2002): 'God, Oil and Country – Changing the Logic of War in Sudan', Report No. 39, Christian Aid, Oxfam, IRC.

3 Rumbek Meeting: The minutes of the 'Confidential Report of the SPLM/A leadership Council Meeting', 29 November–1 December 2004. The most prominent points raised were: no cohesion within leadership/Garang was accused of 'carrying the movement in his suitcase'; rampant corruption; no political system developed for future governance of South Sudan; SPLA ill-equipped, ill-trained; no equitable regional presentation; the chairman is evasive and reluctant to convene the widely demanded South–South Dialogue; and finally the leadership collectively accepted part of the blame because they failed to appropriately advise the chairman (see http://www.southsudannation.com/rumbek%20revelations).

4 This was evident when he met with John Garang on 31 July 1986. Sadiq El Mahdi vehemently rejected the abolition of 'Islamic Laws', which he himself described as 'not worth the time used in its writing' (see Adlan, 2006, p. 350).

5 The broader influence of this declaration should be seen from the point of its overall influence on the direction of public discourse even among the Islamists themselves following the split within the NIF. See for example the memorandum of understanding between the SPLA and Turabi faction following the 17–19 February 2001 meeting in Geneva (Mohy Eldin, 2006, pp. 432–433).

6 I am referring here to the rich debate on the abundance resource curse suggesting that natural resources tend to slow transition to democracy or lack of transparency and accountability associated with a '*rentier*' type of state, leading to a serious reduction in tax-dependence (for an extensive survey see Rosser, 2006, and on taxation impact see Moore, 2007).

7 With the successive peace agreements (DPA 2006 and EPA 2007), this already inflated top-brass structure was excessively enlarged. 'Buying peace with oil' money became the motto of the Khartoum regime.

8 See Sudan Advocacy Report 09-07, 'Seeking a just and lasting peace for Sudan'. *Sudan Advocacy Action Forum: Situation*, 9 April 2007 http://sudanadvocacy.com/situation.htm.

9 ICG (International Crisis Group) (2005): 'Garang's Death: Implications for Peace in Sudan, Update Briefing Africa Briefing No. 30, Nairobi–Brussels, 9 August 2005.

10 *Sudan Tribune*, 15 April 2007.

11 *Sudan Advocacy Action Forum: Situation*, 9 April 2007 http://sudanadvocacy.com/situation.htm. A full report on the serious financial crimes involving unaccounted transfers from central government, fake projects and fictitious bids and contracts was reported the *Sudan Tribune*, 13 April 2007, entitled: 'In South Sudan, "anything goes", as per the rules of corruption', See also the WB report on the GoSS, January 2007.

7 Post-Nivasha

1 The extent of such entrepreneurs and capital flight from war zones in both Southern Sudan and Darfur is enormous. The northern business community in Southern Sudan's memorandum is indicative. Over 5,000 wholesale traders, who are no longer residing in Southern Sudan, are included.

2 This practice found authority in section 560(1) of the 1984 Civil Transaction Act, that ruled that the person who developed the land by tilling it is entitled to such land and acquires legal title (AACM, 1992, p. 246, cited in Harragin, 2003).

3 In the 1970 Unregistered Land Act, ownership of all unregistered land was transferred to the government, and in the 1971 'Native Administration Act', the authority of the tribal chiefs was greatly diminished including the right to allocate land use.

4 Tombe, Mary Justo. 'Kiir to BARI: 7000 SAF Soldiers Refuse to Leave, Becoming the Biggest Problem for GOSS'. *The Juba Post* Volume 3, Issue 11, 23–30 March 2007.

5 The UN had estimated that, in 2006, 680,000 returnees will voluntarily return to the Sudan. Out of this number 366,000 will return to South Sudan. The UNHCR has declared that so far 14,000 refugees have voluntarily repatriated to the Sudan, 350,000 are still waiting to be repatriated from neighbouring countries and around 4 million internally displaced south Sudanese (Southern Sudan Programmes, Sudan Work Plan 2006 http://www.unsudanig.org/workplan/2006/data/plan/WorkPlan2006-low-res.pdf, "UNHCR" South Sudan repatriation operation threatened by funding shortfall', UNHCR, Geneva, 15 September.

6 'A family in Mayo camp returned to the South, and had returned back to Khartoum after one month. Two reasons were identified by the family: 1. the outbreak of meningitis in Juba could cost them their lives; and 2. living in Juba is extremely expensive compared to Khartoum. This family has been advising other IDPs intending to return to stay in Khartoum since they will not be able to cope with the contrasting life in Juba' (Hamimi, 2007, p. 15).

7 Three years after the Nivasha Peace Agreements the high hopes of a massive return of refugees and IDPs did not materialize. See Morris, Tim (2007): 'Slow Return of Displaced Southern Sudanese: Forced Migration Review', July, pp. 38–39, http://www.fmreview.org/FMRpdfs/FMR28/20.pdf see also similar reports at the UNIMIS (United Nation Mission In Sudan) site: http://unsudanig.org/data/annual/Return%20and%20Reintegration%20Assistance2005–2007.pdf

References

AACM (Australian Agriculture Consulting and Management Company) in association with TIRSICO (1992) South Kordofan Agricultural Development Programme – Land Use Survey, Adelaide.

Abbashar, J. (1991) Funding Fundamentalism, Middle East Report, No. 172, Sudan Finding Common Grounds, pp. 14–17.

Abbink, J. (2004) Reconstructing Southern Sudan in the Post-War Era: Challenges and Prospects of 'Quick Impact Programmes', ASC Working Paper 55/2004, African Studies Centre, Leiden, The Netherlands.

Abdel, G. E. (2006) The Islamic Capitalists, *Al-sahafa Daily,* No. 4849, December 10.

Abdel, R. O. (2006) *Al Turabi wa Al Ingaz: Siras Alhawiaa wa Alhawaa* (Turabi and Salvation Revolution: The Conflict of Identity and Interest) (in Arabic), Ekrema Press, Damascus.

Abdel Al-Rahim, M. (1985) Arabism, Africanism and Self-Identification in the Sudan, in Y. F. Hassan (ed.), *Sudan in Africa*, Khartoum University Press, Khartowm.

Abdelgadier, O. (2004) God, Oil and Country: Sudan's Long Road to Peace, paper presented at the Conference on 'Sudan at the Crossroad' at the Fletcher School, 12 March.

Abdel Rahim, M. (1973) Arabism, Africanism, and Self-Identification in the Sudan, in D. Wai (ed.), *The Southern Sudan: The Problem of National Integration*, Frank Cass and Co. Ltd, London, pp. 29–47.

Abdel Salam, A. H., de Waal, A. and Medani, A. M. (eds.) (2001) *The Phoenix State, Civil Society and the Future of Sudan*, The Red Sea Press.

Abdelsalam, S. and Abdelsalam, A. (2005) *Sudan*, RoutledgeCurzon, London and New York.

Abdel-Wahab, A. R. (1976) Development Planning in the Sudan, in A. M. Elhassan (ed.), *An Introduction to Sudan Economy*, Khartoum University Press, Khartoum, pp. 219–220.

Abdulrahman, A. I. (1988) The Impact of Desertification and Urbanization and Urban Growth in Western Sudan, with Reference to Nyala, El Fashir, El Obied and El Nahud, Ph.D. Dissertation, Department of Geography, University of Khartoum, p. 426.

Abu Baker, H. (1995) *Coping with Displacement Among the Sudanese Community in Egypt: The Case of Ten Displaced Sudanese Women in Cairo, Egypt*, The American University in Cairo.

Abu Shoukm, A. I. (2004) *Yusuf Michael Memoirs*, Abdelkarim Mirghani Cultural Centre, Omdurman.

ACR (1970/71) *Africa Contemporary Records: Annual Survey and Documents*, Legum, C. (ed.), African Publishing Company, a Division of Holmes and Meir Publishers, London.

ACR (1973/74) *Africa Contemporary Records: Annual Survey and Documents*, Legum, C. (ed.), African Publishing Company, a Division of Holmes and Meir Publishers, London.

Adam, F. H. (1983) Mechanized Agriculture in the Central Rain Land of the Sudan, in P. Oesterdiekhof and K. Wohlmuth (eds.), *The Development Perspective of the Democratic Republic of the Sudan*, African Studies Series, No. 109, IFO-institut fur Wirtschaftsforschung Munchen, weltforum verlag, Munchen.

Adar, K. G. (2000) Sudan: The Internal and External Contexts of Conflict and Conflict Resolution, UNHCR, Centre for Documentation and Research, WRITENET Paper No. 06/2000, July.

ADB (2003) African Development Bank: Selected Statistics on African Countries, Research Development Department, Tunis.

ADB (2006) African Development Bank: Selected Statistics on African Countries, Volume XXIV, Research Development Department, Tunis.

ADBC (2006) African Development Bank Country Report, Sudan, Development Research Department, Tunis.

Adlan, E. (2006) *Ma Elmanfa wa ma Elwatan* (What is Exile and What is Home?), Mararik Publishers, Cairo.

AFESD (Arab Fund for Economic and Social Development) (1976) Basic Programme for Agricultural Development in the Democratic Republic of the Sudan, 1976–1985, Summary and Conclusion, AFESD, Kuwait.

AFYP (1971) The Amended Five Years Plan for Economic and Social Development, 1970/71–1976/77, MNFP, Khartoum.

Ahmed, A. G. (2002) Changing Systems of Livelihood in Rural Sudan, OSSREA, Addis Ababa.

Ahmed, A. G. M. (2006) The Darfur Crisis: Mapping the Root, Causes, in Abdel Ghaffar, M. Ahmed and Leif Manger (eds.), *Understanding the Crisis in Darfur: Listening to Sudanese Voices*, Centre for Development Studies, Bergen.

Ahorsu, K. E. (2004) The Political Economy of Civil Wars in Sub-Saharan Africa – A Conceptual Framework, paper presented at UNU-WIDER Conference: Making Peace Work, June.

Akec, J. A. (2007) Fragmented Party System in South Sudan May Undermine Peace, *Sudan Tribune*, February 19.

Akol, L. (2001) SPLM/SPLA: Inside an African Revolution, Khartoum University Press, Khartoum, Sudan.

Alexander, J., McGregor, J. and Ranger, T. (2000) Ethnicity and the Politics of Conflict: The Case of Matabeleland, in E. W. Nafziger, F. Stewart and R. Väyrynen (eds.), *The Economic Causes of Humanitarian Emergencies*, Oxford University Press, Oxford, UK.

Ali, A. A. (ed.) (1985) *The Sudan Economy in Disarray: Essays on the Crisis*, Ithaca Press, London.

Ali, A. A. G. (1992a) Structural Adjustment Programs and Poverty Creation: Results from Sudan, *Eastern Africa Social Science Review*, 8(1), 1–24.

Ali, A. A. (1992b) Economic Restructuring and Poverty Alleviation: Some Theoretical and Empirical Results, *Eastern Africa Social Science Review*, 9(2), 33–46.

Ali, A. A. G. (1994) *Structural Adjustment Programs and Poverty in Sudan*, Arab Planning Institute, Kuwait.

Ali, A. A. G. (1998) Dealing with Poverty and Income Distribution Issues in Developing Countries: Cross-regional Experiences, *Journal of African Economies*, 7, AERC Supplement, 77–115.

Ali, A. A. G. (2003) Can the Sudan Reduce Poverty by Half by the Year 2015?, paper prepared for a volume in honour of Heba Handoussa, ERF, Cairo.

Ali, A. A. G. (2004) On Achieving the National and Sub-National Targets for the Sudan, Arab Planning Institute, Kuwait.

Ali, A. A. G. and Elbadawi, I. (2001) Growth Could Be Good for the Poor, unpublished manuscript.

Ali, A. A. G. and Elbadawi, I. A. (2003) Explaining Sudan's Economic Growth Performance, Country Chapter in AERC's Collaborative Project on Explaining Africa's Growth Performance, AERC, Nairobi.

Ali, H. I. (1996) Islamic Movements and Democracy, Centre for Arab Unity Studies, Beirut, October.

Ali, N. (2003) Diaspora and Nation: Displacement and the Politics of Kashmiri Identity in Britain, *Contemporary South Asia*, 12(4), 471–480.

Ali, T. A. (1982) The Cultivation of Hunger: Towards the Political Economy of Agricultural Development in the Sudan: 1956–1964, unpublished Ph.D. thesis, University of Toronto.

Alier, A. (1992) *Sudan: Too Many Agreements Dishonoured*, Ithaca Press, Reading.

Allen, A. (1992) War, Famine and Flight in Sudan, *Disasters*, 15(2), 133–136.

Allen, T. and Turton, D. (1996) 'Introduction', in T. Allen (ed.), *Search for Cool Ground: War, Flight and Homecoming in Northeast Africa I*, UNRISID, London.

Al-Sharmani, M. (2003) Livelihood and Identity Constructions of Somali Refugees in Cairo, Working Paper No. 2, The Forced Migration and Refugees Studies, The American University in Cairo, Egypt.

AMF (Arab Monetary Fund) (1982) Arab Economic Report for 1982, AMF Publications, Kuwait.

Amin, N. E. (1986) Nomadism versus Sedenterization: An Environmental Choice in Western Sudan, the Case of *Gerih Sarha*, Environment Monograph Series, No. 5, Institute of Environmental Studies, University of Khartoum, p. 105.

Anand, S. and Kanbur, R. (1993) Inequality and Development: A Critique, *Journal of Development Economics*, 41(1), 19–43.

Arab Human Development Report (2002): Creating Opportunities for Future Generations, UNIDO, Amman, Jordan.

Assal, M. A. M. (2005) Darfur: An Annotated Bibliography of Social Research on Darfur, University for Development Studies, University of Bergen.

Attas, P. M. and Licklider, R. (1999) Conflict Among Former Allies after Civil War Settlements: Sudan, Zimbabwe, Chad and Lebanon, *Journal of Peace Research*, 36(1), 35–54.

Ayalon, D. (2000) The Spread of Islam and the Nubian Deem, in Haggai Elrich and Israel Gershoni (eds.), *The Nile: Histories, Cultures, Myths*, Lynne Rienner, Boulder, CO.

Azar, (1993) The Theory of Protracted Social Conflict and the Challenges of Transforming Conflict Situation, in D. Zinnes (ed.), *Conflicts Process and the Breakdown of International System*, University of Denver, Denver, CO.

Azarya, V. and Chazan, N. (1987) Disengagement for the State in Africa: Reflections from the Experience of Ghana and Guinea, *Comparative Studies in Society and History*, 29(1), 106–131.

Azzam, J. P. and Hoeffler, A. (2002) Violence against Civilians in Civil Wars: Looting or Terror? *Journal of Peace Research*, 39(4), 461–485.

Babikir, El Tigany El Tayeb (2005) *Elbahth En Elsalam fi Elsudan* (in Arabic); The Search for Peace in the Sudan, Alamya Publishers, Cairo and Khartoum.

Balamoan, G. A. (1981) *Peoples and Economics in the Sudan 1884–1956*, White Friars Press, London.

Ballentine, K. and Sherman, J. (eds.) (2003) *The Political Economy of Armed Conflict: Beyond the Greed and Grievance*, a project of the International Peace Academy, Boulder, London.

Barbour, K. M. (1961) *The Republic of Sudan: A Regional Geography*, University of London Press, London.

Barakat, S. (2005) *After the Conflict: Reconstruction and Development in the Aftermath of War*, I. B. Tauris, London and New York.

Barbara, H. (1973) *Rich Nations and Poor in Peace and War: Continuity and Change in the Development Hierarchy of Seventy Nations from 1913 through 1992*, Lexington Books, London.

Barro, R. (2000) Inequality and Growth in a Panel of Countries, *Journal of Economic Growth*, 5, 5–32.

Bayat, A. (2002) Activism and Social Development in the Middle East, *International Journal of Middle Eastern Studies*, 34(1), 1–28.

Bayat, A. (2003) The 'Street' and Politics of Dissent in the Arab World, in Middle East Report 226, March, Washington D.C.

Behsai, A. A. (1976) *Export Performance and Economic Development in the Sudan: 1900–1967*, Ithaca Press, London.

Bekoe, D. A. (2006) *East Africa and the Horn: Confronting Challenges to Good Governance*, International Peace Academy Occasional Papers, Lynne Rienner Publishers, Boulder, London.

Benjaminsen, T. A. and Lund, C. (2002) Formalization and Informalization of Land and Water Rights in Africa: An Introduction, *European Journal of Development Studies*, 14(2), 1–10.

Benthall, J. and Bellion-Jourdan, J. (2003) *The Charitable Crescent: Politics of Aid in the Muslim World*, I. B. Tauris, London and New York.

Beshir, M. O. (1968) *The Southern Sudan: Background to Conflict*, Khartoum University Press, Khartoum, Sudan.

Beshir, Y. H. B. (1990) *Qadaia Sudania Sakha* (Hot Issues in Sudan), April, Jeddah.

Beyerchen, A. (1992/93) Clausewitz, Nonlinearity, and the Unpredictability of War, *International Security*, 17(3), 59–90.

Bjorkelo, A. (1989) *Prelude to the Mahadiyya: Peasants and Traders in Shendi Region, 1821–1885*, African Studies Series, No. 62, Cambridge University Press, Cambridge.

Boyle, P. (2002) Population Geography: Transnational Women on the Move, *Progress in Human Geography*, 26(4), 531–543.

Bratton, M. and De Walle, N. V. (1994) New Patrimonial Regimes and Political Transitions in Africa, *World Politics*, 46, 453–489.

Brempong, K. G. (1989) Defense Spending and Economic Growth in Sub-Saharan Africa: An Economic Investigation, *Journal of Peace Research*, 20(1), 79–90.

Brockerhoff, M. (2000) An Urbanizing World, *Population Bulletin*, 55(3), 1–44.

Bruck, T. (2002) Ludwig Erhard in Africa: War Finance and Post War Reconstruction in Germany and Mozambique, in J. Brauer and J. P. Dunne (eds.), *Arming the South: The Economics of Military Expenditure, Arms Production and Arms Trade in Developing Countries*, Palgrave, Basingstoke and New York, pp. 235–250.

Bulir, A. (1998) Income Inequality: Does Inflation Matter?, WP/98/7, IMF, Washington D.C.

Burr, J. M. and Collins, R. O. (1995) *Requiem for Sudan: War, Drought, and Disaster Relief on the Nile*, Westview Press, Boulder, San Francisco and Oxford.

Burr, M. (1990) Khartoum Displaced Persons: A Decade of Despair, USAID Committee for Refugees (draft report).

Cairns, E. (1997) *A Safer Future: Reducing the Human Cost of War*, Oxfam Publications, Oxford.

Callaghy, T. M., Kassimir, R. and Latham, R. (2001) *Intervention and Transnationalism in Africa: Global-Local Networks of Power*, Cambridge University Press, Cambridge.

CARE/International Organization for Migration (IOM) (2003) Sudan IDPs and Refugees in Northern Sudan: Findings of an Exploratory Survey, 6–19 September, http://www.idpproject.org (last accessed 30 May 2005).

Casteles, S. and Miller, M. S. (2003) *The Age of Migration*, Macmillan Press Ltd, Houndmills, Basingstoke, Hampshire and London.

CAWTAR (2001) Arab Women Development Report: Globalization and Gender: Arab Women Economic Participation, CAWTAR, Tunis.

Central Bureau of Statistics (CBS) (2001) *Sudan in Figures 1988–2000*, Khartoum.

Chabal, P. and Daloz, J.-P. (1999) *Africa Works: Disorder as Political Instrument*, The International African Institute in association with James Currey, Oxford, and Indiana University Press, Bloomington and Indianapolis.

Christian Aid (2001) The Scorched Earth: Oil and War in Sudan. See also New Sudan Council of Churches, Sudan Civil Society Forum on Good Governance and Reconciliation in Sudan During the Interim Period, Entebbe, Uganda, http//www.reliefweb.int/library/documents/2001/Chr_aid-sud14marl.

Christian Aid (2002) God, Oil and Country – Changing the Logic of War in Sudan, Report No. 39.

Christian Aid, Oxfam, IRC, Tearfund and Save the Children (2002) The Key to Peace: Unlocking the Human Potential of Sudan.

Clapham, C. (1989) *Africa and the International System: The Politics of State Survival*, Cambridge Studies on International Relations, Cambridge University Press, Cambridge.

Clapham, C. (2002) The Challenge to the State in a Globalized World, *Development and Change*, 33(5), 775–795.

Cleaver, F. (2002) Reinventing Institutions: Bricolage and Social Embeddedness of Natural Resources Management, *European Journal of Development Studies*, 14(2), 11–30.

Collier, P. and Gunning, J. (1999) Explaining African Economic Performance, *Journal of Economic Literature*, 37(1), 64–111.

Collier, P. and Dollar, D. (2000) Can the World Cut Poverty in Half? How Policy Reform and Effective Aid Can Meet the International Development Goals, *World Development*, 29(11), 1787–1802.

Collier, P. and Hoeffler, A. (2001) Greed and Grievance in Civil Wars, Manuscript, World Bank (http://www.worldbank.org/research/conflict/papers/greedgrievance.htm).

Collier, P. and Dollar, D. (2002) Aid Allocation and Poverty Reduction, *European Economic Review*, 26, 1475–1500.

Collier, P. and Hoeffler, A. (2003) Breaking the Conflict Trap: Civil War and Development Policy, World Bank Policy Research, May.

Collier, P., Hoeffler, A. and Soderbom, M. (2003) On the Duration of Civil War, Centre for the Study of African Economics, Oxford (available at: http://users.ox.ac.uk-ball0144).

Collier, P., Elliot, V. L., Hegre, Ha'vard, Hoeffler, A., Reynal-Querol, M. and Sambanis, N. (2003) *Breaking the Conflict Trap: Civil War and Development Policy*, a copublication of the World Bank and Oxford University Press, Oxford.

Copson, R. W. (1994) *Africa's Wars and Prospects for Peace*, M. E. Sharpe, Armonk, New York and London.

Cordell, D. D., Gregory, J. W. and Piche, V. (1996) *Hoe and Wage: A Social History of a Circular Migration System in West Africa*, West View Press, Boulder, CO.

Cowen, M. (1982) The British State and the Agrarian Accumulation in Kenya, in M. Fransman (ed.), *Industry and Accumulation in Africa*, Heinemann, London.

Cramer, C. (2004) The Great Post-Conflict Makeover Fantasy, paper presented at WIDER Conference: Making Peace Work, Helsinki, 4–5 June, http://www.wider.unu.edu/confrerence-2004-1-paper.htm.88k

Cramer, C. and Goodhand, J. (2002) Try Again, Fail Again, Fail Better? War, the State, and the 'Post-Conflict' Challenge in Afghanistan, *Development and Change*, 34(5), 885–909.

Crawford, O. G. S. (1951) *The Fung Kingdom of Sennar*, Gloucester.

Cutler, P. (1986) The Response to Drought of Beja Famine Refugees in Sudan, *Disasters*, 10(3), 181–188.

Cutler, P. (1988) Famine and Household Coping Strategies, *Disasters*, 10(3), 181–188.

Daedalus (2000) Multiple Modernities, *Daedalus*, 129(1), 1–29. (Note: the entire issue of *Daedalus*, Winter, 129(1), is devoted to 'Multiple Modernities'.)

Daly, W. (1993) Broken Bridge and Empty Basket: The Political and Economic Background of the Sudanese Civil War, in W. Daly and A. A. Sikainga (eds.), *Civil War in the Sudan*, British Academic Press, London.

Danforth, J. (2002) The Outlook for Peace in Sudan, on the White House website: http://www.whitehouse.gov/news/releases/2002/05/outlook_for_peace_in_ sudan.pdf.

Dasgupta, P. (1993) *The Economics of Destitution*, Cambridge University Press, Cambridge.

De Haas, H. (2003) Migration and Development in Southern Morocco: The Disparate Socio-economic Impact of Out-migration on the Todgha Oasis Valley, unpublished Ph.D. thesis, Radboud University, Nijmegen, Amsterdam.

De Haas, H. (2005) International Migration, Remittances and Development: Myths and Facts, *Third World Quarterly*, 26(8), 1269–1284.

De Haas, H. (2008) Migration and Development: A Theoretical Perspective, International Migration Institute, James Martin 21st Century School, University of Oxford, Working Paper No. 9.

Deininger, K. and Squire, L. (1996) A New Data Set for Measuring Income Inequality, *World Bank Economic Review*, 10(3), 565–591.

Deininger, K., Iba'nez, A. M. and Querubin, P. (2004) Towards Sustainable Return Policies for the Displaced Population: Why Are Some Displaced Households More Willing to Return than Others?, HICN Working Paper No. 7, February.

Deng, F. M. (1973) *Dynamics of Identification: A Baseline for National Integration in the Sudan*, Khartoum University Press, Khartoum.

Deng, F. M. (1995) *War of Visions: Conflict of Identities in the Sudan*, Brookes Institution, Washington D.C.

Deng, L. (2003) Confronting Civil War: A Comparative Study of Household Livelihood Strategies in Southern Sudan during the 1990s, Ph.D. thesis, University of Sussex, Institute of Development Studies (IDS), Brighton.

Deng, L. B. (2004a) The Challenges of Post-Conflict Economic Recovery and Reconstruction in Sudan, Institute of Development, Environment and Agricultural Studies, 24 September (presented at the Woodrow Wilson Center, Washington).

Deng, L. B. (2004b) Are Non-poor Households Always Less Vulnerable? The Case of Households Exposed to Protracted Civil War in Southern Sudan, paper presented at the Conference on Africa: Economic Growth and Poverty, March, Centre for Study of African Economies, Oxford, United Kingdom.

Deng, L. B. (2005) The Comprehensive Peace Agreement: Will It Also Be Dishonoured?, *Forced Migration Review*, 24, November, 15–16 (http://www.reliefweb.int/rw/lib.nsf/db900SID/EVOD-6JMCJ2/$FILE/Forced%20Migration%20Review.pdf? OpenElement).

De Waal, A. (2001) Review of Jeffrey Sachs and others, 'Macroeconomics and Health: Investing in Health for Economic Development', Report of the Commission on Macroeconomics and Health to the Director-General of the World Health Organization, 20 December. See: http://www.radixonline.org/resources_op-ed.htm

De Waal, A. and Ajawin, Y. (eds.) (2000) *When Peace Comes: Civil Society and Development in Sudan*, The Democracy and Development in Transition in Sudan, Conference on Human Rights, Kampala, Uganda.

De Waal, A. and Ajawin, J. (eds.) (2002) *When Peace Comes, Civil Society and Development in Sudan, Eritrea,* Red Sea Press, New Jersey.

Dixon, W. J. and Moon, B. E. (1986) The Military Burden and Basic Human Needs, *Journal of Conflict Resolution*, 30(4), 660–684.

Dollar, D. and Kraay, A. (2002) Growth is Good for the Poor, *Journal of Economic Growth*, 7(3), 195–225.

Doninio, A., Niland, N. and Wermester, K. (eds.) (2004) Nation-Building Unraveled? Aid, Peace and Justice in Afghanistan, a project supported by the International Peace Academy, Kumarian Press, Bloomfield.

Doornbos, M. C. L., Ahmed, A. G. M. and Markakis, J. (1992) *Beyond Conflict in the Horn: The Prospects for Peace, Recovery, and Development in Ethiopia, Somalia, Eritrea and Sudan*, The Red Sea Press, New Jersey.

Doornbos, P. (1988) On Becoming Sudanese, in T. Barnett and A. Abdelkarim (eds.), *Sudan: State, Capital and Transformation*, Croom Helm, London, New York and Sydney, pp. 99–120.

Douglas, J. (1998) The Sudan Liberation Army and the Problem of Factionalism, in C. Clapham (ed.), *African Guerrillas*, Indiana University Press, Oxford and Kampala.

Douglas, J. (2003) *The Root Causes of Civil War in the Sudan*, James Currey, Oxford.

D'Souza, F. and Shoham, J. (1985) The Spread of Famine: Avoiding Worst, *Third World Quarterly*, 7(3), 515–531.

Duffield, M. (1991) From Emergency to Social Security in Sudan, and (1990), *Disasters*, 14(3), 187–203 and 14(4), 322–334.

Duffield, M. (2001) *Global Governance and the New Wars: The Merging of Development and Security*, Zed Books, London and New York.

Dunne, J. P. and Mohammed, N. A. L. (1995) Military Spending in Sub-Saharan Africa: Some Evidence for 1967–1985, *Journal of Peace Research*, 32(3), 331–343.

Dunne, P. J. and Brauer, J. (eds.) (2002) *Arming the South: The Economics of Military Expenditure, Arms Production and Arms Trade in Developing Countries*, Palgrave, Basingstoke and New York.

Economist, EIU (2003) Country Report, Sudan, Main Report, December 2003.

EIU (The Economist Intelligence Unit) (2007) Sudan: Country Outlook, April 2005, ciao/EIU PARTNERSHIP: http://www.ciaonet.org/atlas/SD/Economy/Outlook/20070403_8816.html

El-Affendi, A. W. (1991) *Turabi Revolution: Islam and Power in Sudan*, Grey Seal, London.

El-Affendi, A. (1995) *Al-Thaera wa I-Islah al-Siayassi fi'l-Sudan* (Revolution and Political Reform in Sudan), Alerrees Forum, London.

El-Affendi, A. (2006) On the Removal of www. Subsidies, *Alqudus Al Arabi*, 29 August.

Elbadawi, I. and Sambanis, N. (2000) *External Interventions and the Duration of Civil Wars*, World Bank, Washington, D.C.

Elbadawi, I. and Sambanis, N. (2002) How Much War We Will See? Explaining the Prevalence of Civil War, *Journal of Conflict Resolution*, 43(3), 307–334.

El Basher, A. and Idris, B. (1983) Impact of Marketing and Pricing Policies on Production of Groundnuts, a paper presented at the agricultural price policy in the Sudan, Paper No. 4, Khartoum.

El-Battahani (1996) The Social and Political Impact of Economic Liberalization and Social Welfare in Sudan, Working paper 6/96, Institute of Development Studies, University of Helsinki, Helsinki.

Eleditsch, N. P. (1998) Armed Conflict and the Environment: A Critique of the Literature, *Journal of Peace Resolution*, 35(3), 341–400.

El Gadal, M. S. (1993) *The History of Modern Sudan: 1820–1955*, Amal Publishers, Khartoum.

El-Imam, El-Tom, A. and Egemi, O. (2005) *Addressing Land Question in Nuba Mountain*, JAM, htttp://www.unsudanig.org/JAM

El Mahadi, S. (1997) On Sudan's Current Affairs, unpublished lecture notes, El Rayaam Daily, Cairo.

Elnur, I. (1998) Stabilization, Growth and Equity: Towards a Framework for Macro Policy for Alternative Development Strategy for Sudan, GAPS' DP presented to GAPS' Working Group on Macroeconomic Policies.

Elnur, I. (2002) The Second Boat of African New Diaspora: Looking at the Other Side of the Global Divide with Emphasis on Sudan, African Issues, Special Issue of the African Association's Journal, 'The Pitfalls and Possibilities of the African "Brain Drain" to the North'.

Elnur, I. (2003) War, Flight and Destitution and New Urbanity in the Sudan: Some Implications to Post-Conflict Reconstruction, paper presented to The Middle East Awards Program in Population and the Social Sciences (MEAwards): Workshop on 'The Socio-economic Dimensions of Poverty in West Asia and North Africa', Rabat, Morocco, 13–16 May.

Elnur, I. *et al.* (1993) Some Aspects of Survival: Strategies among the Southern Sudan Displaced People in Greater Khartoum, in H. G. Bohle (ed.), *Coping with Vulnerability and Criticality: Case Studies on Food-Insecure People and Places*, Verlag Breitenbach Publishers, Saarbucken, Germany.

Elnur, I., Elrasheed, F. and Yacoub, Y. (1994) *Resource Guide to Displaced and Refugees Studies in the Sudan*, Khartoum University Press, Khartoum.

Elnur, I. *et al.* (1994a) Dynamics of Internal Displacement: Socio-economic Changes among Southern Sudan Displaced Persons in Greater Khartoum, together with the DPSG, University of Juba.

Elnur, I. *et al.* (1994b) *Resource Guide to Displaced and Refugees Studies in the Sudan*, Khartoum University Press, Khartoum.

El Rasheed, F. A. R. (1991) Commercial Activities and Socio-Economic Dynamism in Darfur, Brussels: Royal Academy of Sciences of Overseas, Memories; T. 51, fasc. 2. Classify Sciences Morals and Policies [Collection], p. 228.

Elrich, H. and Gershoni, I. (eds.) (2000) *The Nile: Histories, Cultures, Myths*, Lynne Rienner Publishers, Colorado and London.

Elsawi, A. A. H. (1993) On the Issues of Arabism, Sudanism and Democracy: Exploratory Comments, paper presented at Workshop on the Assessment of the Democratic

Experiences in Sudan, jointly organized by the Sudanese Studies Centre and Al Ahram Centre for Political and Strategic Studies, Cairo, 4–6 July.

Elsheikh, F. A. (1981) Investment Encouragement Act in the Sudan, paper presented at the Conference on Investment Legislations organized by the Sudanese Lawyers Association, Khartoum.

Elturabi, M. (1993) The Democratic Unionist Party: Reflections on the Ideological Dimensions, paper presented at Workshop on the Assessment of the Democratic Experiences in Sudan, jointly organized by the Sudanese Studies Centre and Al Ahram Centre for Political and Strategic Studies, Cairo, 4–6 July.

El Zein Abdeen, E. (2003) *Magalat Un Elharaka El Islamia fi El Sudan* (in Arabic), Sudan's Islamic Movements Discourses, Sudanese Books House, Khartoum.

Enough (The Project to Abolish Genocide and Mass Atrocities) (2007) The Answer to Darfur: How to Resolve the World's Hottest War, by John Prendergast, International Crisis Group, Strategy Paper 1, http://www.enoughproject.org.

Eriksson, J. R. (1998) An Institutional Framework for Learning from Failed State, in R. Piccioto and E. Wiesner (eds.), *Evaluation and Development: The Institutional Dimensions*, World Bank, New York, pp. 218–234.

Esposito, D. and Crocker, B. (2004) To Guarantee the Peace: An Action Strategy for a Post-Conflict Sudan, Report for the Secretary of the States, January.

Fagen, P. W. and Bump, M. N. (2006) Remittances in Conflict and Crises: How Remittances Sustain Livelihoods in War, Crises, and Transitions to Peace, International Peace Academy, http://www.ipacademy.org/ProgramsLResearch/ProgReseDev_Pub.htm.

Fageer, M. K. and Merghany, A. B. *et al.* (2002) Poverty and Social Development in Sudan, mimeo.

Faist, T. (2004) *The Volume and Dynamics of International Migration and Transnational Social Spaces*, Oxford University Press, Oxford.

Faki, H. (1982) Economics and Management of Irrigation in the Sudan Gezira Scheme, unpublished doctoral thesis, university of Hohenheim.

FAO (Food and Agricultural Organization) (1973) Perspective Study of the Agricultural Development for the Democratic Republic of the Sudan, FAO, Rome.

FAO/WFP (2002) Crop and Food Supply Assessment, January.

Fawcett, J. T. (1989) Networks, Linkages, and Migration Systems, *International Migration Review*, 23, 671–680.

Fearon, J. D. (2004) Why Do Some Civil Wars Last So Much Longer Than Others?, *Journal of Peace Research*, 41(3), 275–301.

Flint, J. and De Waal, A. (2005) *Darfur,* Zed Books, London and New York.

Frankman, M. J. (1971) Urbanization and Development in Latin America, *Cahiers de Geographie de Que'bec*, 15, 341–350.

Friedrichs, J. (2001) The Meaning of New Medievalism, *European Journal of International Relations*, 7, 475–501.

Fusato, M. (2003) Disarmament, Demobilization, and Reintegration of Ex-Combatants, in G. Burgess and H. Burgess (eds.), *Beyond Intractability*. Conflict Research Consortium, University of Colorado, Boulder. Posted: July 2003 (http://www.beyondintractability.org/essay/demobilization/).

FYP (1970) The Five Year Plan for Economic and Social Development for the Democratic Republic of the Sudan: 1970/71–1974/75, Vols. I and II, Ministry of National Finance and Planning, Khartoum, 1.

Gadal, M. S. (1993) *Modern History of Sudan 1820–1955* (in Arabic), Amal Publishing Company, Cairo.

Galandar, M. M. (2005) *Sanwat El Nimeiri* (in Arabic), (The Years of Nimeiri: Documentation and Analysis of Years of May Regime in Sudan), Abdel Karim Mirghani Cultural Centre, Omdurman, Sudan.

GAPS (2003) Executive Summary of GAPS Second Health Workshop, Cairo.

Garang, J. (1992) *The Call for Democracy in the Sudan*, M. Khalid (ed.), Kegan Paul New York, London.

Garang, J. (1994) This Convention is Sovereign: Opening and Closing Speeches to the First National SPLM/SPLA National Convention, April, SPLA Publications.

Garang, J. (1998) The Vision of the New Sudan: Questions of Unity and Identity, Kameir, E. Consortium for Policy and Development (COPADES), Cairo.

Garang, J. (2005) John Garang addresses delegates at the South–South Meeting, Nairobi, 19 April (AFP: http://www.sudantribune.com).

Gelabi, M. A. and Elshafie, S. A. (1986) Main Programmes and Projects for the Implementation of the Strategy for Agricultural Development (in Arabic), paper presented at the National Economic Conference, February, Khartoum.

Gelal, E. M. E. (1985) Remittances from Sudanese Emigrant to Oil-Producing Countries: Factors Determining Size, and Uses of Remittances, Bulletin No. 64, Development Research Centre, University of Khartoum.

Ghai, D. (2002a) *Decent Work: Concepts, Models and Indicators*, International Institute for Labour Studies, DP 139/2002, Geneva.

Ghai, D. (2002b) ILO (2001) Reducing the Decent Work Deficit, Report of the Director General, Geneva.

Girodano, M. F., Giordano, M. A. and Wolf, A. T. (2005) International Resource Conflict and Mitigation, *Journal of Peace Research*, 42(1), 47–65.

Gleditsch, N. P. (1998) Armed Conflict and the Environment: A Critique of the Literature, *Journal of Peace Resolution*, 35(3), 341–400.

Gliek, J. (1987) *Chaos: Making a New Science*, New York.

Global IDP, Database, http://www.idproject.org

GNU and GoSS (2006) Framework for Sustained Peace, Development and Poverty Eradication: Progress Monitoring Note, Khartoum.

Goldman, M. L. (1983) *U.S.S.R. in Crisis: The Failure of an Economic System*, W.W. Norton & Company, New York and London.

GoS and UN (2004) Sudan's Millennium Development Goals, Interim Unified Report, United Nations Country Team.

Green, D. (1999) *Gender Violence in Africa: African Women's Responses*, St. Martin's Press, New York.

Green, R. H. and Thompson, C. B. (1986) Political Economics in Conflict: SADCC, South Africa and Sanctions, in Phyllis and Martin (eds.).

Gresh, A. (2003) Introduction, Rosano, Didar Fawzy (2003) *Al Sudan Ila Ein,* Third World Publisher, Cairo, translated from French by Mourad Fahmy (Le Soudan: En Question, La Table, Paris, 2002).

Grossmann, S. and Mayer-Kress, G. (1989) Chaos in the International Arms Race, *Nature*, February, 701–704.

Guha-Sair, D. (2006) Counting the Deaths in Darfur: Estimating Mortality from Multiple Survey Data, HICN Working Paper No. 15.

Gurak, D. T. and Caces, F. (1992) Migration Networks and the Shaping of International Migration Systems, in M. M. Kritz, L. L. Lim and H. Zlotnik (eds.), *International Migration Systems: A Global Approach*, Clarendon Press, Oxford.

Gurr, T. R. (2000) *Peoples Versus States: Minorities at Risk in the New Century*, United States Institute of Peace, Washington, DC.

Gyimah-Brempong, K. and Corley, M. E. (2005) Civil Wars and Economic Growth in Sub-Saharan Africa, *Journal of African Economies*, 14(2), 270–311.

Hale, S. (2001) Liberated but Not Free: Women in Post-War Eritrea, in S. Meintjes, A. Pillay and M. Turshen (eds.), *The Aftermath: Women in Post-Conflict Transformation*, Zed Books, London and New York, pp. 122–140.

Hall, P. and Pfeiffer, U. (2000) *Urban Future 21: A Global Agenda for Twenty-First Century Cities*, E&FN Spon, London and New York.

Hamad, M. A. E. G. (1996) *Al Sudan: El Mazag El Tarikhi wa Afag El Mustagbal* (Sudan: Historical Impasse and Future Prospects; in Arabic), International Studies & Research Bureau, British West Indies (vols. I and II).

Hamid, G. M. (2000) Local Level Authorities and Local Actors in Greater Khartoum, Sudan, ME Awards Regional Paper No. 47, Population Council, Cairo.

Hamimi, N. H. (2007) Challenge to Return, Reintegration and Reconstruction of Refugees and Internally Displaced Persons: The Case of South Sudan, MA thesis, AUC, May.

Hammond, L. (2004) *The Place Will Become Home: Refugee Repatriation to Ethiopia*, Cornell University Press, Ithaca.

Harabeson, J. W. (1987) *The Military in African Politics*, Praeger, New York, Westport, Connecticut and London.

Harir, S. and Tvedt, T. (eds.) (1994) *Short Cut to Decay: The Case of the Sudan*, Nordiska Afirkainstituet, Uppsala.

Harragain, S. (2003) Nuba Mountains and Natural Resources Study, Part 1: Land Study, a study funded by USAID and Nuba Mountain Programme for advancing conflict transformation.

Harrison, P. (1985) *Inside the Inner City: Life Under the Cutting Edge*, Penguin Books, revised edition 1985, first published 1983, Penguin Group, London.

Hassan, A. I. (1991) *Mohammed Ali Pasha fi al-Sudan*, Khartoum University Press, Khartoum, p. 25.

Hauge, W. (1998) Beyond Environment Scarcity, *Journal of Peace Resolution*, 35(3), 299–317.

Håvard, H. and Sambanis, N. (2005) Sensitivity Analysis of the Empirical Literature on Civil War Onset, paper presented at the 46th annual meeting of the International Studies Association, http://www.prio.no/page/Publication_details/Publications_other_2003/9429/46409.html

Hecht, R. M. (1985) Immigration, Land Transfer and Tenure Changes in Divo Ivory Coast, 1940–80, *Africa*, 55(3), 319–336.

Herbst, J. (2000) *States and Power in Africa: Comparative Lessons in Authority and Control*, Princeton University Press, Princeton, New Jersey.

Herge, H. and Sandler, T. (2002) Economic Analysis of Civil Wars, *Defence and Peace Economics*, 13(6), 429–433.

Hill, R. (1959) *Egypt in Sudan: 1820–1881*, Oxford University Press, Oxford.

Hobson, J. and Phillipson, R. (2006) The Urban Transition: Challenges and Opportunities, *Rural Economic Development*, 13(2), (http://www.rural-development.de/2263.0.html).

Holt, P. M. (1958) *The Mahadist State in the Sudan*, Clarendon Press, Oxford.

Holt, P. M. (1961) *A Modern History of the Sudan: From Funj Sultanates to the Present Day*, Weidenfeld & Nicolson, London.

HTS (1977) Hunting Technical Services: Agricultural Development in Jebel Mara Area, HTS, London.

Hughes, J. and Sasse, G. (2001) Conflict and Accommodation in the Former Soviet Union: The Role of Institutions and Regimes, in J. Hughes and G. Sasse (eds.), *Ethnicity and Territory in the Former Soviet Union: Regions in Conflict*, pp. 220–240.

Human Rights Watch (2005) Sudan: Entrenching Impunity. Government Responsibility for International Crimes in Darfur, *Human Rights Watch*, 17(17)(A).

Humeida, B. K. (1983) *Some Features from Sudan History During Ismael Rule* (in Arabic), Graduate School Publications, University of Khartoum.

Hurreiz, S. H. and Abdelsalam, E. A. (eds.) (1989) *Ethnicity, Conflict and National Integration in Sudan*, Institute of African and Asian Studies, University of Khartoum, Khartoum.

Ibrahim, B. E. A. (2003) Poverty via Islamic Banking Finance to Micro-Enterprises (MEs) in Sudan: Some Lessons for Poor Countries, Sudan Economy Research Group, Institute for World Economics and International Management (IWIM), University of Bremen.

Ibrahim, F. (1978) The Problem of Desertification in the Republic of Sudan with Special Reference to North Darfur Province, DSRC Monograph Series No. 8, Khartoum University Press, Khartoum, p. 42.

Ibrahim, F. (1982) The Role of Women Peasants in the Desertification in Western Sudan, *Geojournal*, 6(1), 25–29.

Ibrahim, F. (1984) The Problem of Overstocking and the Ecological Degradation in the Republic of Sudan, *Al-Tasahhur: Sudan Journal of Desertification*, 2, 12–21.

Ibrahim, F. (1998) The Zaghawa and the Midob of North Darfur: A Comparison of Migration Behaviour, *Geojournal*, 46(2), 135–141.

Ibrahim, H. A. (1991) *Mohammed Ali Pasha fi al-Sudan*, Khartoum University Press, Khartoum, p. 25.

Ibrahim, S. E. (1990) War Displacement: The Socio-Cultural Dimension, paper presented at the Conference on Internal Migration and Displacement Issues in the Sudan, University of Gezira.

ICG (International Crisis Group) (2005) Garang's Death: Implications for Peace in Sudan, Update Briefing, Africa Briefing No. 30, Nairobi-Brussels, 9 August.

IDMC (2006) Internal Displacement Monitoring Centre: Slow Return to the South while Darfur Crisis Stay Unabated, http://www.internal-displacement.org/8025708F004CE90B/(httpCountrySummaries)/AA1D687D6D477153C12571C600364BD0?OpenDocument&count=10000

ILO (1976) Growth, Employment and Equity: A Comprehensive Stategy for the Sudan, Report of the ILO/UNDP Employment Mission to the Sudan, ILO, Geneva.

IMF, UN and World Bank (2006) Framework for Sustainable Peace, Development and Poverty Eradication, Staff Assessment of Progress.

International Crisis Group (2006) Beyond Victimhood: Women's Peace-building in Sudan, Congo and Uganda, Africa Report No. 112–128, June, International Crisis Group.

IOM (2006) IDPs Intention Survey, Survey Results, September.

Ioyob, R. and Khadiagala, G. M. (2006) *Sudan: The Elusive Quest for Peace*, International Peace Academy Occasional Paper Series, Lynne Rienner Publishers, Boulder, London.

IRC (International Rescue Committee) (2004) Freedom from Fear. Promoting Human Security for the Return and Reintegration of Displaced Persons in Sudan: A Protection Reassessment, May.

IRIN (1999) United Nations Integrated Regional Information (IRIN), Sudan pages: http://www.irinews.org/frontpage?selklectRegion=East_Africa&SelectCountry=Sudan.

ISS (2002) International Crisis Group Report 'God, Oil and Country – Changing the Logic of War in Sudan', Report No. 39.

ISS (2004) The South Sudan Defense Force – A Challenge to the Peace Process: ISS Think-Tank.

Issawi, C. (1954) Egypt at Mid-Century: An Economic Survey.

Jabar, F. A. (2000) Shaykhs and Ideology: Detribalization and Retribalization of Iraq, 1968–1986, Middle East Report, No. 215.

Jackson, R. (1990) *Quasi-state: Sovereignty. International Relations and Third World*, Cambridge University Press, Cambridge.

JAM Sudan (2004) A National Poverty Eradication Strategy Concept Note, Khartoum.

JAM (2005) Cluster Reports, Volume I, March.

JAM (2005) Cluster Reports, Volume II, March.

JAM (2005) Cluster Reports, Volume III, March.

JAM (2005) Cluster, Costing and Matrices, Khartoum.

JAM (2005) *Framework for Sustained Peace, Development and Poverty Eradication*, Vol. I, Khartoum.

JAM (2005) Sudan. Peace Dividend Launched: The Development Plan for New Era, Nairobi.

Jha, S. K. (1996) The Kuznets Curve: A Reassessment, *World Development*, 24(4), 773–780.

Johnson, D. H. (1998) The Sudan People's Liberation Army and the Problem of Factionalism, in C. Clapham (ed.), *African Guerrillas*, James Currey, Indiana Publishers.

Johnson, D. H. (2003) *The Root Causes of Sudan's Civil Wars*, African Issues, The International African Institute in association with James Currey, Oxford, Indiana University Press, Bloomington and Indianapolis, and Fountain Publishers, Kampala.

Junne, G. and Verkoren, W. (2004) *Postconflict Development: Meeting New Challenges*, Lynne Rienner Publishers, Boulder, London.

Kabaj, M. Ibrahim A. (2006) *Al Sudan: Igitisad Al Ingaz wa Al Ifgar Alshamil*, Sudan: The Salvation Policies and Impoverishment (in Arabic), sponsored by the Institute for African Alternative, London, Azza for Publication and Distribution, Khartoum.

Kaplan, R. D. (1996) *The Ends of the Earth*, Random House.

Kapur, D. (2001) Diasporas and Technology Transfer, *Journal of Human Development*, 2(2), 265–286.

Kapur, D. and McHale, J. (2003) Migration New Payoff, *Foreign Policy*, 139(Nov.–Dec.), 48–57.

Karbo, T. and Mutisi (2006) Post-Conflict Elections and Democracy: A Comparative Analysis of the Mozambique and Angolan Elections, *Conflict Trends*, 2, 19–23.

Karshenas, M. (2001) Measurement and Nature of Poverty in Least Developed Countries, Background Paper for the Least Developed Countries Report 2002, UNCTAD, Geneva.

Kaufmann, C. (1996) Possible and Impossible Solutions to Ethnic Civil Wars, *International Security*, 20(4), 136–175.

Keith, G. A. R. K. and Ickowitz, A. (2002) Poverty and Distribution of Land, *Journal of Agrarian Change*, 3, 279–330.

Kelly, R. C. (1985) *The Nuer Conquest: The Structure and Development of an Expansionist System*, University of Michigan Press, Michigan.

Khalafalla (1981) Capital Accumulation and the Consolidation of a Bourgeoisie Dependent State in the Sudan, 1898–1978, *Research in Political Economy*, 4, 29–80.

Khalid, M. (1990) *The Government They Deserve: The Role of the Elite in Sudan Political Education*, Kegan Paul International, London.

Khalid, M. (1993) *Eknukhba AlSudanyya wa Idman Elfashal* (in the English edition (1990): The Government They Deserve: The Role of the Elite in Sudan Political Evolution, Kegan Paul International, London and New York), vol. 2, Elamin Publishers, Cairo.

Khalid, M. (2003) *War and Peace in Sudan: A Tale of Two Countries*, Kegan Paul, London.

Khalid, M. (2005) On the CPA, Sudaneseonline (http://www.Sudaneseonline.com/articl): last accessed 21 May 2005.

Khogali, M. M. (1979) Nomads and Their Sedentarization in the Sudan, http://www.unu. edu/unupress/unupbooks/80044e/80044E08.htm-31k

Kireyev, A. (2001) Financial Reforms in Sudan: Streamlining Bank Intermediation, IMF Working Paper WP/01/53.

Kiss, J. (1977) Will Sudan be an Agricultural Power? Studies in Developing Countries No. 94, Institute for World Economy of the Hungarian Academy of Sciences, Budapest.

Klak, T. and Holtzclaw, M. (1993) The Housing, Geography, and Mobility of Latin American Urban Poor: The Prevailing Model and the Case of Quito, Ecuador, *Growth and Change*, 24(2), 247.

Klugman, J. and Kallaur, E. G. (2005) Developmental Transformation and Peace Consolidation in Southern Sudan, *Forced Migration Review*, 24.

Knight, M. N. and Villanueva, D. (1995) The Peace Dividend: Military Spending and Economic Growth, unpublished mimeo, The International Monetary Fund, Middle Eastern Development, April (cited in Elbadawi, 1997).

Korbin, S. J. (1998) Back to the Future: Neomedievalism and the Post Modern Digital World Economy, *Journal of International Affairs*, 51, 361–386.

Kritz, T. S., Lim, L. I. and Zlotnik, H. (eds.) (1992) *International Migration System: A Global Approach*, Clarendon Press, Oxford.

Kurita, Y. (1989) The Concept of Nationalism in the White Flag League Movement, in Mahasin Abdelgadir Hag Alsafi (ed.), *The Nationalist Movement in the Sudan*, Sudan Library Series No. 15, Institute of African and Asian Studies, University of Khartoum.

Kurita, Y. (1993) The Role of the 'Negroid but Detribalized' People in Sudanese Society: 1920–1940, paper presented at the Sudanese Studies Conference, Durham, Vol. 3, pp. 107–120.

Kurita, Y. (1994) The Social Bases of Regional Movement in Sudan: 1960s–1980s, in Katsuyoshi Fukui and John Marakis (eds.), *Ethnicity and Conflict in the Horn of Africa*, James Currey, London.

Kuznets, S. (1955) Economic Growth and Income Inequality, *American Economic Review*, 45(1), 1–28.

Lado, J. (1996) Women as Refugees: Change through Displacement among Southern Sudanese Women in Cairo, Egypt, The American University in Cairo.

Lake, A. (ed.) (1990) *After the Wars: Reconstruction in Afghanistan, Indo-China, Central America, Southern Africa and the Horn of Africa*, New Brunswick, USA, and Oxford, UK.

Lebon, J. H. G. (1965) Land Use in Sudan, The World Land Use Survey, Monograph 4, Geographical Publication Ltd, London.

Lesch, A. M. (1998) *The Sudan: Contested National Identities*, Indiana University Press, Bloomington, and James Currey, Oxford.

Lewis, W. A. (1954) Economic Development with Unlimited Supplies of Labour, *Manchester School of Economic and Social Studies*, 22, 139–191.

Licklider, R. (1995) The Consequence of Negotiated Settlement in Civil Wars, 1945–1993, *The American Political Science Review*, 89(3), 681–690.

Lipton, M. (1970) Interdisciplinary Studies in Less Developed Countries, *Journal of Development Studies*, 9(1), 5–18.

Looney, R. E. (1989) Internal and External Factors in Effecting Third World Military Expenditures, *Journal of Peace Research*, 20(1), 33–46.

Mabogunje, A. L. (1970) System Approach to a Theory of Rural-Urban Migration, *Geographical Analysis*, 2, 1–18.

Madam R. De M. (2006) Briefing to the Sudanese in Nashville, Tennessee, 11 February Nashville, Tennessee, USA.

Magar, N. (1993) *Misr wa Binnaa El Dulwa Elhaditha fi El Sudan* (Egypt and Building of Modern Sudan), Centre for Egypt's Documents and Contemporary History, Egyptian Public Authority for Book, Cairo.

Mahmoud, M. (2001) Mahmud Muhammad Taha and the Rise and Demise of the Jumhuri Movement, *New Political Science*, 23(1), 65–88.

Mahmud, U. and Baldo, S. (1987) Al Daien Massacre: Slavery in Sudan, Khartoum.

Manchanda, R. (2001) Ambivalent Gains in South Asian Conflicts, in S. Meintjes, A. Pillay and M. Turshen (eds.), *The Aftermath: Women in Post-Conflict Transformation*, Zed Books, London and New York, pp. 99–121.

Manger, L. (2005) Understanding Resource Management in Western Sudan, in Q. Gausset, M. A. Whyte and T. Birch-Thomsen (eds.), *Beyond Territory and Scarcity: Exploring Conflicts over Natural Resource Management*, Nordiska Afrikainstitutet, Elander Gotab, Stockholm.

Martin, C., Badri, B. and Atif, J. (eds.) (2005) *Inter-Communal Conflict in Sudan: Causes, Resolution Mechanisms and Transformation: Introduction and Summary*, Ahfad University for Women, Building Peace Through Diversity Series, Ahfad University, Omdurman.

Martin, D. (2005) *On Secularization: Toward a Revised General Theory*, Ashgate, Hants and Burlington.

Martin, R. (2002) *Sudan's Perfect War*, Foreign Affairs, March/April.

Mazrui, A. M. (1971) The Multiple Marginality of the Sudan, in Yusuf Fadl Hassan (ed.), *Sudan in Africa*, Khartoum University Press, Khartoum.

Mazrui, A. M. (1973) The Black Arabs in Comparative Perspective: The Political Sociology of Race Mixture, in D. Wai (ed.), *The Southern Sudan: The Problem of National Integration*, Frank Cass, London.

Mbiti, J. S. (1969) *African Religions and Philosophy*, Heinemann, Ibadan, Nairobi and London.

Meintjes, S., Pillay, A. and Turshen, M. (2001) There is No Aftermath for Women, in S. Meintjes, A. Pillay and M. Turshen (eds.), *The Aftermath: Women in Post-Conflict Transformation*, Zed Books, London and New York, pp. 3–18.

Melvin, N. (2001) Introduction, *Civil Wars*, 4(4), 1–10.

Migdal, J. (1988) *Strong Societies and Weak States: State-Society Relations and State Capabilities in the Third World*, Princeton University Press, Princeton, NJ.

Milliken, J. and Krause, K. (2002) State Failure, State Collapse, and State Reconstruction: Concepts, Lessons and Strategies, *Development and Change*, 33(5), 753–774.

Mills, L. R. (1977) Population and Manpower in Southern Sudan, Research Paper No. 1, Population and Manpower Unit, University of Juba, Juba, Sudan.

Mills, L. R. (1982) Trends and Implications of Recent Population Distribution and Urban Growth in Southern Sudan. The Case of Juba: The Regional Capita', paper presented at the International Geographical Union Symposium, Khartoum, 8–12 March.

Ministry of Manpower (1997) Trends and Profiles of Poverty in Sudan: 1990–1996, unpublished report in collaboration with the ILO, Khartoum, Sudan.

Mintz, A. and Stevenson, R. T. (1995) Defense Expenditures, Economic Growth, and the 'Peace Dividend', *Journal of Peace Research*, 39(2), 283–305.

Miraghani, I. (2002) *Sudanese Army and Politics* (in Arabic), Sudanese Studies Centre, Cairo.

Mitchell, C. R. (1989) Conflict Resolution and CW: Reflections on the Sudanese Settlement of 1972, Working Paper No. 3, Centre for Conflict Analysis and Resolution, George Mason University, UA.

Mitchell, T. (1991) The Limit of the State: Beyond the Statist Approaches and their Critics, *The American Political Science Review*, 85(1), 77–96.

MNFP (1982) Prospects, Programmes and Policies for Economic Development: 1982/83–1984/85, MNFP, Khartoum, World Bank.

Mohamed, N. A. (1993) The Development Trap: Militarization – Environmental Degradation and Poverty and Prospects of Military Conversion, MacArthur Post Doctoral Thesis, The Global Security Programme, Faculty of Social and Political Sciences, University of Cambridge.

Mohammed, A. E. Z. (2004) Indigenous Institutions and Practices Promoting Peace and/or Mitigating Conflict: The Case of Southern Darfur of the Sudan, paper presented at the Workshop by University for Peace of the United Nations, in collaboration with the Peace Institute, University of Khartoum.

Mohammed, N. A. L. (1992) Military Expenditure in Sub-Saharan Africa: A Comparative Analysis and Case Study of the Sudan, Ph.D. dissertation, Cambridge University.

Mohy, E. and Abdel, R. O. (2006) *Al Turabi wa Al Ingaz: Siras Alhawiaa wa Alhawaa* (Turabi and Salvation Revolution: The Conflict of Identity and Interest) (in Arabic), Ekrema Press, Damascus.

Monsutti, A. (2005) *War and Migration: Social Networks and Economic Strategies of the Hazaras of Afghanistan*, Routledge, New York and London.

Moore, M. (2007) How Does Taxation Affect the Quality of Governance?, IDS Working Paper, No. 240.

Mustafa, M. E. (1983) Development Planning, Urban Labour Market and International Migration in the Sudan, in Peter Oesterdiekhoff and Karl Wohlmuth (eds.), *The Development Perspectives of the Democratic Republic of the Sudan: The Limits of the Breadbasket Strategy*, Ifo-institut Fur Wirtschaftsforschung Munchen Abteilung Entwicklungslader, Munchen.

Nafziger, E. W. and Auvinen, J. (1997) War, Hunger and Displacement: An Econometric Investigation into the Sources of Humanitarian Emergencies, Working Paper No. 142, World Institute for Development Economics Research, United Nations University, Helsinki.

Nashashibi, K. (1979) A Supply Framework for Exchange Reform in Developing Countries: The Experience of the Sudan, *IMF Staff Papers*, 27(1), 24–79.

National Population Committee (NPC) (1992) Care International Sudan and Commissioner for Displaced: The Registration System, Socio-Economic and Demographic Characteristics of Al-Salam Omdurman and Jebel Awliya Displaced Camps, Final Report, December.

Nimeiri, S. M. (1976) Industry in the Sudan, in A. Elhassan, (ed.), *An Introduction to Sudan Economy*, Khartoum University Press, Khartoum.

Nugud, M. I. (1995) *Slavery, Religion in Sudanese Society*, Khartoum.

Nyaba, P. A. (1997) *The Politics of Liberation in South Sudan: An Insider's View*, Fountain Publishers, Kampala, Uganda.

Nyoka, C. M. (1999) Southern Sudanese Women in Refuge: Experiences in Egypt, thesis (MA), The American University in Cairo.

O'Brien, J. (1984) Sowing the Seeds of Famine: The Political Economy of Food Deficit in Sudan, paper presented at the Conference on the World Recession and the Crisis in Africa organized by the *Review of African Economy Journal* and the Department of Economics of the University of Keele, Staffordshire.

O'Fahey, R. S. (1995) Islamism and Ethnicity in Sudan, in Hayder Ibrahim Ali (ed.), *Cultural Diversity: The Formation of National State in Sudan*, Sudanese Studies Centre, Cairo.

Okuk, J. (2007) Dilemmas of the Comprehensive Peace Agreement, *Sudan Tribune*, 5 June.

Omotola, S. J. (2006) Post-Election Reconstruction in Liberia: The Challenges of Security Sector Reforms, *Conflict Trends*, 2, 42–46.

Osman, M. A. (2004) Transition from War to Peace in Sudan, University for Peace.

Osterdiekhoff, P. and Wohlmuth, K. (eds.) (1983) *The Development Perspective of the Democratic Republic of the Sudan*, African Studies Series, No. 109, IFO-institut fur Wirtschaftsforschung Munchen, Weltforum Verlag, Munchen.

Outram, Q. (2002) The Demographic Impact of Early Modern Warfare, *Social Science History*, 26(2), 245–275.

Owns, G. and Stedman, S. J. (2002) Evaluating Issues in Peace Implementation, in S. J. Stedman, D. Rothchild and E. M. Cousens (eds.), *Ending Civil Wars: The Implementation of Peace Agreements*, Lynne Rienner Publishers, Boulder, London, pp. 43–70.

Phelan, J. and Wood, G. (2006) An Uncertain Return, Report on the Current and Potential Impact of Displaced People Returning to Southern Sudan, Ockenden International UK.

Phyllis, J. and Martin, D. (1996) Destruction Engagement: Southern Africa at War, Publishing House for the Southern African Research and Documentation Center, Harare.

Pollani, D. (2005) Conflict Analysis Guidelines, JAM: http://www.unsudanig.org/JAM

Pollard, N. (1984) The Sudan's Gezira Scheme: A Study in Failure, in E. Goldsmith and N. Hildyard (eds.), *The Social and Environmental Effects of Large Dams*, vol. 2, Case Studies, Wadebridge Ecological Centre, Cornwall.

Portes, A. and Borocz, J. (1987) Contemporary Immigration: Theoretical Perspectives on its Determinants and Modes of Incorporation, *International Migration Review*, 23: 606–630.

Prest, A. R. (1948) *War Economics of Primary Producing Countries*, Cambridge University Press, Cambridge.

Programme of Action (1972) Published by the General Secretariat of the Sudanese Socialist Union (SSU), Khartoum.

Pugh, M. and Cooper, N. (2004) *War Economies in Regional Context*, Macmillan Press Ltd, London.

Radi, N. M. (1982) *Studies in the History of Sudanese Egyptian Relations, 1964–1956*, Ansar Publishing House, Cairo.

Raeymaekers, T. (2005) Collapse or Order? Questioning State Collapse in Africa, HiCN Working Paper, No. 10, http://www.hicn.org.

Rapley, J. (2006) State Capacity and Development in a Post-Modern Age, *Progress in Development Studies*, 6(2), 167–172.

Ravallion, M. (1998) Poverty Lines in Theory and Practice, LSMS Working Paper No. 133, World Bank, Washington D.C.

Rayaam Daily: http://www.rayaam.net/sysia/syasa3.htm – 02/07/2005.

Rayaam Daily: http://www.rayaam.net/sysia/syasa3.htm – 04/07/2005.

Reno, W. (1997) African Weak States and Commercial Alliances, in *African Affairs*, 96, William Research Centre, Cairo, Egypt (in Arabic), pp. 165–185.

Richards, D. (1990) Is Strategic Decision Making Chaotic?, *Behavioral Science*, 35(3), 219–232.

Riehl, V. (2001) Who is Ruling in South Sudan? The Role of NGOs in Rebuilding Socio-Political Order, Studies on Emergencies and Disaster Relief, No. 9, Nordiska Afrikainstitutet, Lynne Rienner Publishers, Colorado and London.

Rosano, D. F. (2003) *Al Sudan Ila Ein*. Third World Publisher, Cairo, translated from French by Mourad Fahmy (Le Soudan: En Question, La Table, Paris, 2002).

Rose, M. (1993) The Management of Conflict: Interpretation in *Comparative Perspective*, Yale University Press, New Haven.

Rose, W. and Dusen, E. (2002) Sudan's Civil Wars as a Cause of Foreign Intervention in its Wars: Insights from Balance of Threat Theory, *Civil Wars*, 5(3), 1–64.

Ross, L. M. (2003) Oil, Drugs and Diamond: The Varying Roles of Natural Resources in Civil Wars, in K. Ballentine and J. Sherman, (eds.), *The Political Economy of Armed Conflict: Beyond the Greed & Grievance*, a project of the International Peace Academy, Boulder, London.

Rosser, A. (2006) Escaping the Resource Curse: A Review Essay, *New Political Economy*, 11(4), 557–570.

Rotberg, R. I. (ed.) (2003) *State Failure and State Weakness in a Time of Terror*, World Peace Foundation, Cambridge, Massachusetts, Brookings Institution Press, Washington, D.C.

Rothchild and Cousens, E. M. (eds.) (2002) *Ending Civil Wars: The Implementation of Peace Agreements*, Lynne Rienner Publishers, Boulder, London, pp. 43–70.

Rothchild, D. and Groth, A. J. (1995) Pathological Dimensions of Domestic and International Ethnicity, *Political Science Quarterly*, 110(1), 69–82.

Roy, A. (2003) *City Requiem, Calcutta: Gender and the Politics of Poverty*, University of Minnesota Press, Minnesota.

Rumbek Meeting (2004) The minutes of the 'Confidential Report of the SPLM/A Leadership Council Meeting', 29 November–1 December http://www.southsudannation.com/rumbek%20revelations

Sachs, J. and others (2001) Macroeconomics and Health: Investing in Health for Economic Development, Report of the Commission on Macroeconomics and Health to the Director-General of the World Health Organization, 20 December.

Salih, M. A. M. (1985) Pastoralist in Town: Some Recent Trends in Pastoralism in the North West of Omdurman District, ODI, Pastoral Development Network, August.

Salih, M. A. M. (2003) Islamic NGOs in Africa: The Promise and Peril of Islam, in de Waal (ed.), *The Islamic Project and its Enemies: Jihad, Civil Society and Humanitarianism in North East Africa*, C. Hurst, London.

Sassen, S. (2001) Cities in the Global Economy, in R. Paddison (ed.), *Handbook of Urban Studies*, Sage Publications, London, pp. 256–272.

Sattar, A. (1982) A Study of the Cost of Production and Comparative Advantage of Crops Under Different Farming Systems in Sudan, UNDP/IBRB Planning Assistance and Training Project, MNFP, Khartoum.

Savage, P. (2003) The Crisis of Governance and the Challenge to Peace in Sudan, Christian Aid and Policy Analysis, April, http://212.2.6.41/indepth/035.suda/sudan.pdf

Sayed, H. A. (1971) *Ja'aliyyin Folktales: An Interplay of African, Arabian and Islamic Elements,* Indiana Press.

Seers, D. (1972) What are We Trying to Measure?, *Journal of Development Studies*, 8(2), 21–36.

Sen, A. K. (1999) *Development as Freedom*, Anchor Books, New York.

Shaaeldin, F. and Brown, R. (1985) Towards an Understanding of Islamic Banking in Sudan: The Case of Faisal Islamic Bank in Sudan, Monograph Series No. 21, DSRC, University of Khartoum.

Sidahmed, A. S. and Sidahed, A. (2005) *Sudan: The Contemporary Middle East*, RoutledgeCurzon, London and New York.

Sigma One Corporation (1982) The Structure of Incentives in Sudan Rainfed Agricultural Sector, Raleigh.

Sikainga, A. A. (1996) *Slaves into Workers: Emancipation and Labor in Colonial Sudan*, University of Texas Press, Austin.

Simone, A. (1994) *In Whose Image? Political Islam and Urban Practices in Sudan*, University of Chicago Press, Chicago and London.

Slatin, R. (1986) *Fire and Sword in the Sudan*, Edward Arnold, London.

Small, M. and Singer, J. D. (1982) *Resort to Arms: International and Civil Wars: 1816–1980*, 2nd ed., Sage, Beverly Hills.

Sorbo, G. M. (1977) How to Survive Development, DSRC Monograph Series No. 6, DSRC, University of Khartoum.

Sorbo, G. M. (2004) Peacebuilding in Post-War Situations: Lessons from Sudan, Report No. 13, Chr. Michelsen Institute, CMI, Bergen.

Sörensen, Stilhoff, J. (2003) War as Social Transformation: Wealth, Class, Power and an Illiberal Economy in Serbia, *Civil Wars*, 6(4), 55–82.

Stark, O. (1978) Economic-Demographic Interactions in Agricultural Development: The Case of Rural-to-Urban Migration, FAO, Rome.

Stark, O. (1991) *The Migration of Labour*, Blackwell, Cambridge and Oxford.

Stark, O. and Bloom, D. E. (1985) The New Economics of Labour Migration, *The American Economic Review*, 75(2), 173–178, papers and proceedings of the Ninety-seventh Annual Meeting of the American Economic Association.

Stewart, F. (1993) War and Underdevelopment: Can Economic Analysis Help Reduce the Costs? Development Studies Working Paper, International Development Centre, Oxford.

Stewart, F. and Fitzgerald, V. (2001) The Economics and Social Consequences, Vol. II *Country Experiences*, Oxford University Press, Oxford.

Sudanese Writers Union (2006) Towards a Democratic Scheme of Peaceful Acculturation, General Conference Proceedings (in Arabic), Sharga Hall, Khartoum.

Suhrke, A., Harpviken, K. B., Knudsen, A., Ofstad, A. and Strand, A. (2002) Peace Building: Lessons from Afghanistan, Chr. Michelsen Institute, Bergen.

Suhrke, E. V. and Woodward, S. L. (2005) Economic Aid to Post-Conflict Countries: A Methodological Critique of Collier and Hoeffler, Chr. Michelsen Institute, Bergen (CMI Working Paper No. 4), 26.

Suliman, A. A. (1975) *Issues in the Economic Development of the Sudan*, Khartoum University Press, Khartoum.

Suliman, M. (1993) Civil War in the Sudan: From Ethnic to Ecological Conflict, *The Ecologist*, 23(May–June), 104–109.

Suliman, M. (1999) *Brecht: The Poet of Dialectics*, Arabic Translation of Selected Poems, El Farabi House, Beirut.

Suliman, M. (2000) *Sudan Civil Wars: New Perspective*, Cambridge Academic Press, Cambridge.

Suliman, M. (2004) *Darfur: New Perspective*, Cambridge Academic Press, Cambridge.

SYP (1977) The Six Years Plan for Economic and Social Development, 1977/78–1982/83, Vols. I and II, MNFP, Khartoum.

Taha, H. (1993) *Al Ikhwan wal Asker* (The Brotherhood and the Military: The Narrative of Islamic Front and Power in Sudan) (in Arabic), Arab Civilization Information and Publication Centre, Cairo.

Taylor, C. (2004) *Modern Social Imaginaries*, Duke University Press, Drham, NC.

Taylor, J. E. (1999) The New Economics of Labour Migration, *International Migration*, 37(1), 65–85.

Tearfund and Save the Children (2002) The Key to Peace: Unlocking the Human Potential of Sudan.

The Act (1976) The Development and Promotion of Agricultural Investment Act for 1976, Gazette 1196, No. 19, Khartoum.

The Act (1980) The Encouragement of Investment Act 1976, Gazette 1272, 1980 Provisional Order No. 17, Khartoum.

The Economist (EIU) (1986) Sudan in Transition, Country Outlook, The Economist Intelligence Unit, London.

The International Fund for Agricultural Development (1999) The Republic of Sudan: Thematic Study on Rainfed Agriculture, Report No. 1021-SD, October.

Todaro, M. P. (1969) A Model of Labor Migration and Urban Unemployment in Less Developed Countries, *American Economic Review*, 60(March), 138–148.

Todaro, M. P. (1976) *Internal Migration in Developing Countries*, ILO, Geneva.

Todaro, M. P. (1977; 3rd edition, 1993) *Economics for Developing World: An Introduction to Principles, Problems and Policies for Development*, Longman, London.

Todaro, M. P. (1997) *Economic Development*, Longman, London and New York (6th edition).

Tordoff, W. (1993) *Government and Politics in Africa*, 2nd edition, Indiana University Press, Bloomington and Indianapolis.

Trainor, B. (1998) The Origin and End of Modernity, *Journal of Applied Philosophy*, 15(2), 133–144.

Trimingham, J. S. (1949) *Islam in the Sudan*, Oxford University Press, London and New York.

Tronvoll, K. (1998) The Process of Nation Building in Post-War Eritrea: Created from Below or Directed from Above, *The Journal of Modern African Studies*, 36(3), 461–482.

Turabi, H. (1991) *The Islamic Movement in Sudan: Progress, Gains and Methods*, El Furgan Publishers, Rabat, 2nd edition.

Turner, J. C. (1968) Housing Priorities, Settlement Patterns, and Urban Development in Modernizing Countries, *Journal of the American Institute Planners*, 34, 354–363.

Tvedt, T. (1998) *Angels of Mercy or Development Diplomats? NGOs and Foreign Aid*, James Currey Publishers, Oxford; Africa World Press, Trinton, NJ.

Tvedt, T. (2004) *Southern Sudan: An Annotated Bibliography*, I. B. Tauris, London and New York.

UN (2002) Implementation of the United Nations Millennium Declaration: Report of the Secretary-General; report no. A/57/270; http://www.un.org

UN (2006) United Nations and Partners: Work Plan for the Sudan, November.

UNDP (2002) Research on Roots of Conflict and Traditional Conflict Transformation Mechanisms: Transhumance Rates in North Darfur, UNDP Project, Reduction of Natural Resources-Based Conflict Among Pastoralists and Farmers.

UN-Habitat (2005) Urbanization Challenges in Sub-Saharan Africa, http://www.unhabitat.org

UNHCR (2006) South Sudan Operation: Achievements in South Sudan in 2005, Khartoum, March.

UNICEF (1989) Children on the Front Line, Annex A, 'Economic Cost of Destabilization and Warfare, 1980–1988: A Note', pp. 35–40, UNICEF, New York.

UNICEF (2003) Sudan: Annual Report, http://www.unicef.org/publications/files/Annual_Report_2001.pdf

UPA (1971) *Sudan Today*, Ministry of Information and Culture of the Democratic Republic of Sudan, UPA, Nairobi.

Utterwulghe, S. (1999) Rwanda's Protracted Social Conflict: Considering the Subjective Perspective in Conflict Resolution Strategies, *The Online Journal of Peace and Conflict*, 2(3), August (http://www.trinstitute.org/jpcr/2.3utter.htm).

Van Hear, N. (2004) Diasporas, Remittances, Development and Conflict, Migration Information Source, June v1, 2003.

Verdery, K. (1993) Ethnic Relations in the Economies of Shortage and Transition in Eastern Europe, in C. H. Han (ed.), *Socialism, Ideals, Ideology and Local Practice*, ASA Monograph, Routledge, London.

Vertovec, S. (1999) Conceiving and Researching Transnationalism, *Ethnic and Racial Studies*, 22, 445–462.

Voll, J. O. (1991) Northern Muslim Perspectives, in John V. Montville (ed.), *Conflict and Peacemaking in Multiethnic Societies*, Lexington Books, Lexington, MA, p. 339.

Wagner, P. (2000) Modernity – One or Many?, in J. Blau (ed.), *The Blackwell Companion to Sociology*, Blackwell, Oxford.

Wallerstein, I. (1989) Elegy and Requiem for Ideology of National Development, F. Braidal Papers, University of Binghamton, New York.

Walter, B. (2004) Does Conflict Beget Conflict? Explaining Recurring Civil War, *Journal of Peace Research*, 41(3), 371–388.

Warburg, G. (1995) Mahadism and Islam in Sudan, *Journal of Middle East Studies*, 27(2), 219–236.

Warren, K. (ed.) (1993) *The Violence from Within: Cultural and Political Opposition in Divided Nations*, Westview Press, Boulder.

Weida, W. J. and Gertcher, F. L. (1987) *The Political Economy of National Defense*, Westview Press, Boulder and London.

Willis, C. A. (ed.) (1985) *Slaves and Slavery in Muslim Africa*, Frank Cass, London.

Winsor, C. Jr. (2007) Saudi Arabia, Wahhabism and the Spread of Sunni Theofascism, *Mideast Monitor*, 2(1), June/July.

Woodward, P. (1990) *Sudan, 1898–1989: The Unstable State*, Lynne Rienner, Boulder.

World Bank (1991) World Development Report, Oxford University Press, Oxford.

World Bank (2000) World Development Report 2000/2001: Attacking Poverty, Oxford University Press, Oxford.

World Bank (2003) Sudan: Stabilization and Reconstruction, Country Economic Memorandum, 30 July.

World Bank (2004) The Role of the World Bank in Conflict and Development: An Evolving Agenda, World Bank, Washington, D.C.

World Bank (2006) The Sudan Consortium, http://siteresources.worldbank.org/CDFINTRANET/Overview/21011131/Sudan07–31-06.doc

Wunsch J. S. and Olowu, D. (1990) The Failure of the Centralized State: Institutions and Self-Governance in Africa, Westview Press, Boulder, San Francisco and Oxford.

Xiushi, Y. (1999) Gender Differences in Determinants of Temporary Labor Migration in China: A Multilevel Analysis, *International Migration Review*, 33(4), 954–987.

Yath, Y. A. (1993) The Proportional Importance of Most Needed Items at Suq. el Markazi as Appreciated by the Dinka Migrants, *GeoJournal*, 36(1), 93–101.

Yeung, Y. M. (2000) Globalization and Networked Societies: Urban-Regional Change in Pacific Asia, University of Hawaii Press, Honolulu.

Young, C. (1994) *The African Colonial State in Comparative Perspective*, Yale University Press.

Young, J. (2005) John Garang's Legacy to the Peace Process, the SPLM/A and the South, *Review of African Political Economy*, 106, 535–548.

Young, J. (2006) *The South Sudan Defense Forces in the Wake of Juba Declaration*, Department of International Development, The Small Arms Survey, The Graduate Institute of International Studies in Geneva, Switzerland.

Index

Diagrams and tables are given in italics